Business and Microeconomics is a concise introduction to microeconomics, specifically designed to provide students and practitioners of business with an understanding of the workings of the market system. Thus, the focus of attention is 'the market' itself, rather than the individual company, although it is recognised that the 'strategic' firm can and does play an important part in the operation of markets. Markets are not static, but driven and shaped by the dynamics of inter-firm rivalries.

The main purpose of this book is to examine key aspects of market demand and supply, market structure, conduct and performance both in terms of relevance to the achievement of corporate success and the efficient use of economic resources to the benefit of society at large. A main emphasis throughout the book is to show how an understanding of microeconomics is relevant to modern decision-makers. In this way, importance is placed on application, using illustrative 'boxes' of microeconomic concepts in 'real world' business situations.

Written in a clear, accessible way by two experienced teachers of economics and business studies, this book is an important addition to the Elements of Business series. Including questions at the end of each chapter and text examples throughout, this text will be ideal for both MBA and DMS students, as well as undergraduate management and business studies students.

Christopher Pass is a Lecturer in Managerial Economics at the University of Bradford's Management Centre. **Bryan Lowes** is a Senior Lecturer in Managerial Economics, also at Bradford.

Elements of Business Series
Series editor: David Weir
University of Bradford Management Centre

This important new series is designed to cover the core topics taught at MBA level with an approach suited to the modular teaching and shorter time frames that apply in the MBA sector. Based on current courses and teaching experience, these texts are tailor-made to the needs of today's MBA student.

Other titles in the series:

Business and Society
Edmund Marshall

Management Accounting
Leslie Chadwick

Financial Accounting
Iain Ward-Campbell

Managing Human Resources
Christopher Molander and Jonathan Winterton

Managerial Leadership
Peter Wright

Financial Management
Leslie Chadwick and Donald Kirby

Business and Microeconomics

An introduction to the market economy

Christopher Pass and Bryan Lowes

INTERNATIONAL THOMSON BUSINESS PRESS
I(T)P An International Thomson Publishing Company

London • Bonn • Boston • Johannesburg • Madrid • Melbourne • Mexico City • New York • Paris
Singapore • Tokyo • Toronto • Albany, NY • Belmont, CA • Cincinnati, OH • Detroit, MI

Business and Microeconomics

Copyright © 1994 Christopher Pass and Bryan Lowes

 A division of International Thomson Publishing Inc.
The ITP logo is a trademark under licence

British Library Cataloguing-in-Publication Data
A catalogue record for this book is available from the British Library

First published 1994 by Routledge, reprinted 1996
Reprinted by International Thomson Business Press 1997

Printed in Italy by Legoprint srl

ISBN 1-86152-347-5

International Thomson Business Press
Berkshire House
168–173 High Holborn
London WC1V 7AA
UK

International Thomson Business Press
20 Park Plaza
13th Floor
Boston MA 02116
USA

http://www.itbp.com

Contents

Figures

Tables

Boxes

Preface

Markets constitute the particular arenas in which companies 'do business'. A company's strategic choice of which business activities or markets to operate in and how to compete in these markets depends, in part, on the underlying characteristics of those markets and the 'attractiveness' of the market in offering scope for profit gain. The objective of this book is to provide students and practitioners of business with an understanding of the functioning of markets. Thus, the focus of attention is 'the market' itself, rather than the individual company, although it is recognised that the 'strategic' firm can and does play an important part in the operation of the market – markets are not static, but are driven and shaped by the dynamics of inter-firm rivalries. The main purpose of the book is to examine key aspects of market demand and cost conditions, market structure, market conduct and market performance, in terms of both their relevance to the achievement of corporate success and the efficient use of economic resources to the benefit of society at large.

The book is primarily intended to cater for the needs of MBA, DMS and other business students who have not studied economics before and who are seeking a relevant, straightforward and relatively non-technical introduction to microeconomics. Some of the material will also be useful to students taking courses in the areas of industrial economics and business policy.

Acknowledgements

We would like to thank Sylvia Bentley and Chris Barkby for their patience and efficiency in typing drafts of the manuscript, and Rosemary Nixon, Gabi Woolgar and Leigh Wilson for their enthusiastic support of the work.

Christopher Pass, Bryan Lowes

Chapter 1

Microeconomics and the market environment of business

An overview

1.1 WHY STUDY MARKETS?

Markets constitute the particular arenas in which companies 'do business'. No matter how few or how many business activities a company undertakes, its corporate prosperity will depend fundamentally on how well it succeeds in the individual product markets making up its business. It is thus important for companies to understand the underlying characteristics of the markets in which they operate (or which they are likely to enter) and the forces driving competition in those markets in order to become 'corporate winners', achieving above-average profit returns on their investments.

Markets form a core analytical focus of economics, specifically 'microeconomics'. The ultimate purpose of economic endeavour is to satisfy human wants for goods and services. The problem is that whereas wants are virtually without limit, the resources – natural resources, labour and capital – available at any one time to make goods and services, are limited in supply; that is, resources are scarce relative to the demands they are called upon to satisfy. The fact of economic scarcity means that resources need to be allocated amongst competing end uses as efficiently as possible, so as to attain the maximum fulfilment of society's demand for goods and services. Microeconomics studies the behaviour of consumers, firms, workers and resource owners, and the determination of the market prices and quantities transacted of goods, services and factor inputs, and seeks to identify the strategic determinants of an optimally efficient use of resources.

1.2 SCARCITY AND CHOICE

Economic activity involves combining natural resources (agricultural and mineral commodities), labour and capital in order to produce goods and services for ultimate consumption. However, in all societies, from the most primitive, isolated village community to the most sophisticated, industrialised nation state, resources are finite and the wants to be satisfied from these resources are unlimited. This gives rise to the fundamental economic problem of scarcity and the need to attempt to match resources and wants to the greatest possible extent. The mismatch between resources and wants can be seen in its most acute form in many third world countries whose resources are inadequate to provide even the most basic food, clothing and shelter for much of the population, so that many of their needs go unmet. However, even in sophisticated industrialised countries, where improving productivity often enables more wants to be satisfied each year from available resources as living standards rise, it is generally the case that people's wants grow more quickly than the economy's ability to satisfy them.

Scarcity poses a number of economic problems which must be addressed. First, it is important to attempt to increase available resources and to improve the productivity with which they are used, since such economic growth enables more wants to be satisfied. Second, it is important to keep available resources fully utilised in producing goods and services – unemployment is very wasteful in terms of lost output, as well as having adverse effects upon those who are unfortunate enough to be unemployed. However, rapid growth and full employment can only partially alleviate, rather than solve, the problem of economic scarcity. Choices still have to be made about what goods and services to produce with limited resources, what resource combinations to use in producing goods and services, and how the resulting goods and services are to be distributed. In making these choices, alternatives must be evaluated in terms of their opportunity cost – the value of resources in their next best alternative use – in order to weigh carefully the implications of using scarce resources for a particular purpose.

The concept of choice and opportunity cost can be illustrated in terms of production possibility curves which show the combinations of particular products (goods and services) which can be produced from given, finite resources. Figure 1.1 shows two such curves, the first (a) showing combinations of military products and civilian products and the second (b) showing capital products and consumer products.

The curve in Figure 1.1(a) shows the maximum amount of military and/or civilian products that can be made by an economy at a given time with available resources and technology, assuming all resources are fully employed in the most efficient way. Point W represents the maximum output of military goods if no civilian products are made, while point X represents the maximum output of civilian goods if no military products are made. At any point along the boundary, such as B or J, there is a trade-off between the two products, so that in moving from B to J, output of civilian goods can be expanded only by taking resources away from making military products. The boundary is curved rather than a straight line, because not all resources are equally efficient in the production of the two products.

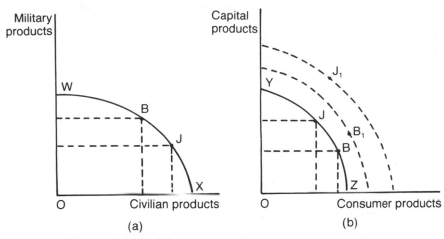

Figure 1.1 Production possibility curves

Over the past few decades Britain and the USA have devoted 5 per cent or more of their total resources to making military goods, placing them on a point like B in Figure 1.1(a). By contrast, Japan and Germany have devoted only 2 per cent or less of their total resources to making military goods, placing them on a point like J in Figure 1.1(a). As a consequence, Japan and Germany have been able to make proportionately more civilian products – both consumer products and capital products – than Britain or the USA. However, with the easing of political tensions between the Western and Eastern countries, it is becoming possible for countries such as Britain and the USA to gain a 'peace dividend' by cutting back on their military spending and channelling the resources released into making more civilian products, effectively moving from B to J on the production possibility curve.

Point Y on the curve in Figure 1.1(b) shows the maximum amount of capital products (factories, offices, machinery, etc.) that could be made by an economy if all resources were devoted to making capital products, while point Z shows the maximum amount of consumer products (food, consumer durables, entertainment, etc.) if all resources were devoted to making consumer products. Over the past few decades Japan (and Germany) have devoted around 20 per cent or more of their resources to making capital goods, placing them at point J in Figure 1.1(b). By contrast Britain (and the USA) have devoted 15 per cent or less of their resources to making capital goods, placing them at point B in Figure 1.1(b). These proportions have implications for the growth of these economies because, given the link between investment in capital products, productivity and rates of economic growth, we would expect the total output of countries like Japan to grow quickly, pushing the production possibility boundary outward over time and leaving Japan with a much larger output of both kinds of products at a point such as J_1 compared with slower-growing Britain which would be left in a position such as B_1 after an equivalent time period. This is borne out by the evidence which shows Japan to be achieving an average annual growth in output of over 5 per cent in recent decades, compared with under 2 per cent in Britain.

1.3 PLANNED AND MARKET ECONOMIES

In dealing with the economic problems of scarcity and choice, countries have tended to adopt one of two broad socio-political systems for allocating scarce resources: planned economies and free enterprise or (market-based) economies. In planned economies the State collectively owns all natural and capital resources and directs resources into the production of particular goods and services. The State, through its economic planning agencies, is responsible for estimating the wants of the population, establishing priorities and directing resources to meet these wants. Managers of production units – farms, mines, factories, etc. – are given output quotas which they are required to meet and are allocated resources to produce output.

Planned economies can be an effective means for allocating resources in subsistence economies where living standards are low and wants are very basic, for it is comparatively easy for the State to estimate needs. For example, if a country's target is merely to provide everyone with one pair of shoes per year, then wants are easy to estimate and associated output targets easy to set. However, as living standards rise and a country's population becomes wealthy enough to afford a wider range of products and to exercise choice, it becomes more difficult for the State to estimate wants. For example, once people become wealthy enough to afford more than one pair of shoes and begin to decide whether they want black or brown coloured shoes, then it becomes more difficult for the State to estimate how many pairs of shoes of each colour to produce and, as consumer preferences change from, say, black to brown shoes, the State can be slow to respond, producing too many black shoes and too few brown shoes, with a resulting waste of resources. Again, as living standards rise, people begin to prefer higher quality, more reliable products, but in planned economies, where output quotas are set largely in quantitative terms, production units have little incentive to expend resources on improving product quality. Finally, planned economies are poor at providing incentives to managers and workers to work hard or move jobs or transfer their skills from making products which are no longer needed to new ones that are required. In subsistence level planned economies it is possible to direct and redirect workers from one job to another or from one part of the country to another as required. However, as living standards rise, appropriate wage differentials or other financial inducements are necessary to encourage workers to work harder or to change jobs.

The weaknesses of state planning as a resource allocation mechanism in economies with rising living standards has led many communist countries, like the former USSR and the Eastern European countries, to abandon their planning systems and turn instead to market systems as the primary means of allocating resources. Market systems have been widely used by Western governments for many centuries and though markets also have their problems, as we shall see later, on balance they appear to be the better resource allocation mechanism of the two. Market economies place heavy reliance upon the institution of private, rather than collective, ownership of resources; and on the freedom of individual producers to deploy their privately owned resources in making whatever products they wish to, guided by profit opportunities – hence the term 'free enterprise'. In market economies, resource allocation is generally more decentralised. Though the State still usually takes responsibility for allocating some national resources to uses like military defence and the police, many of the economy's resources are allocated as a result of the decisions made by many thousands of consumers about how to allocate their scarce income amongst the competing consumer products on offer in order to satisfy their wants; and many thousands of producers deciding how to deploy their resources to satisfy the demands of consumers. The manner in which markets allow consumers to signal their preferences and provide incentives to businesses to deploy their resources to meet consumer wants is described in more detail in section 1.5.

1.4 WHAT ARE MARKETS?

Economically, a market may be defined as an 'exchange mechanism' which brings together the suppliers and buyers of a particular product, for example beer. In practice, however, it is often difficult to identify the boundaries of a market, since a range of products rather than one specific type of product may satisfy a consumer demand. For example, although beer may constitute a discrete market, viewed narrowly, beer may also be regarded as being part of a bigger market for alcoholic beverages, competing within this market alongside wines and spirits. Thus, there is a problem of how narrowly or widely a market is specified. Economic analysis suggests that this issue can be resolved by using the *cross-elasticity of demand* test (see Chapter 2), that is, products can be regarded as *substitutes* for one another if a change in the price of a given product has a discernible impact on the demand for some other product. Thus, if the price of beer increases and this causes the demand for beer to fall and the demand for, say, whisky to rise, then buyers regard the two products as being substitutes, and hence these two products can be seen to be part of the 'same' market. In practice, however, cross-elasticity of demand data are not usually available, so that markets tend to be identified by more pragmatic criteria, such as trade and buyer opinion and customary use. The picture is further complicated by spatial factors. Depending upon transportation costs, regional and country differences in buyer preferences, etc. markets may be local, regional, national or international in scope. An additional factor which is also important in the context of business practice is that of market segmentation. Apart from some commodity-type products (coal, iron ore, etc.), most markets are capable of being segmented such that distinct 'pockets' of buyers can be identified and targeted with 'customised' versions of the generic products.

The above considerations enable us to look at market profiles from a number of angles and how companies might choose to 'position' themselves in the market, either as broad-range suppliers or niche specialists, and as international suppliers or as suppliers solely to their own domestic markets. To take two examples: Box 1.1 considers the market for alcoholic drinks and the market for pharmaceuticals. The resource and skill requirements for different segments of the market may be markedly different. For example, to compete successfully in the 'patent-based' sector of the pharmaceutical market requires companies to spend millions of pounds annually on research and development; in the 'generic' sector, where firms produce 'copy-cat' versions of off-patent drugs, low-cost production is an essential competitive requirement. Similarly, leading alcoholic drink producers spend millions of pounds on international brand-building and marketing, whereas small niche producers, with minimal distribution and marketing costs, are able to supply local retail outlets at low wholesale prices.

1.5 HOW DO MARKETS 'WORK'?

In a private enterprise market economy, the basic decisions about what goods and services to produce, the quantities of each to produce and their relative prices are determined by the interaction of buyers and sellers in product and factor markets, as indicated in Figure 1.2. The firm is a key element in the market system, operating in product markets where it sells products and factor markets where it buys or hires resources. The market system thus acts to allocate resources in the production of goods and services in accordance with consumer demand.

Box 1.1   Market segments in the alcoholic drinks and pharmaceutical markets and the strategic positioning of selected companies

Alcoholic drinks

Market segment

		Companies			
		Allied (UK)	Goose Eye (UK)	Grolsch (Dutch)	Seagram (Canada)
Product group	• Ales	√	√	√	
	• Lagers	√		√	
	• Wines	√			√
	• Spirits	√			√
Geographic spread:		Worldwide manufacturing and sales subsidiaries	Local, UK	Exports to 40 countries, production in UK and Germany	Worldwide manufacturing and sales subsidiaries

Pharmaceuticals

Market segment

		Companies			
		Merck (USA)	Glaxo (UK)	Norgine (UK)	Atochem (Canada)
Product group:	• Patent-protected branded 'prescription-only' drugs	√	√		
	• Off-patent branded 'over the counter' drugs	√	√	√	
	• Generics	√			√
Geographic spread:		Worldwide manufacturing and sales subsidiaries	Worldwide manufacturing and sales subsidiaries	Limited export coverage	Canada only

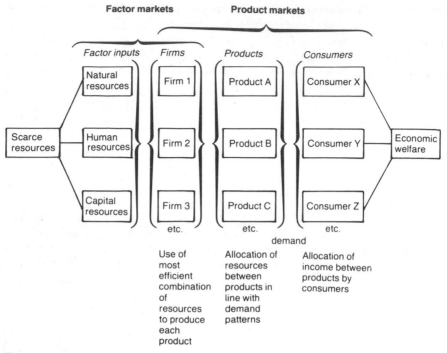

Figure 1.2 The market system

In a market system, a pivotal role is played by the price mechanism which operates to synchronise the actions of buyers and sellers. The following simplified example of the carrot and pea markets explains how the price mechanism works to this end. Suppose initially that carrot and pea prices were such as to equate supply and demand for these products in their respective markets, but that then there was a change in consumer demand away from carrots and towards peas, as indicated in Figure 1.3. The increased demand for peas, coupled with unchanged pea supply in the short run, would result in an excess demand for peas at the prevailing price and price would rise to ration the scarce peas amongst consumers. The decreased demand for carrots, coupled with unchanged carrot supply in the short run, would initially give rise to an excess market supply at the prevailing price, and the price of carrots would fall as suppliers sought to clear unsold stocks.

These changes in prices will affect the profits of carrot and pea suppliers. As demand and prices rise in the pea market, pea growers will experience increased profits, while carrot growers, faced with falling demand and prices, will find their profits declining. Over the long term, pea producers will invest in additional land and machinery and hire more labour to expand supply, and new firms will be tempted by high profits to enter the pea market. The resulting expansion in pea supply will force high prices back down to a lower level, leaving firms producing peas making 'normal' profits, at which level there will be no further incentives for new firms to enter the pea market or for total supply to expand. By contrast, as demand and prices fall in the carrot market, suppliers will find their profits falling and less efficient producers will go out of business as they experience losses, while other producers curtail their carrot output. The resulting decline in carrot supply will continue until carrot supply adjusts to the lower demand and firms left in the carrot market are earning a normal profit.

Changes in product markets will have repercussions in factor markets, as Figure 1.3 indicates. In order to expand pea supply, extra natural, human and capital resources must be drawn into pea production and this can only be achieved by offering them a higher return than they receive elsewhere. The increased demand for peas will result in an increased derived demand for factor inputs in pea production and this excess demand for factor inputs in the pea industry will increase the returns to factors employed there. By contrast, the carrot industry will be releasing resources as firms leave the industry, and unemployment of factors of production in the carrot trade will reduce factor returns as the derived demand for them falls. These forces serve to shape the distribution of income between those working in pea and carrot production.

The above example shows how the price system results in a reallocation of resources in response to signals given out by consumers about their changed demand for products, which in turn affects the prices of factor inputs. However, autonomous changes in the prices of factor inputs can themselves affect product prices and consumer demand patterns through the price system. For example, assume that carrot production is a relatively labour-intensive process while the growing and picking of peas is highly automated.

Consequently, a sharp upward shift in wage rates would affect the two industries differently, the cost and price of carrots rising substantially while peas costs and prices change little. Since carrots are now more expensive, while peas are much the same price, consumers will tend to alter their consumption patterns, buying less relatively expensive carrots and more relatively cheap peas. Consequently output and employment in the carrot industry will tend to fall while output of peas expands, and a reallocation of resources from carrots to peas might be expected. The process of reallocation may be more direct than this though, for, as firms seek to produce carrots at minimum cost through the most efficient combination of factor inputs, faced then with an increase in wage rates they will alter production methods using less relatively expensive labour inputs and more relatively cheap capital. Increasing wage rates are thus likely to accelerate automation in the carrot industry reducing the demand for labour there.

	Product markets		Factor markets	
	Pea market	*Carrot market*	*Pea inputs*	*Carrot inputs*
Short run	D=S	D=S	DF=SF	DF=SF
	D ↑	D ↓		
	D>S	D<S		
	P ↑	P ↓		
	Pr ↑	Pr ↓		
Long run	market entry	market exit	DF ↑	DF ↓
	S ↑	S ↓	DF>SF	DF<SF
	P ↓	P ↑	Pf ↑	Pf ↓
	Pr ↓	Pr ↑		
	D=S	D=S		

Key: D = product demand; S = product supply; P = price of products; Pr = profits of suppliers; Pf = price of factor input; SF = factor supply; DF = factor demand

Figure 1.3 Demand, supply and market prices

1.5 Limitations of the market

The operation of market forces can also affect national and regional prosperity as changes in technology and consumer preferences lead to the growth and decline of particular industries. For example, north-east England which was formerly heavily dependent upon coal-mining, shipbuilding and heavy engineering suffered badly from job losses as these industries have declined; whilst south-east England, which relied more upon commercial services, distribution and light engineering, prospered with the growth of these industries. Market forces could, in principle, deal with this problem if unemployed or poorly paid coal-miners and shipyard workers were to retrain for jobs in commerce and distribution and move from the north-east to south-east England, attracted by the better job prospects, wages and conditions there. However, in practice workers may be less occupationally and geographically mobile than this, so that unemployment differentials can persist. Again market forces could operate through capital mobility to deal with such disparities, companies building new offices, warehouses and factories in north-east England in order to lower their costs by taking advantage of the plentiful, comparatively cheap labour there. Again though, in practice companies may be reluctant to relocate, so that disparities can persist.

Box 1.2 shows how market forces have led to changes in industrial structure over time as a consequence of changes in demand and technology.

The price system can provide a sophisticated mechanism for allocating resources in an automatic way. However, it is not necessarily as perfect a resource allocator as it may appear. First, the response of supply within

Box 1.2 Market forces and changes in industrial structure

	Percentage distribution of gross domestic product					
	Agriculture		Industry		Services	
	1960	*1990*	*1960*	*1990*	*1960*	*1990*
UK	3	2	43	36	54	62
US	4	2	38	29	58	69
Japan	13	4	45	41	42	55
West Germany	6	2	53	39	41	59

Source: World Bank (1992)

The goods and services produced in an economy can be classified into three broad groups or sectors:

1 the primary sector, embracing agricultural products and other raw materials;
2 the secondary or industrial sector, including manufactured goods, construction, etc.;
3 the tertiary or service sector, comprising retailing, banking, tourism, etc.

In turn, each of these sectors can be subdivided more narrowly on an industry-by-industry basis.

Changes in technology and consumer demand patterns cause the relative importance of these sectors to change as economies expand over time. Thus developing countries are characterised by large primary sectors and small industrial and service sectors, while developed countries like those in the table above tend to have small primary sectors and large industrial and service sectors.

Within these sectors particular industries have grown significantly in developed economies like the UK, for example, banking, finance and insurance, whilst others have declined dramatically, for example, coal and coke extraction and manufacturing in the UK.

the price system to changes in consumer demand may be very slow and painful, because less efficient firms are not eliminated quickly but linger on, making losses. Second, resources are not always as occupationally or geographically mobile as the model implies, especially where workers require significant training to acquire appropriate skills. Third, the price system cannot ensure the provision of certain collective products, like defence, which are enjoyed in common by all consumers, because no markets for such products exist. Fourth, markets price products only on the basis of the resource costs incurred by suppliers so that they do not allow for the (external) pollution costs involved in their production or consumption. Fifth, the distribution of income and wealth in a market economy depends upon the resources which each household owns and the scarcity and value of these resources, which can give rise to gross disparities in income levels which may need to be modified by government by means of taxation and social security benefits. Finally, the efficient functioning of the price system depends crucially upon the structural characteristics of product and factor markets. With perfect competition in product and factor markets, the price system might well operate along the lines of the previous example. By contrast, where markets are characterised by monopoly or oligopoly, with high barriers to entry, then firms are not free to enter or leave product markets at will in response to profit opportunities. For example, if our earlier pea market was dominated by a monopoly supplier, then faced with an increase in demand the monopolist may decide not to expand pea supply but to exploit the increased demand by raising the selling price. Consequently in the long run, the monopolist earns above-normal profit and no extra factor inputs are devoted to pea production as consumer demand requires (see Chapter 5).

Because of the problems of 'market failure' noted above, governments often attempt to improve the resource allocation process by direct intervention in the market system. For example, *industrial policy* can be used to reorganise markets suffering from excess capacity, by providing financial inducements to firms to leave the market or by encouraging firms to merge and close down redundant plant; industrial policy can be used to foster innovation by providing grants and tax benefits to firms investing in research and development, and it can involve the provision of retraining facilities to improve the occupational mobility of the labour force. *Competition policy* can be used to prevent monopolistic firms from profiteering at the expense of consumers and it can be used to outlaw price-fixing cartels between firms and other arrangements between firms which limit competition. Similarly, competition policy can involve the prohibition of mergers and takeovers likely to have anti-competitive consequences (see Chapter 9).

1.6 WHAT DETERMINES MARKET PERFORMANCE?

Conventional market analysis is primarily concerned with the efficiency of markets in utilising scarce economic resources to meet consumers' demands for goods and services; that is, how well markets have *performed* in contributing to the enhancement of economic welfare. Market performance does not arise in a vacuum but derives fundamentally from the interaction of *structural* and *conduct* variables – see Figure 1.4. Market analysis is particularly concerned with elements of market structure and market conduct that have a strategic importance in determining market performance.

Market structure parameters considered to have a key influence on market conduct and performance include:

- *Market concentration*: the number and size distribution of sellers and buyers (whether there are many sellers/buyers, or a few, or only one).
- *Nature of the product*: whether it is a standardised product, or capable of being differentiated.
- *Condition of entry*: the ease or difficulty (because of barriers to entry) of new firms entering the market.
- *Condition of exit*: the ease or difficulty (because of barriers to exit) of existing firms leaving the market.
- *Vertical integration*: the extent to which firms operate also in the markets which supply their inputs or buy their outputs.
- *Diversification*: the extent to which firms operate in other product markets.
- *Internationalisation*: the extent to which firms are engaged in buying and selling in a number of geographic markets.

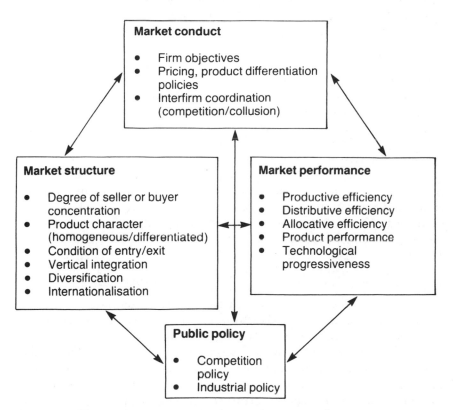

Figure 1.4 The market structure-conduct-performance schema

Market conduct elements considered to have a strategic influence on market structure and performance include:

- *Firm objectives*: the goals firms set for themselves in terms of profits, sales, growth of assets, etc.
- *Marketing-mix policies*: the instruments used by firms to achieve competitive success – pricing, advertising and sales promotion.
- *Interfirm coordination*: the nature and intensity of the use of the above instruments as influenced by competitive and collaborative tendencies between sellers.

Market performance itself can be judged in a number of ways. Ideally, a good performance in the round is typified by:

- *Productive efficiency*: the production of the market's output at the lowest possible cost.
- *Selling efficiency*: the use of cost-effective advertising and selling techniques.
- *Allocative efficiency*: the compatibility of market prices with the real economic costs of supplying the product, including a 'normal' profit return to suppliers – that is, prices charged should be 'fair', not 'excessive'.
- *Product performance*: the satisfaction of consumers' demands for product variety and sophistication.
- *Technological progressiveness*: the invention and innovation of new process technologies which enable supply costs to be cut, and new products which are superior to existing offerings.

The market structure-conduct-performance schema provides a useful analytical framework both for companies seeking to formulate appropriate competitive strategies and for public policy makers responsible for promoting economic efficiency. For example, structure and conduct patterns enable an analysis to be made of the forces driving competition in a market, which, together with observation of market performance results, enables a company to assess the 'attractiveness' of the market in terms of growth and profit potential and the actual and potential strengths and weaknesses of established suppliers. Some established firms may be relatively cost-inefficient, because of their failure to exploit economies of scale, or, because of inertia or limited marketing vision, may neglect potentially lucrative market niches. Consideration of such factors may allow a new company to successfully enter this market by establishing an optimal scale plant (giving it cost advantages over existing suppliers) or by segmenting the market (focusing on underexploited segments of the market). The schema is relevant also to government competition and industrial policy makers in applying appropriate remedial measures to correct poor market performance. For example, structural initiatives involving mergers and rationalisation schemes may be the preferred means of reorganising markets to eliminate excess capacity; alternatively, mergers between the leading firms in a market may be vetoed because they would lead to an undesirable degree of monopolisation. Likewise, conduct measures may be used to improve cost efficiency and lower 'excessive' market prices and profit levels by, for example, the prohibition of price-fixing cartels.

The key elements of market structure, market conduct and market performance and their inter-relationships are examined in detail in Chapters 5–8, and various competition policy concerns (market dominance, cartels and takeovers and mergers) are looked at in Chapters 9 and 10. First, however, the basic forces of supply and demand, and their interactions in determining market prices and quantities transacted, are highlighted in Chapters 2–4.

Chapter 2

Demand

Businesses operate in markets. The quantity of output a business produces, together with the combined output of other firms in the market, will determine market supply. How much output will be supplied in total depends fundamentally on the costs of producing that output and, crucially, on whether the level of market demand is such that the product can be sold at a profit. Market demand itself depends on a range of factors, including the availability and the prices of substitute products, income levels and, crucially, the product's own price. Since the product's own price is determined in large measure by supply costs it will be readily apparent that cost-price linkages are fundamental to an understanding of market demand and market supply and their interactions. These interactions will determine the 'attractiveness' of a market to a firm and will influence its decision to enter a market, stay in the market or leave the market. Before these issues are addressed it is necessary to examine certain basic demand and supply concepts as portrayed in conventional market analysis.

2.1 DEMAND : BASIC CONCEPTS

In economic analysis, 'demand' reflects people's desire (backed by a willingness and ability to pay) to consume a particular product which yields them satisfaction, for example, a basic food product or a luxury holiday. However, in a private enterprise economy such products are not 'free' – they are available to be bought only at a price. This price may be high or low, depending on the resource cost of supplying the product and its relative scarcity.

2.1.1 Factors affecting demand

Many factors affect the amount of a good which consumers wish to buy. The demand function is used to indicate all of the factors affecting demand, and is written, notationally as:

$$Qd = f(P,Y,Ps,Pc,A,D,C,B,Q,S \text{ etc.})$$

where Qd is the quantity of the product demanded, the dependent variable, which is affected by various independent variables, namely: P which is the product's own price; Y which is the level of consumers' disposable income; Ps which are the prices of substitute products; Pc which are the prices of complementary products conventionally consumed with the product in question; A which is advertising; D which is the size of the population; C which is consumer credit terms (particularly important for consumer durable products); B which is product packaging; Q which is product quality; and S which is stocks of the product held by consumers.

Changes in any of these factors will affect Qd but it is possible to isolate the effect of any one variable upon Qd by assuming that all the other factors affecting demand are held constant (the so-called *ceteris paribus*, other things equal, assumption).

For example, if we wish to study the effects of variations in product price upon quantity of the product demanded then assuming that the other terms in the demand function do not change, we can concentrate attention upon the particular effect of price variations upon demand, thus:

$$\overset{\uparrow}{\underset{\downarrow}{Qd}} = f(\overset{\uparrow}{\underset{\downarrow}{P}},Y,Ps,Pc,A,D,C,B,Q,S)$$

Similarly we could study the effects of variations in disposable income upon quantity of the product demanded by holding constant product price, prices of substitutes, etc. in order to focus attention upon the income-demand relationship, thus:

$$\overset{\uparrow}{\underset{\downarrow}{Qd}} = f(P,\overset{\uparrow}{\underset{\downarrow}{Y}},Ps,Pc,A,D,C,B,Q,S$$

By applying the statistical technique of multiple regression analysis to data about the dependent variable, quantity demanded, and the various independent variables which may affect demand – price, disposable income, etc., it is possible to hold the effects of other variables constant and investigate the effects of any particular independent variable (see demand forecasting section).

2.1.2. The market demand curve

Given a possible range of prices for a product, a demand curve can be drawn for the product which plots the total market demand for the product against the products' own price. Figure 2.1 depicts a 'normal' market demand curve for a product. The curve slopes downwards from left to right, indicating that as the price of the product falls (from OP₁ to OP₂), the quantity demanded will increase (from OQ₁ to OQ₂). See Boxes 2.1 and 2.2.

In Figure 2.1 the quantity demanded is determined by the product's own price. The demand curve is drawn on the assumption that all other factors affecting demand are held constant.

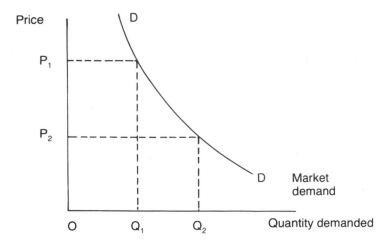

Figure 2.1 Market demand

Demand curves for normal products slope downward from left to right, indicating that as the price of the product falls, more of it is demanded, and vice versa. This happens because as its price falls, the product becomes cheaper relative to other goods that consumers could buy so that con-sumers will tend to substitute this new, cheaper product for others. In addition, where purchase of a product accounts for a sizeable proportion of consumers' disposable income, then a fall in its price will effectively increase consumers' real income, leaving them with more income to spend on buying more of this product or more of other products.

A few products tend to have unusual demand curves, like those in Figure 2.2, where part of their demand curve may not be downward-sloping. Figure 2.2(a) shows the demand curve for an inferior product where the bottom of its demand curve is upward sloping. Here further cuts in price below price OP₁ cause consumers to have misgivings about the quality of the product because it is priced below the price that they expect to pay

Box 2.1   Why demand curves slope downward

In demand theory, the consumer's economic 'problem' is that he or she has only a limited amount of income to spend and, therefore, cannot buy all of the products they would like to consume. Given a fixed income and faced by known product prices, rational consumers will allocate their purchases between products in such a way as to maximise their satisfaction. If the price of a particlar product falls, this is equivalent to an increase in their real income, that is, the consumer's income now has greater purchasing power, so that at the lower price more of the product can be purchased.

In Figure (a) the 'budget line' AB shows the quantities of two products, X and Y, which can be bought with a given income Z and known prices for the two products. 'Indifference curve' I_1 shows combinations of X and Y which yield equal satisfaction to the consumer and, therefore, between which the consumer is indifferent. The consumer will choose to buy quantities OX_1 and OY_1 which yield the greatest satisfaction consistent with his or her limited income. If the price of product Y were to fall from PY_1 to PY_2 then this allows the consumer to buy more of product Y, shifting the budget line outward from AB to AC. This enables the consumer to achieve a higher level of satisfaction on indifference curve I_2 and the consumer will now buy OX_2 of product X and OY_2 of product Y. It can be seen that this change in purchasing patterns generally involves buying more of product Y, whose price has fallen, and less of X, which is now comparatively more expensive. The resulting demand curve for product Y in Figure (b) indicates that as the price of Y falls from PY_1 to PY_2, quantity demanded increases from quantity OY_1 to OY_2.

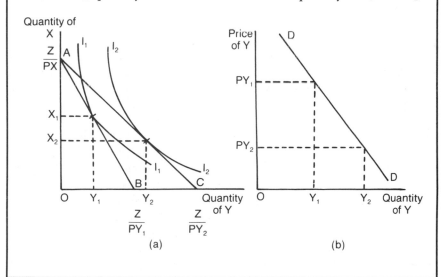

Box 2.2   Consumer surplus

The downward-sloping nature of most demand curves reflects the fact that consumers' desire for a product varies, some consumers attaching a high priority to purchases of the product and being prepared to pay a high price for it, whilst for others the product is less important, so that they would be prepared to pay only a lower price. For example, in the figure consumer A who attaches most importance to the product would be prepared to pay a high price, OP_1, for the first unit offered for sale; by contrast, consumer B would only be prepared to pay a price of OP. If suppliers offer the quantity SS, so that the equilibrium market price is OP, then consumer B will pay a price which exactly reflects his or her valuation of the product, while consumer A who would have been prepared to pay a price of OP_1 for the product pays only the same price, OP, and secures a 'consumer surplus' equal to PP_1 for that unit. The shaded area shows the total consumer surplus secured by all consumers who would have been prepared to pay a price for the product above OP.

Where firms are able to distinguish between consumers or groups of consumers and supply them separately, then they may be able to charge different prices to each consumer or group of consumers, rather than a single common price. Such price discrimination enables supplies to reduce consumer surplus and appropriate this surplus for themselves in the form of increased revenues.

See Section 2.2.

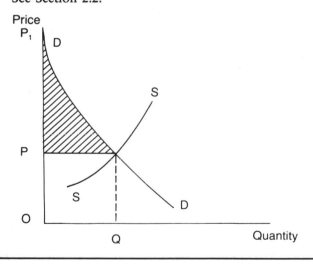

for such a product, causing them to buy less of it as its price falls.* By contrast Figure 2.2(b) shows the demand curve for a superior product where the top part of the demand curve is upward-sloping. Here rises in price above price OP$_2$ reinforce the 'exclusiveness' and the quality of the product, causing consumers to buy more of it rather than less. This demand pattern may be detected for certain very expensive motor cars, perfumes and cosmetics, where consumers indulge in conspicuous consumption of the products – buying them in order to reinforce and enhance their image amongst their peers. Both these examples serve to remind us that, in making their buying decisions, consumers are influenced not only by the price of the product but by their perceptions of the attributes of that product, so that both product and price must be considered together in any pricing decision.

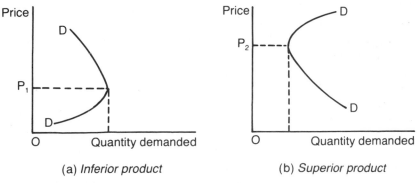

(a) *Inferior product*   (b) *Superior product*

Figure 2.2 Unusual demand curves

The two-dimensional presentation of the demand curve, as shown in Figure 2.1, is done partly because of expository focus (that is, market analysis is concerned primarily with price-output relationships) and partly because a product's price is usually the chief determinant of demand. However, changes in the other variables affecting demand can easily be accommodated in the analysis by moving the position of the demand curve, specifically *shifting* the demand curve at *all* price levels. For example, if consumers' disposable income increases, the demand curve will shift to the

*Economists often restrict the use of the term 'inferior product' to those products whose demand curve is upward-sloping over most price ranges, usually cheap products which take up a large proportion of consumers' incomes and which are regarded as inferior to alternative products. In such cases rises in the product's price forces consumers to buy more of the inferior product because the price rise reduces their real income and forces them to curtail consumption of more expensive, superior alternatives. However, any rise in the disposable incomes of such consumers will cause them to reject inferior products in favour of alternatives. For example, in certain African countries which traditionally grow and consume maize as their staple food product, growing affluence amongst urban consumers has caused a switch to more expensive, imported, wheat.

right, so that more is demanded at each price than formerly. In Figure 2.3 an increase in income shifts the demand curve from DD to D_1D_1, increasing the quantity demanded from OQ to OQ_1. The magnitude of this shift will depend upon the *income-elasticity of demand* (see below).

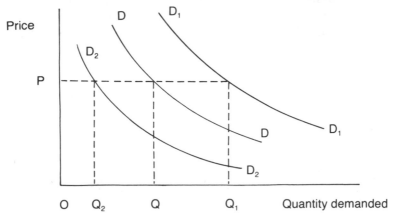

Figure 2.3 Shifts in market demand

By contrast, a fall in the price of a substitute product will serve to shift the demand curve to the left, so that less is demanded at each price than formerly. In Figure 2.2, a fall in the price of a substitute product shifts the demand curve from DD to D_2D_2, reducing the quantity demanded from OQ to OQ_2. The magnitude of this shift will depend upon the *cross-elasticity of demand* (see below).

2.1.3. The income demand curve

An income demand curve, or Engels curve, shows the amount of product demanded at various levels of disposable income. The curve is drawn on the assumption that all other factors affecting demand are held constant, including product price. Figure 2.4 shows the income demand curves for a number of products. The curve labelled A shows the income demand curve for a normal product where quantity demanded increases proportionately with disposable income, so that the curve is a straight line. The curve labelled B shows the income demand curve for a superior product, with a decreasing slope such that increases in disposable income lead to greater than proportionate changes in demand. Finally the curve labelled C shows the income demand curve for an inferior product, with increases in disposable income up to income level Y_1 leading to less than proportionate increases in quantity demanded, while demand declines at income levels above OY_1.

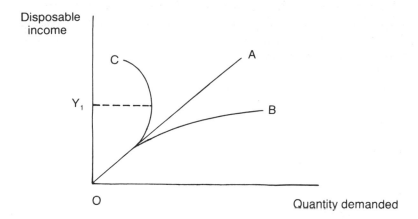

Figure 2.4 Income demand curves

2.1.4 Demand and revenue

Demand is important to a business, since it is the firm's source of *revenue* (no sales – no revenue). There are three demand-revenue concepts of relevance to market analysis: total revenue, average revenue and marginal revenue.

Total revenue

Total revenue is the aggregate revenue obtained by a firm from the sale of a particular quantity of output, equal to price times quantity sold. Under conditions of perfect competition (see Chapter 5), the firm faces a horizontal demand curve at the going market price. Each extra unit of output sold (marginal revenue) adds exactly the same amount to total revenue as previous units. Hence, total revenue is a straight upward-sloping line (Figure 2.5(a)). By contrast, under conditions of imperfect competition the firm faces a downward-sloping demand curve and price has to be lowered to sell more units. As price is lowered, each extra unit of output sold adds successively smaller amounts to total revenue than previous units. Thus, total revenue rises by a decreasing rate, and eventually falls (Figure 2.5(b)).

The significance of total revenue in market analysis is that it, in combination with *total cost*, determines the level of output at which the firm achieves *profit maximisation* (see Chapter 5).

Average revenue

Average revenue is the total revenue received (price times number of units sold) divided by the number of units. Price and average revenue are in fact

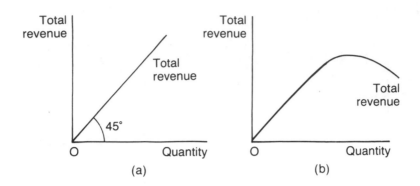

Figure 2.5 Total revenue

equal, as shown in Figure 2.6: the price £10 = average revenue = (£10 × 10 units) ÷ 10 units = £10. It follows that the demand curve is also the average revenue facing the firm.

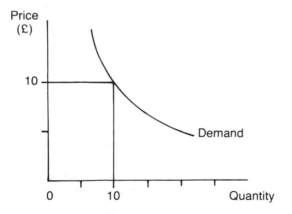

Figure 2.6 Average revenue

Marginal revenue

Marginal revenue is the addition to total revenue from the sale of one extra unit of output. Under conditions of perfect competition, as noted above, each extra unit of output sold adds exactly the same amount to total revenue as previous units (Figure 2.7(a)). Under conditions of imperfect competition the firm faces a downward-sloping demand curve and price has to be lowered in order to sell more units. Marginal revenue is less than price – as price is lowered, each extra unit sold adds successively smaller amounts than previous units (Figure 2.7(b)).

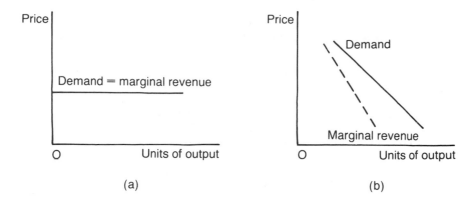

Figure 2.7 Marginal revenue

2.1.5 Elasticity of demand

Demand elasticity measures the degree of responsiveness of quantity demanded of a particular product to a given change in one of the independent variables which affect demand for that product. The responsiveness of demand to a change in the product's own price is referred to as price-elasticity of demand; the responsiveness of demand to a change in income is known as income-elasticity of demand; and the responsiveness of demand for a particular product to changes in the price of other related products is called cross-elasticity of demand.

Price-elasticity of demand

Price-elasticity of demand measures the sensitivity of demand to a given change in the product's own price.

$$\text{price-elasticity of demand} = \frac{\%\ \text{change in quantity demanded}}{\%\ \text{change in product's price}}$$

If a change in price results in a more than proportionate change in quantity demanded, as shown in Figure 2.8(a), then demand is *price-elastic*; if a change in price leads to a less than proportionate change in the quantity demanded, as in Figure 2.8(b), then demand is *price-inelastic*.

At the extremes, demand can be perfectly price-inelastic, that is, price changes have no effect at all on quantity demanded, which shows up as a straight-line vertical demand curve; or demand can be perfectly price-elastic, that is, any amount will be demanded at the prevailing price but nothing at all at a slightly higher price, which shows up as a straight-line horizontal demand curve.

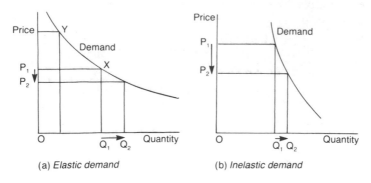

(a) *Elastic demand*　　　　　(b) *Inelastic demand*

Figure 2.8 Price-elasticity of demand

Total revenue (price times quantity demand) will be affected by price changes. Where demand is price-elastic, a small cut in price will generate a large increase in quantity demanded, so that a price cut will serve to increase total revenue (while a price rise serves to reduce total revenue). By contrast, where demand is price-inelastic, a large cut in price will generate only a small increase in quantity demanded so that the price cut will serve to reduce total revenue (while a price rise serves to increase total revenue). Where demand has unitary elasticity then the percentage price cut (increase) will be matched by an exactly offsetting percentage change in quantity demanded so that total revenue remains the same.

It must be stressed, however, that the price-elasticity of demand can vary along the length of a given market demand curve. For example, although in Figure 2.8(a) the demand curve as a whole is elastic in configuration, it is more elastic at point X than it is at point Y. What factors determine the price-elasticity of market demand for a product? The principal determinant is the availability and price of substitute products. If a generic product, such as oil, has no close substitutes (although in some uses gas and electricity, for example, can be substituted for oil) then the market demand for the product will be highly price-inelastic. By contrast, where two generic products, for example tea and coffee, are closely substitutable in terms of use and have similar product prices, then the demand for these products will be relatively price-elastic.

Cross-elasticity of demand

The consideration of substitutability between products is relevant to the degree of price-elasticity which exists not only *between* product markets, but also *within a particular* product market. Outside monopoly markets, account must be taken of the fact that each supplier offering a single or a number of versions (or 'brands') of the product will have its own *individual demand curve*. Typically, the demand for each of the individual brands making up the market is likely to be much more elastic, because they face competitive substitutes within the market. Thus, even if overall market demand is price inelastic (for example, the elasticity value for cigarettes in the UK is around 0.3), the demand for an individual brand such as Marlboro or Benson and Hedges is likely to be price-elastic (that is, over 1.0) since consumers can readily switch to another brand if the price of a particular brand is increased.

The extent to which market demand for a product and the demand for an individual brand is affected by a change in the price of a *substitute* product or brand can be measured in terms of the *cross-elasticity* of demand:

$$\frac{\% \text{ change in quantity demanded of product (brand) A}}{\% \text{ change in price of product (brand) B}}$$

If a given change in the price of product B (tea, for example) results in some change in the quantity demanded of product A (coffee, for example) then consumers regard the two products as substitutes; specifically, if a small change in the price of B (tea) results in a large change in the quantity of product A (coffee) indicating a high cross-elasticity value, then A and B can be regarded as close substitutes. In the case of substitute products, the cross-elasticity measure will be positive, since as the price of product (or brand) B rises there will be an increase in demand for its substitute product (or brand) A.

Cross-elasticities are also helpful in analysing relationships between complementary products (products whose demands are interrelated – for example, motor vehicles and petrol, tennis rackets and tennis balls). Thus, if the price of tennis rackets increases, this will not only reduce the demand for rackets but will also tend to reduce the demand for tennis balls. In the case of complementary products the cross-elasticity measure will be negative, since as the price of product (or brand) B rises, there will be a decrease in demand for the product (or brand) and a decrease in the demand for its complementary product (or brand) A.

There are practical difficulties in the way of measuring price-elasticity and cross-elasticity values. For example, there is usually insufficient data available to construct a comprehensive 'market demand curve' covering a wide range of price-quantity demanded combinations and to isolate individual brand cross-elasticity effects in a multi-brand setting, particularly where competing suppliers use product differentiation techniques (advertising, etc.) to build brand-loyalty and 'dampen down' brand-switching tendencies.

Income-elasticity of demand

Income-elasticity of demand measures the sensitivity of demand to a change in the level of consumers' disposable income:

$$\text{income-elasticity of demand} = \frac{\%\ \text{change in quantity demanded}}{\%\ \text{change in disposable income}}$$

If a given change in disposable income results in a more than proportionate change in quantity demanded, then demand is income-elastic, while if a given change in disposable income results in a less than proportional change in quantity demanded, then demand is income-inelastic.

Income-elasticity is positive for a 'normal' product and negative for a so-called 'inferior' product (that is, a product, say home-made wine, whose demand tends to fall absolutely as consumers' income rises and they can afford to buy better quality branded wines). Products which have income-elasticity of demand of less than one are referred to as 'staple' products (bread, potatoes) while products with an income-elasticity of more than one are called 'luxury' products (electrical appliances, motor cars).

Increases in consumers' disposable income will increase demand for most products. The effect of this on product prices is looked at later in this chapter. Additionally the concept is of importance to company managers in indicating which markets are likely to decline or expand over time and, hence, is relevant to the formulation of business strategies (diversification and divestment). Box 2.3 shows income elasticity of demand for a range of products in the UK.

Box 2.3 Income elasticity of demand

UK consumers' expenditure at 1985 market prices					
	£ million at 1985 prices			% change in volume 1981–91	Income elasticity of demand %
	1981	1986	1991		
Durable goods:					
Cars, motorcycles and other vehicles	7,754	10,735	10,657	37.44	1.25
Furniture and floor coverings	4,031	4,336	4,893	21.38	0.72

Other goods:

Food	30,217	31,541	33,409	10.56	0.35
Beer	8,561	8,406	8,211	−4.09	−0.14
Other alcoholic drink	6,363	7,293	7,616	19.69	0.66
Tobacco	8,167	6,813	6,569	−19.57	−0.66
Clothing	9,563	13,327	14,410	50.21	1.68
Footwear	2,195	2,893	2,895	31.89	1.07
Energy products	17,319	19,299	21,331	23.16	0.78

				% change 1981–91
Real national disposable income (£m. at 1985 prices)	318,462	370,721	413,556	29.86

$$\text{income-elasticity of demand} = \frac{\text{\% change in demand volume}}{\text{\% change in real disposable income}}$$

Source: National Income Blue Book (1992) CSO

Some products, such as clothing, cars and footwear have income elasticity figures greater than one, indicating that demand for these products has grown more rapidly than disposable incomes. These income-sensitive products are likely to experience rapid demand growth as disposable incomes rise, but equally will tend to suffer rapid decline in demand as disposable incomes fall. Other products such as food, furniture and energy products have income elasticities less than one, indicating that demand for these products has grown less rapidly than disposable incomes. These income-insensitive products are likely to experience slow demand growth as disposable incomes rise, but tend to be more recession-proof insofar as they tend to suffer smaller declines in demand as disposable incomes fall. Yet other products, such as tobacco and beer, have negative elasticities, demand for these products falling despite rising disposable income.

2.2 SEGMENTING DEMAND

In some markets, 'the product' supplied is completely standardised or homogeneous and offered to the whole of the market. More usually, suppliers will offer 'differentiated' products which may be broadly similar or significantly different. Where market demand is non- uniform, it is possible to divide a market into identifiable submarkets or segments, each having their own particular customer profile and buyer characteristics. For example, the UK beer market (see Box 2.4) can be segmented by *type* of beer, the *form* in which it is supplied, and the *distribution channels* used to retail it.

Box 2.4 Segmentation of demand in the UK beer market, 1991

Beer category	% of market demand	Product format	% of market demand	Retail outlet	% of market demand
Ales (bitter, mild, stout, etc.)	49	*Draught* (on tap)	71	*On-sale outlets* (public houses, hotels, etc.)	80
Lagers	51	*Packaged* (cans/bottles)	29	*Off-sale outlets* (supermarkets, off-licences etc.)	20

Source: Brewers Society and HM Customs and Excise

Firms may choose to operate in all segments of the market, or they may choose to 'position' themselves in a particular segment (see Chapter 1). In conventional market analysis the significance of different market segments, each with their own particular demand curves, is the opportunity this presents to firms to practise price discrimination between market segments. Strictly speaking, price discrimination refers to the ability of a supplier to sell the *same* product in a number of *separate* markets at *different* prices. Markets can be separated in a number of ways, such as by different consumer requirements (for example, bulk and low-volume gas supplies to industrial and household consumers, respectively); by the nature of the product itself (for example, original and replacement components for motor cars, and hardback and paperback books) and by geographical location (for example, domestic and foreign markets). In order for price discrimination to be viable, markets must differ in their demand profiles (that is, exhibit different demand elasticities, so that higher prices can be charged where demand is more price-inelastic and lower prices charged when demand is more price-elastic), and the supplier must be able to 'seal off' each market, so that customers in lower-priced markets cannot resell the product to customers in higher-priced markets.

Figure 2.9 shows how price discrimination may be employed to increase the total revenue from a segmented market. Market 1 is characterised by inelastic demand, as indicated by the steep slope of the demand curve, while consumers in market 2 are much more price sensitive, as indicated by the shallow slope of the demand curve. By charging the same price OP in both markets, the supplier would yield a total revenue equal to the two areas, namely the sum of $OPAQ_1$ and $OPBQ_2$. However, by charging a higher price OP3 in the less price sensitive market 1 and a lower price OP4 in the more price sensitive market 2, the supplier can secure a much larger total revenue equal to the sum of OP_3CQ_3 and OP_4DQ_4.

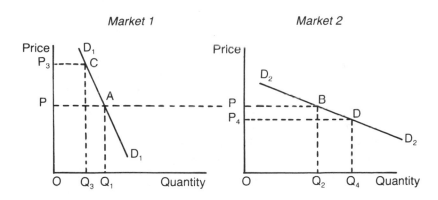

Figure 2.9 Price discrimination

The concept of differential pricing can be applied more broadly to encompass segmentation of demand based upon variations in, for example, product format and means of delivery, each offering different degrees of value added. Thus, for example, bitter beer sold in can form may be more expensive than the equivalent draught version, and bitter sold in can form may be cheaper when sold by a supermarket for drinking at home, compared to the same can sold in a public house for consumption on the premises, where the customer is also paying for the drinking facilities provided.

2.3 MARKET SIZE AND DEMAND TRENDS OVER TIME

The current overall size of a market and the relative size of various market segments, together with changes in primary market demand and shifts in sector shares, including the creation of new market segments, are important factors determining the 'attractiveness' of a market over time. Although conventional market analysis ignores such considerations, they are critical to an understanding of market processes viewed as a *dynamic* phenomenon.

A useful starting point in looking at these issues is the concept of the *industry/product life cycle*. This hypothesises that industries and the individual products and brands making up the market typically go through a dynamic sequence of change characterised by four phases: birth or introduction, growth, maturity/saturation and decline. Each of these phases has different implications for firm behaviour and market competition (see Box 2.5). Studies of industries and brands tend to confirm the broad configuration of change postulated by life cycle analysis although, of course, there is nothing definitive about the overall length of the cycle, nor of its individual phases. For example, the UK brewing industry has been around for many centuries. Initially it was a 'cottage' industry, but the eighteenth century saw the dawn of large-scale brewing, facilitated by the development of new brewing techniques, the spread of industrialisation which raised per capita incomes and stimulated consumption, and later the development of new transportation modes (particularly the railway) which widened distribution networks. However, between the 1870s and the 1950s beer consumption went into decline, primarily as a result of a 'clamp-down' on drinking by the application of governmental licensing restrictions on retail outlets, and the spread of other leisure activities. Between 1960 and the end of the 1980s, however, beer consumption rose strongly (from 27.6 million bulk barrels in 1960 to 40.7 million barrels in 1980), but consumption has since fallen (to 36 million barrels in 1993). Nevertheless, the beer market remains a big market in terms of sales value (around £13 billion in 1993).

Box 2.5 The product life cycle

The product life cycle depicts the typical sales pattern followed by a product over time as changing consumer tastes and technological innovation cause new products to emerge which supersede existing products. The typical life cycle followed by a product introduced into a market is depicted in the figure below. It consists of four main phases:

1   Product launch, which follows the successful development of a new product and its national launch. When the product is first put on the market, sales volume will be low until consumer resistance has been overcome. At this stage the market is frequently limited to high-income consumers with more adventurous buying habits.

2   Product growth phase, where the product gains market acceptance and sales grow rapidly as the product reaches the mass market. During this phase competitors may begin to enter the field with rival products, so that the distinctiveness of the original product fades.

3   Product maturity, where sales are largely limited to repeat purchases by existing customers, since the majority of potential customers have already made their first purchases. At this stage the market is saturated, so that competitors are unable to benefit from market growth and must compete intensely to maintain or increase their share of the constant market.

4   Product decline, where sales begin to decline as consumer tastes change or superior products are launched. If left to follow this downward trend the product will eventually die as sales fall to low levels, though long before this managers may decide to phase out the product.

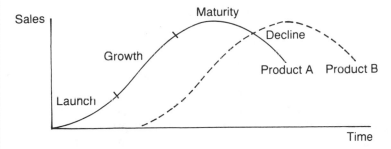

Most companies market a number of different products and must formulate a product-range strategy, providing for a regulated process of new product launches, with new products like B in the figure growing as older products like A reach maturity, so as to maintain an appropriate product mix of newly launched products, growth products and mature lines.

A company's pricing policy for a product may be related to the stages of the product's life cycle. During the launch phase, managers will tend to opt for a high skimming price which capitalises on the new and distinctive nature of the product and the temporary monopoly power which this conveys. In this early stage, demand for the product is likely to be less price-elastic, for high prices will not deter high-income pioneer consumers. Furthermore, a high price will reinforce the quality image of the largely untried product, as well as recouping research and development and heavy promotion expenditures. During the growth phase managers may change to a low penetration price, lowering price to bring the product within reach of the mass of consumers. At this stage demand is likely to be more price-elastic, for the average consumer is more price-conscious than the pioneer consumer. By lowering price the firm can expand sales appreciably, gaining cost-savings from large-scale production and can maintain a large market share in the face of entry by competitors. Once the maturity phase is reached with several similar products firmly established in the market, then prices will tend to stay in line with one another, for any attempt by one firm to reduce its price and expand its market share will provoke retaliation as competitors fight to maintain their market share.

Similarly, other elements of the marketing mix, such as advertising and sales promotion, need to be adapted to the phases of the product life cycle.

Other British industries of great longevity which are now in secular decline include coal-mining, steel and textiles, while shipbuilding has almost disappeared. In recent years a number of new industries have been established as a result of the synthesis of a perceived consumer demand and technological advance. For example, the frozen food market in the United Kingdom began to expand rapidly in the 1960s with the increase in the number of working women, which led to a growth in the demand for convenience foods. Market demand has continued to increase strongly (total sales in 1992 were £2 billion), facilitated by the spread of household freezers (ownership increased from 33 per cent of UK households in 1976 to 84 per cent in 1991); the promotion of frozen products by the major supermarket groups (including own-label brands), and a substantial increase in the range of food items supplied in frozen form (ready-made meals, pizzas, burgers, cakes and desserts, etc.). The invention of the computer and advances in consumer electronics have spawned a whole range of new industries including personal computers, electronic games and toys, and audio systems such as compact discs. The personal computer market in the United Kingdom, which began in 1983 when the IBM PC became widely available, has grown spectacularly, PC hardware sales totalling £765 million in 1986 and £1.9 billion in 1990, while software sales in 1990 totalled £325 million. The audio software market (cassettes, CDs – see below) likewise has exhibited high growth rates, market sales rising from £288 million in 1983 to over £703 million in 1992. Some other products (most notably consumer durable goods such as televisions, videos, washing machines, vacuum cleaners, etc.) have similarly enjoyed rapid, but short-lived, growth to be followed by maturity/saturation and a dependency on replacement sales to sustain market size.

Within markets, whether declining or expanding, new product development and changing consumer preferences can cause major shifts in the relative importance of various market segments, including the establishment of new ones. For example, in the last thirty years there has been a major switch in consumer demand preferences in the UK beer market in favour of lager brands. In 1960 lager accounted for under 1 per cent of total UK beer sales; there was no indigenous lager production, and UK demand was satisfied largely by imported premium lagers from Germany and Denmark. In 1970 lager still only accounted for 7 per cent of total demand. By 1980 lager sales had shown spectacular growth, accounting for 31 per cent of market sales in that year and by 1991 lager had overtaken the industry's traditional ale products (bitter, mild and stout beers), accounting for 51 per cent of total market sales. This increase in lager consumption in turn has accelerated the underlying trend towards greater seller concentration in the industry (lager production is capital-intensive and the promotion of national lager brands needs to be supported by large advertising budgets).

Radical shifts in the importance of market segments have been characteristic of many other industries. For example, as Table 2.1 shows, the compact disc, which was first introduced into the UK record market in 1983, has expanded rapidly at the expense of the vinyl long-playing record and, latterly, the cassette format.

Table 2.1   UK sales of audio software, 1983–92

Year	Singles	LPs	Cassettes £m.	CDs	Total sales
1983	65.1	138.0	84.0	1.5	288.6
1986	76.1	140.6	152.1	56.5	425.3
1989	80.3	108.0	251.8	230.7	670.8
1992	78.7	36.6	229.7	358.4	703.4

Source: Retail Business, vol. 419, 1993

Fluctuations in demand associated with the business cycle may also have a significant impact on some markets. As Table 2.2 shows, demand in the United Kingdom for audio products (music centres, cassette and CD players, personal stereos, etc.) declined substantially in 1991 and 1992 after expanding strongly in the 1970s and 1980s.

This is particularly the case in capital intensive industries where fixed costs constitute a high proportion of total supply costs and hence break-even throughput rates are required to maintain viable output levels. Any large shortfall in demand relative to installed capacity will thus have adverse effects on firm and market profitability. For example, the protracted slump in the housing market in the United Kingdom in the late 1980s and early 1990s has left many construction companies with sizeable losses and has also led to losses and low profitability in related markets, particularly building materials markets (bricks, roofing tiles, concrete, etc.) as well as estate agencies. Similarly, in 1991, the recession in the Japanese car market resulted in Nissan posting its first loss since 1946.

Table 2.2   UK sales of audio products, 1986–92

Year	Sales £m.
1986	1040
1987	1125
1988	1210
1989	1265
1990	1335
1991	1075
1992	975

Source: *Retail Business*

In sum, secular (and cyclical) changes in demand can have a profound effect on market viability and industry price and profit levels. Expanding market demand tends to attract new suppliers, while market maturity and decline tend to produce rationalisation of capacity and the exit of uneconomic suppliers. However, the effective adjustment of supply to demand conditions may be impaired by the existence of barriers to entry and exit (see Chapter 6). From the firm's perspective, demand changes over time have an important influence on its diversification and divestment strategies.

2.4 DEMAND FORECASTING

In order to plan changes in plant capacity, managers need to forecast what future long-term demand for their product is likely to be (and what market share their particular brands are likely to gain). Also, in order to schedule production and plan their levels of finished product stock, managers need to be able to predict short-term changes in demand. Various forecasting methods can be used to estimate future demand conditions, varying greatly in terms of their subjectivity, sophistication, data requirements and cost.

One method employs survey techniques involving the use of interviews or mailed questionnaires asking consumers or industrial buyers about their future buying intentions. Alternatively, members of the sales force may provide estimates of future market sales; or industry experts can offer scenario-type forecasts about future market developments.

A second method employs time-series analysis, using past sales data to predict future demand trends. These methods implicitly assume that the historical relationships which have held in the past will continue to hold in the future. Time-series data usually comprise a long-run secular trend, with certain medium-term cyclical fluctuations and short-term seasonal variations, affected by irregular, random influences.

Figure 2.10 shows a typical time-series analysis. The fluctuations in time-series data, which inevitably show up when such series are plotted on a graph, can be classified into four basic types of variation which act simultaneously to influence the time-series.

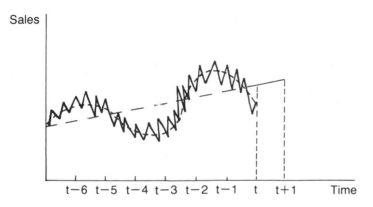

Figure 2.10 Time-series analysis

These components of a time series are:

- *secular trend,* which shows the relatively smooth, regular movement of the time series over the long term;
- *cyclical variation,* which consists of medium-term regular repeating patterns, generally associated with business cycles. The recurring upswings and downswings in economic activity are superimposed upon the secular trend;
- *seasonal variation,* which consists of short-term, regular repeating patterns, generally associated with different seasons of the year. These seasonal variations are superimposed upon the secular trend and cyclical variations;
- *irregular variations,* which are erratic fluctuations in the time series caused by unpredictable, chance events. These irregular variations are superimposed upon the secular trend, cyclical variations and seasonal variations.

Time-series analysis is concerned with isolating the effect of each of these four influences upon a time-series with a view to using them to project this past experience into the future. In order to identify the underlying secular trend in a time series, it is possible to use regression analysis to fit a line to the time-series observations. Alternatively, a moving average can be used to smooth the time series and help identify the underlying trend. For example, a five-period moving average could be used, replacing each consecutive observation by the average of that observation and the two preceding and two succeeding observations. Exponential smoothing provides yet another technique which can be used to smooth time-series data. It is similar to the moving-average method, but gives greater weight to more recent observations in calculating the average.

In order to identify the seasonal variations we can construct a measure of seasonal variation (called the 'seasonal index') and use this to deseasonalise the time- series data and show how the time series would look if there were no seasonal fluctuations.

Once the trend has been identified it is possible to extrapolate that trend and estimate trend values for time periods beyond the present time period. In Figure 2.10, for example, the trend for time periods up to and including time t can be extrapolated to time t + 1. Extrapolating thus becomes a method of making predictions or forecasts, though the accuracy of these forecasts will depend critically upon whether underlying forces which affected the time series in the past will continue to operate in the same way in the future. Specifically, time-series analysis is generally unable to predict sharp upturns or downturns in demand associated with rapid changes in demand-influencing variables like price or income.

A third (econometric) method of predicting future levels of demand examines other variables which are causally related to demand. Econometric models link variables in the form of equations which can be estimated statistically and then used as a basis for forecasting. Judgement has to be exercised in identifying the independent variables which causally affect the dependent variable to be forecast. For example, in order to predict future quantity of a product demanded (Qd) we would formulate an equation linking it to product price (P) and disposable income (Y):

$$Qd = a + bP + cY$$

then use past data on sales, prices and income to estimate the regression coefficients a, b and c. Box 2.6 shows an econometric model which was used to forecast demand for cigarettes.

No forecasting method will generate completely accurate predictions, so when making any forecast we must allow for a margin of error in that forecast. Consequently forecasters need to exercise judgement in predicting future demand conditions, both in choosing which forecasting methods to use and in combining information from different forecasts.

Box 2.6   Forecasting cigarette demand in the United Kingdom

A model for cigarette demand (single equation, linear relationship):

$$\frac{Q_t}{P_t} = \alpha_0 + \alpha_1 C_t + \alpha_2 \frac{Y_t}{P_t} + \alpha_3 \frac{A_t}{P_t} + \text{health scare variables}$$

where Q_t is the number of (manufactured) cigarettes consumed in
   year t
   P_t is the UK population over fifteen years of age in year t
   C_t is the real price of cigarettes in year t
   Y_t is UK real personal disposable income in year t
   A_t is real advertising expenditure in year t
and $\alpha_0 \ldots \alpha_3$ are parameters to be estimated.

Three major health scares were identified as:

HSA = First report by Royal College of Physicians in 1962
HSB = Report by US Surgeon-General's Advisory Committee in
   1964
HSC = Second report by Royal College of Physicians in 1971.

Each of these health scares is suggested as having had a depressing
effect upon demand.

Data
The model was estimated by ordinary least squares regression, using
annual data on cigarette consumption, price, disposable income,
advertising and population for each of the twenty-one years from
1955 to 1975, so that in the model t=1, . . . 21 where 1=1955, . . . 21=
1975.

Empirical results
The equation below shows the estimated equation which results when
the data is incorporated in the above model:

$$\frac{Q}{P} = 7.27 - 0.32C + 0.13\frac{Y}{P} + 0.07\frac{A}{P} - 0.04\text{HSA} - 0.07\text{HSB} - 0.03\text{HSC}$$

R^2 (coefficient of determination) = 0.96, suggesting that the independent variables explain 96 per cent of variations in cigarette consumption.
   The estimated parameters attaching to the price, income and advertising variables indicate the responsiveness of the dependent variable
(cigarettes consumed) to changes in these independent variables. From
the equation, price elasticity is -0.32, whilst income elasticity is 0.13.
Thus it appears that the demand for cigarettes is highly price and
income-inelastic. Advertising has a small but significant effect on

cigarette consumption. Putting data for estimated future price, income, advertising and population into the above equation made it possible to forecast future cigarette consumption for years after 1975.

Source: Witt, S. F. and Pass, C. L. (1981) 'The effects of health warnings and advertising on the demand for cigarettes', *Scottish Journal of Political Economy*, vol. 28.

QUESTIONS

1 What is meant by the term 'effective demand'? Indicate some of the main determinants of the demand for a product.
2 Distinguish between a change in demand (that is, a shift in the demand curve) and a change in the quantity demanded (that is, a movement along an existing demand curve).
3 Examine the concept of demand elasticity for:
   (a) company pricing policies;
   (b) government indirect taxes.
4 (a) What is measured by price-elasticity of demand?
   (b) Outline the factors which usually affect the price-elasticity of demand.
   (c) Assess the relative significance of the factors identified in (b) to veterinary surgeons seeking to boost their income by reducing treatment prices.
5 (a) Define income-elasticity of demand and show how it may be used to identify normal, inferior and luxury products.
   (b) Why is income-elasticity of importance to a firm?
6 Explain what is meant by cross-elasticity of demand; indicate how it might be measured and discuss how information concerning cross-elasticity of demand might be used by a firm producing beer.
7 What is meant by market segmentation? How can markets be segmented?
8 Outline the concept of the 'product life cycle' and examine its significance to a firm.

Chapter 3

Supply and costs

In economic analysis, 'supply' is the amount of a product which firms are prepared to offer for sale in the market at a particular price. Supply depends largely upon the price which firms obtain for their product, the prices which firms must pay for the factor inputs which they need to buy or hire in order to make the product, and the manufacturing technology employed. The goals pursued by firms also influence supply. Insofar as firms are motivated mainly by profit considerations, then they will only be prepared to supply additional units of product if the price is high enough to cover the costs involved and increase profits. A fundamental assumption made in supply analysis is that firms seek to maximise their profits.

3.1 THE MARKET SUPPLY CURVE

The total market supply of a product is reflected in the supply curve. Given a possible range of prices for a product, a supply curve can be drawn for the product which plots the total market supply of the product against the product's price. Figure 3.1 depicts a market supply curve. The typical market supply curve slopes upwards from left to right, indicating that as price rises more of the product will be supplied. Thus, if price rises, from OP_1 to OP_2, the quantity supplied will increase from OQ_1 to OQ_2.

Figure 3.1 shows the supply curve for the market as a whole. This curve is derived by *aggregating* the individual supply curves of all of the producers of the product, which in turn are derived from the producers' *cost curves*. Most supply curves slope upwards because, as the price of the product rises, producers will find it more profitable to supply it, using their existing production facilities, and because any increase in short-run marginal costs (see below) associated with increasing output will be covered by the higher price obtained.

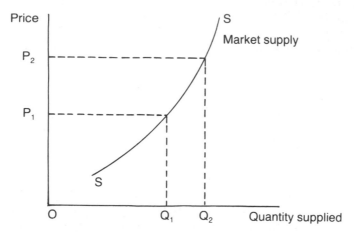

Figure 3.1 Market supply

3.2 THE PRODUCTION FUNCTION AND THE COST FUNCTION

Firms' *physical* ability to supply output will depend on the existing capacity of their plants (see below), the relationship between factor inputs (raw materials, labour, etc.) used in the productive process and the resulting output of finished products.

The *production function* shows for a given state of technological knowledge the relationship between physical quantities of factor inputs and the physical quantities of output involved in producing a good or service. Since the quantity of output depends upon the quantities of inputs used, the relationship can be depicted, notationally as:

$$Q = f(I_1, I_2 \ldots I_n)$$

where Q = output of a product and I_1, I_2, etc. are quantities of the various factor inputs 1, 2 etc, used in producing that output.

It is important to emphasise that factor inputs can be combined in a number of different ways to produce the same amount of output. One method may use only small amounts of labour and large amounts of capital equipment, while another method may employ large quantities of labour and only a little capital. In physical terms, the method which is technically the most efficient is the one which uses the fewest inputs.

However, whether it is *economically viable* to supply the product depends not so much on the physical input-output relationship, but on the *costs* of producing the output. Thus, market analysis focuses on the least costly way of producing a given output. The *cost function* depicts the general relationship between the costs of factor inputs and the cost of output in a firm. In order to determine the cost of producing a particular output, it is necessary to know not only the required quantities of the various inputs but also their prices. The cost function can be derived from the production function by adding the information about factor prices. It takes the general form:

$$Qc = f(p_1 I_1, p_2 I_2, \ldots p_n I_n)$$

where Qc is the cost of producing a particular output Q, and p_1, p_2, etc., are the prices of the various factors used, while I_1, I_2, etc., are the quantities of factors 1, 2, etc., required. The factor prices p_1, p_2 etc., which a firm must pay in order to attract units of these factors will depend upon the interaction of the forces of demand and supply in factor markets.

Changes in factor input costs will affect the position of the supply curve. The market supply curve plots the amount supplied against product price on the assumption that all of the other elements affecting the supply curve are held constant. If any of these other elements change, however, then this will bring about a shift in the supply curve. For example, if costs of production inputs fall, the supply curve will shift to the right, so that more is supplied at each price than formerly. In Figure 3.2 a fall in production input costs shifts the market supply curve S_1S_1 to S_2S_2, increasing the quantity supplied at price OP from OQ_1 to OQ_2.

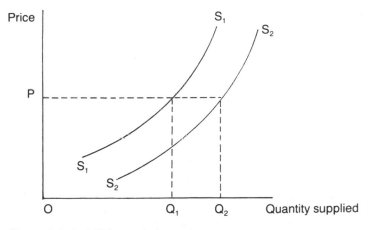

Figure 3.2 A shift in market supply

3.3 ELASTICITY OF SUPPLY

The price-elasticity of supply measures the degree of responsiveness of supply to a given change in the product's price:

$$\text{elasticity of supply} = \frac{\%\ \text{change in quantity supplied}}{\%\ \text{change in product price}}$$

If a change in price results in a more than proportionate change in quantity supplied, then supply is price-elastic. Figure 3.3(a) shows a price increase from OP_1 to OP_2 which results in a more than proportionate increase in quantity supplied, from OQ_1 to OQ_2. By contrast, if a change in price produces a less than proportionate change in quantity supplied, then supply is price-inelastic. In Figure 3.3(b) a price increase from OP_1 to OP_2 results in a less than proportionate increase in the quantity supplied, from OQ_1 to OQ_2.

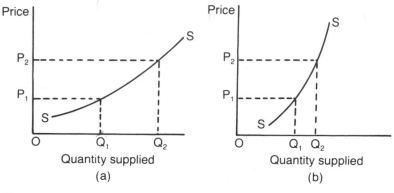

Figure 3.3 Price-elasticity of supply

At the extremes, supply can be perfectly price-inelastic, that is, price changes have no effect at all on quantity supplied, which shows up as a straight-line vertical supply curve; or supply can be perfectly price-elastic, that is, any amount will be supplied at the prevailing price, but nothing at all at a slightly lower price, which shows up as a straight-line horizontal supply curve.

The degree of responsiveness of supply to changes in price is affected by the time horizon involved. In the short-run (see next section), supply can only be increased in response to an increase in demand/price by working firms' existing plant more intensively, but this usually adds only marginally to total market supply. Thus, in the short run the market supply curve tends to be price-inelastic. In the long-run, firms are able to enlarge their supply capacities by building additional plants and by extending existing ones so that supply conditions in the long run tend to be more price-elastic. However, in some cases, for example, petrochemicals production, the long-run supply responses can be five years or more.

3.4 SOME IMPORTANT COST CONCEPTS

Before we analyse cost-price-output interactions as they affect supply conditions, it is necessary to highlight a number of cost concepts which form
the basis of supply analysis. By way of preliminaries it is important to
note that a conceptual distinction is made in cost analysis between the
short-run (defined as a time period in which some factor inputs and
associated costs are variable, but others are fixed) and the long-run (defined
as a time period in which all factor inputs can be varied). All of the cost
concepts explained below specifically define costs as including a 'normal'
profit return to enterprise owners for supplying risk capital; that is, profit
itself is seen as an integral part of economic supply costs, rather than as a
'residual'.

- *Fixed costs (overheads)*: costs which in the short-run do not vary with
  the level of output (see Figure 3.4(a)). They represent payments made
  for the use of fixed factor inputs (interest payments, rent charges on
  fixed plant and equipment) which are incurred irrespective of whether
  current output is high or low. In the short-run, average fixed costs (see
  Figure 3.4(b)) decline continuously as output rises, as a given amount
  of fixed cost is spread over a greater number of units.

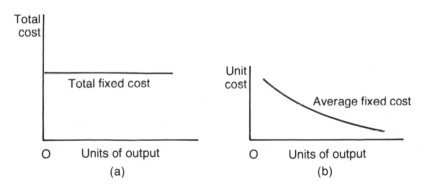

Figure 3.4 Fixed costs: short-run

- *Variable costs*: costs which in the short-run vary directly with the level
  of output. They represent payments made for the use of variable factor
  inputs (raw materials, heating and lighting, labour) which increase as
  output is expanded and fall as output is reduced. If output expands in
  exact proportion to the units of input employed, then total average cost
  will be as shown in Figure 3.5(a) and average variable cost will be
  constant as in Figure 3.5(b).

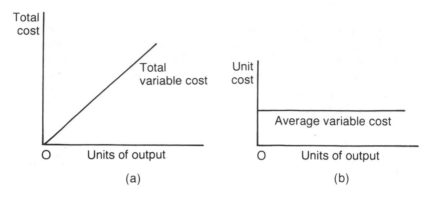

Figure 3.5 Variable costs: short-run

- *Total cost*: the aggregate sum in the short-run of a firm's total fixed cost and total variable cost in producing a particular level of output. Figure 3.6(a) shows total cost, which is equal to fixed cost at zero output then increases thereafter as variable costs increase from zero. Figure 3.6(b) shows average total cost, which is the sum of average fixed and average variable cost. Linear fixed and variable costs are usually embodied in break-even charts (see Box 3.1).

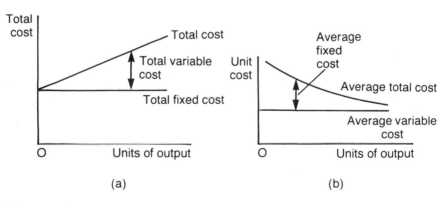

Figure 3.6 Total cost: short-run

- *Marginal cost*: the extra cost (addition to total cost) that is incurred in the short-run in increasing output by one unit. Since fixed costs do not vary with output, marginal costs (MC) are entirely variable costs. If variable costs are constant then these will be the same as the unit marginal cost.

Box 3.1   The basic break-even chart

The break-even chart seeks to bring together cost and demand concepts in order to show the effects of short-run variations in output
upon a firm's profitability. The figure shows a typical break-even
chart.

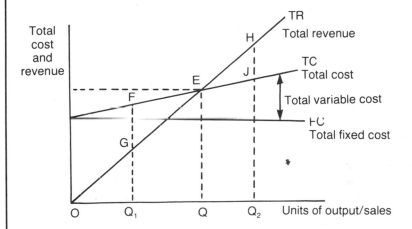

Total fixed costs are constant over a range of output, while total
variable costs start at zero when output is zero and increase with
output thereafter. Total costs are the sum of fixed and variable costs.
The total revenue line starts at zero and increases proportionately
with output and sales volume, if selling price is constant.

The firm breaks even – makes neither a profit nor a loss – at
output OQ. At outputs less than this, say OQ_1, total costs FQ_1
exceed revenues GQ_1, resulting in a loss of FG. At outputs greater
than the break-even output, say OQ_2, total revenues HQ_2 exceed
revenues JQ_2, resulting in a profit of HJ. Profits or losses at other
output levels can be similarly determined.

Break-even charts can be used to explore the effects upon profits
of changes in:

1   sales/output volumes;
2   fixed cost (which move FC vertically up or down);
3   unit variable cost (which alter the slope of TC);
4   selling price (which alter the slope of TR).

Linear fixed and variable costs, as portrayed above, imply that there is a
constant proportionate relationship between variable factor inputs and
product output, each unit of variable input yielding constant amounts
of product. However, in practice such constant returns to the variable

input occur only for modest ranges of output and if we consider a wide range of possible outputs, then returns to the variable input can vary, with consequences for the shape of the cost curves.

3.5 RETURNS TO THE VARIABLE FACTOR INPUT AND SHORT-RUN COSTS

In the short run, a firm can change its rate of output only by combining more or less of the variable factors with the fixed factors; that is, by changing the proportions in which the factor inputs are used. As more and more of a variable input is used in conjunction with a given quantity of fixed input:

1 Initially, as Figure 3.7(a) shows, there are increasing returns to the variable input: output increases more than proportionately to the increase in the variable input, so that the total physical product curve (showing the total amount of output produced) rises steadily and both marginal physical product (the quantity of output produced by each extra unit of variable factor input) and average physical product (the average quantity of output produced by each extra unit of variable factor input) also increase.

2 Constant returns are then experienced, with the increase in output being exactly proportional to the increase in the variable input (marginal physical product and average physical product being constant).

3 Diminishing returns to the variable input are then experienced (see Figure 3.7(b)), with the increase in output being less than proportional to the increase in the variable input (the total physical product curve flattens out and both marginal physical product and average physical product decrease).

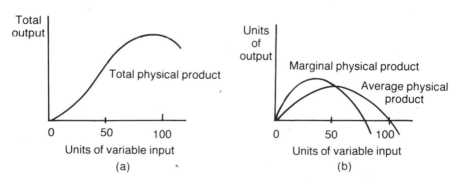

Figure 3.7 Returns to the variable factor input

Changing returns to the variable factor input affect the shape of the short-run cost curves. If each unit of variable input costs the same to buy, then inputs which yield proportionately large quantities of product output will lead to lower input costs per unit of output. By contrast, inputs which yield proportionately small quantities of product output will lead to higher input costs per unit of output.

- *Variable costs*: in the short run, total variable costs (Figure 3.8(a)) may rise slowly at first (reflecting increasing returns to the variable factor input) but then rise quickly (reflecting diminishing returns to the variable factor input). Likewise, average variable costs (Figure 3.8(b)) may fall at first (reflecting increasing returns to the variable factor input) but then may rise (reflecting diminishing returns to the variable factor input). Thus, a typical short-run average variable cost curve is U-shaped.

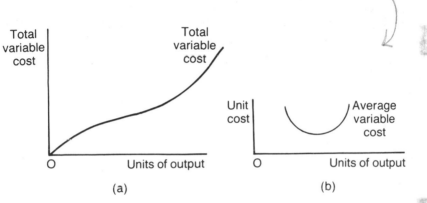

Figure 3.8 Short-run variable costs

- *Total cost*: changes in variable cost, in turn, impact on total cost. Figure 3.9(a) shows a short-run total cost curve consisting of the (constant) total fixed costs and the total variable cost. It has an 's' shape because, as indicated above, at low levels of output total variable costs rise slowly (reflecting the influence of increasing returns to the variable factor input), while at higher output levels total variable costs rise more rapidly (reflecting the influence of diminishing returns to the variable factor input).

The respective influences of increasing and diminishing returns to the variable factor input gives rise to a U-shaped average total cost curve (ATC). Average total cost (the unit cost of producing particular volumes of output) is split into average fixed cost (AFC) and average variable cost (AVC) – Figure 3.9(b). AFC declines continuously as output rises, as a given total amount of fixed cost is spread over a greater number of units.

AVC, as noted above, falls at first (serving to reduce ATC) but then rises (leading to an increase in ATC).

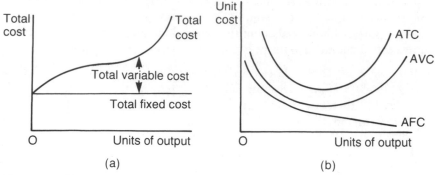

Figure 3.9 Short-run total cost

- *Marginal cost*: in the short run, marginal cost will also be affected by increasing and diminishing returns to the variable factor input, falling at first but then rising as diminishing returns set in (Figure 3.10).

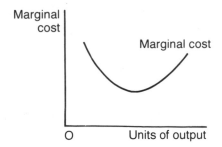

Figure 3.10 Marginal cost

Short-run production decisions are concerned with making the best use of available fixed factor inputs. By contrast, long-run production (where *all* factor inputs can be varied) is concerned with establishing the most appropriate scale of production (see Box 3.2).

Box 3.2   Short- and long-run production and cost conditions

Within a short-run period a firm can only expand output by adding more variable inputs to its fixed inputs. For example, $SATC_1$ in the figure shows unit costs at varying levels of output within the output range up to 100 units of output per week. This corresponds to a given level of fixed plant capacity. Similarly, $SATC_2$ shows unit costs at varying levels of output within the output range from 100 to 200 units of output per week. This corresponds with a larger fixed plant capacity. In each of these cases the firm is combining variable inputs with its fixed inputs in order to secure the best utilisation of its fixed plant input. Only at output level OQ_1 in the first case and output OQ_2 in the second case does the firm achieve an optimum combination of fixed and variable inputs which minimises its unit cost.

Over the longer term, if the firm were able to continuously adjust *all* of its factor inputs, including plant capacity, then it would always be able to achieve the optimum mix of factor inputs, avoiding diminishing returns to the variable factor input and minimising its unit cost. The long-run average cost curve LATC in the figure shows what unit costs would be if continuous fine adjustment of all inputs were possible. Thus, the long-run average cost curve is an 'envelope curve' linking all the possible short-run averages.

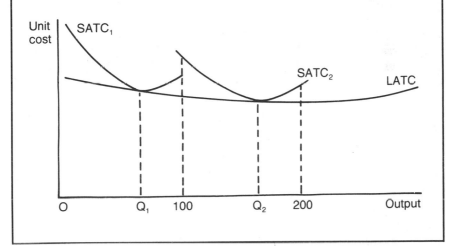

3.6 LONG-RUN COST AND SUPPLY CONDITIONS

The 'long-run' in market analysis is defined as an economic time period long enough for all factor inputs to be varied, but within an existing technological framework (known production methods). Thus, the firm's plant size, which is fixed in the short run, can now be altered to allow for an increased scale of operations.

By increasing the scale of its operations a firm may be able to take advantage of the existence of economies of large scale production and distribution and as a consequence lower its average total costs. On an industry-wide basis, economies of scale may have a profound effect on the level of market supply costs.

Economies of scale may operate both at the level of the individual plant and the firm (operating a number of plants) and arise due to:

1 indivisibilities in machinery and equipment, especially where a number of processes are linked together;
2 economies of increased dimensions – for many types of capital equipment (tankers, boilers), both set-up and operating costs increase less rapidly than capacity;
3 economies of specialisation – at larger outputs there is more scope for using specialist labour and capital equipment;
4 superior techniques or organisation of production – as scale is increased, automatic machinery may be used instead of manually operated items, or it may be possible to substitute continuous mass production for batch production;
5 economies of bulk-buying of raw materials and supplies;
6 marketing economies resulting from the use of mass advertising media and greater density of deployment of sales forces;
7 financial economies which arise from the ability of large firms to raise capital on more advantageous terms;
8 managerial economies from the use of specialist management techniques like work study, operational research and critical path analysis.

Unit costs may not fall continuously as the scale of the firm's operations is increased, and they may level off at some point – the *minimum efficient scale* of operation (OX in Figure 3.11) and remain relatively constant thereafter (BD) – see Box 3.3; or they may rise because of the growing complexities of managing a larger organisation – diseconomies of scale (BC). Diseconomies of scale arise from communications problems in large organisations with many management levels and long chains of command; from the more formal, bureaucratic systems large organisations need to employ; and from the demotivation and possible alienation which employees in large organisations often experience.

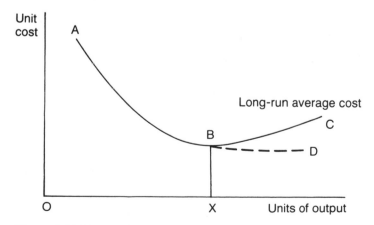

Figure 3.11 Economies of scale

Box 3.3   Minimum efficient scale in the UK brewing and soft drinks industries

- *Beer production*: A leading UK national brewer indicated to the MMC 'that the size of brewery at which production costs might be expected to reach minimum feasible levels would be 4 million barrels per annum' (equivalent to around 14 per cent of UK beer production in 1988). 'Unit production costs would tend to be constant thereafter, whilst unit distribution costs increased' (*Beer Report 1989*, Monopolies and Mergers Commission, para. 4.16). No brewer in fact operated such a scale of plant. The brewer cited above indicated that while the size of the leading *companies* (each operating, currently, a number of breweries) was sufficient to encourage plant size to move closer to 4 million barrels, various factors mitigated against this, particularly the need to brew a wide range of different types of beer and the long operating life of existing assets (para. 4.17).

- *Carbonated drink production* (colas etc.): Britvic estimated the MES for a soft drinks production plant (utilising high-speed equipment) at around 400 million litres per year, equivalent to some 10 per cent of UK soft drink production in 1990 (*Carbonated Drinks Report 1991*, MMC, para. 3.142).

Estimated economies of scale in the production of soft drinks, 1990

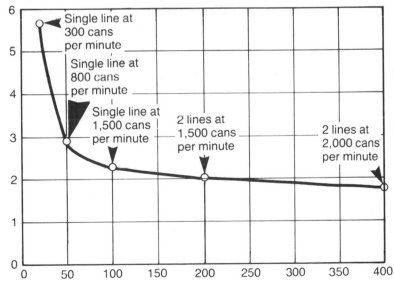

Pence per litre

Million litres per year

See also Chapter 10, Plasterboard, section 10.1.5.

The potential to realise economies of scale can be limited for a variety of reasons. In some industries the nature of the product and the processes of manufacture, or technology, may be such that diseconomies of scale are encountered at modest output levels. On the demand side, total market demand may be insufficient to permit firms to attain minimal efficient scale, or firms' individual market shares may be too small. Where consumers demand a wide variety of products this mitigates against standardisation and long production runs.

Where economies of scale are substantial, seller concentration tends to be high, as for example in petrochemicals and motor vehicles, for only in this way can industry output be produced as efficiently as possible. In such industries firms may undertake horizontal integration, particularly through mergers and takeovers, to eliminate high-cost plants and to rationalise production so as fully to exploit economies of scale.

In some industries flexible manufacturing systems can enable small quantities of a variety of products to be manufactured at unit costs which match those achievable with large-scale production, thus lowering the minimum efficient scale.

Firm and industry cost levels may be further reduced by economies of scope and dynamic 'learning curve' effects. A firm may achieve cost reductions through economies of scope by sharing common factor inputs over a range of its activities, or by jointly promoting or distributing its products. For example, a building society could use its existing branches and staff not only to sell mortgages but also to offer customers other financial services, such as banking and insurance. The learning curve relates to the process whereby managers and operators learn from experience how to operate new technologies more efficiently over time, such that increased familiarity with the technology enables unit costs of production to be progressively reduced.

Over the very long run, market analysis allows for the fact that the technological framework (known production methods) under which firms currently operate can itself change as a result of new process invention and innovation. Thus, technological advance may facilitate a reduction in market supply curves by shifting the cost structures of firms to a new lower level. In Figure 3.12, the firm's cost structure is moved down from ATC_1 to ATC_2, such that costs are reduced at all levels of output, which enables market supply to be expanded at existing price levels.

3.7 COSTS, REVENUE AND SHORT-RUN AND LONG-RUN MARKET SUPPLY

It has been demonstrated that the existence of increasing and diminishing returns to the variable factor input results in U-shaped average total cost

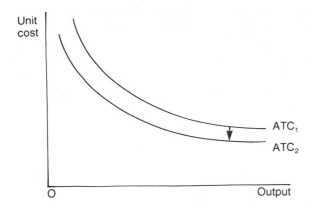

Figure 3.12 Cost reduction through technological advance

and marginal cost curves. How much of a product firms will supply in the short run will depend not only on their costs but also on the price, and hence revenue, they receive from selling their outputs. A profit-maximising firm will seek to produce a quantity of output where total revenue exceeds total cost by the greatest amount and where marginal cost is equal to marginal revenue (see Box 3.4).

Box 3.4 Profit maximisation

A key assumption of conventional market analysis is that firms seek to maximise their profits. The achievement of profit maximisation can be depicted in two ways:

1 First, where total revenue (TR) exceeds total cost (TC) by the greatest amount. In the figure this occurs at the output level where the slope of the two curves is identical, and tangents to each curve are consequently parallel, as at Q_e. At any output level below Q_e the relevant tangents would be diverging – the TR and TC curves would still be moving further apart and profits would still be rising. At any output level beyond Q_e, on the other hand, the relevant tangents would be converging and the profit surplus of TR over TC would be falling. Thus, Q_e is the optimum point, for here the distance between the total revenue and total cost curves is maximised (equal to AB). The difference between the two curves shows up in the total profit curve, which becomes positive at output OQ_1, reaches a maximum at output OQ_e (where profit CD = AB), and becomes negative beyond output OQ_2.

2   Second, profit maximisation can be shown to occur where mar-
    ginal revenue (MR) equals marginal cost (MC) – at output OQ_e
    in the figure. At all output rates above OQ_e additional units add
    more to cost than revenue, so that total profits are reduced. At
    all output rates less than OQ_e additional units add more to rev-
    enue than cost, thereby expanding total profits. Only where MR =
    MC are profits maximised.

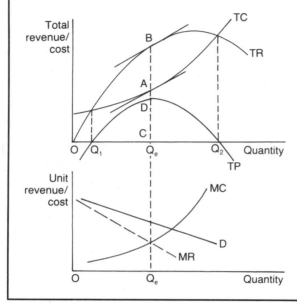

3.7.1. Firms' short-run costs, revenue and profit-maximising levels of supply

In Figure 3.13, ATC = average total cost, AVC = average variable cost,
AFC = average fixed cost and MC = marginal cost. The marginal
cost curve, it will be noted, cuts the ATC curve at its *minimum* point.
(This relationship is a purely mathematical one – when ATC is falling, MC
is always below it – that is, if the extra cost of an extra unit of output
lowers ATC, it must itself be less than ATC in order to drag the average
down; when ATC is rising, MC is above it – that is, if an extra unit of
output increases ATC, its cost must be more than ATC in order to pull
the average up.)

The figure depicts a number of positions. If price is OA then at output
OQ the firm fully covers its total costs (including a *'normal' profit* return).
If price is OB then the firm incurs a *loss*. However, it will remain in the
market in the *short run* since at price OB it earns sufficient revenue to
cover its average variable costs and make some *contribution* towards its

fixed costs. At price OC, however, revenues are insufficient to cover the average variable costs of producing current output, and therefore the firm will exit the market. By contrast, if price is OD the firm will be encouraged to expand its output, moving up its marginal cost curve as long as the extra unit costs of producing additional units of output are less than the extra marginal revenues received (see Box 3.4). It follows that the marginal cost curve is the firm's short-run supply curve, and that the market supply curve itself is derived from a horizontal summation of all of the individual firm's marginal cost curves.

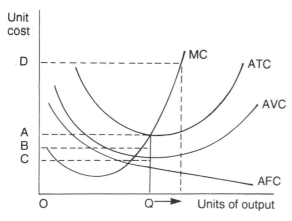

Figure 3.13 Firm's costs and revenue: short-run

3.7.2 Long-run supply adjustments

Firms' marginal revenues and marginal costs together play a fundamental role in *adjusting market supply* over the longer term. Specifically, if current average revenues are insufficient to cover average total costs (that is, both AVC and AFC in the long-run), then firms will *exit* the market, thus reducing long-run market supply. By contrast if current average revenues exceed ATC (including a normal profit return to suppliers) then this will encourage existing firms to expand their outputs and new firms to enter the market, thus expanding long-run market supply.

This process of dynamic supply adjustment is demonstrated, briefly, for a perfectly competitive market (see Chapter 5). In Figure 3.14(a) equilibrium market price and output levels in the *short run* are shown as PM and QM, where the market demand and market supply curves intersect. The profit-maximising price-output combination for the individual firm is given by PF (the firm is a 'price-taker' and must sell at the market price) and QF (where the firm's marginal cost curve (MC) intersects the marginal revenue curve (MR)). In this case the firm realises above-normal unit profits, shown

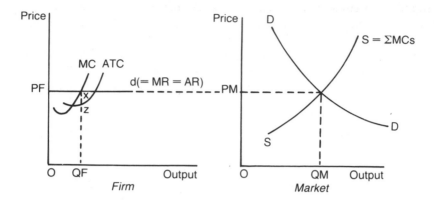

(a) Short-run

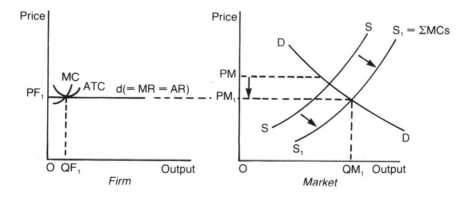

(b) Long-run

Figure 3.14 Perfect competition

by the distance XZ. However, these short-run excess profits will encourage new suppliers to enter the market, shifting the market supply curve to the right and increasing market output (see Figure 3.14(b)). The extra output on the market serves to reduce market price (to PM_1), so that a new long-run equilibrium market price-output combination is attained, with firms now only securing normal profits.

3.8 THE DYNAMICS OF SUPPLY

Supply cannot be looked at in isolation – the 'adequacy' of market supply has to be viewed in relation to movements in market demand. Essentially, demand is the prime mover of the market system – there is no point in producing something that nobody wants to buy, although suppliers can, and do, 'create' demand through new product development.

Figure 3.15 indicates a number of possible market supply-market demand configurations over time. In case 1, market supply rises 'smoothly' in line with the secular expansion of market demand, maintaining a close balance between industry capacity and market demand, thereby ensuring high levels of capacity utilisation. In case 2, suppliers have invested in new capacity ahead of demand only to find that they now have too much capacity on hand because of a failure of demand to reach projected growth rates, leading to an adverse effect on capacity utilisation rates. This may be an acute problem, as the fertiliser case demonstrates (see Box 3.5), in industries where fixed costs account for a high proportion of total production costs and high throughput rates are required for firms to break even and secure profits. In case 3, the market has gone into secular decline, so again under-utilised capacity poses a problem of maintaining plant viability. In both cases 2 and 3, plant rationalisation will be required to eliminate surplus capacity. This could be achieved either by mergers and takeovers, or by the exit of firms from the industry, both involving the closure of high-cost, inefficient plant.

Cyclical demand fluctuations arising from exposure to the business cycle can also pose problems: in upswings, firms may find themselves with inadequate capacity to meet current demand, while in downturns plant is under-utilised.

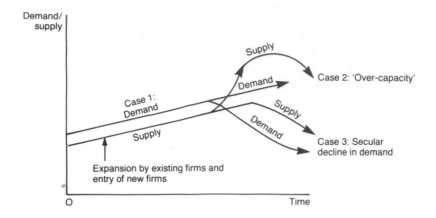

Figure 3.15 The 'balance' of supply and demand

Box 3.5   The UK fertiliser market

In 1990 ICI (29 per cent market share) proposed to sell its fertiliser division to one of only two UK rivals, the Finnish concern Kemira Oy (18 per cent market share), after posting losses for a number of years. The deal, however, was vetoed by the Monopolies and Mergers Commission. The background to the proposed sale was the need to restructure the UK fertiliser industry, which was suffering from over-capacity. A substantial amount of new plant had been installed during an era of growing demand for fertiliser between 1960 and the early 1980s, but 'the end of that growth, combined with a rising degree of import penetration (34 per cent market share) has resulted not only in plant closures, but also in low rates of capacity utilisation (industry average – 69 per cent in 1989/90) for those plants which have remained in operation' (para. 3.39). On acquiring ICI's assets, Kemira proposed to close down ICI's main plant at Billingham and add ICI's sales to its own output, thereby boosting throughput rates. This 'neat' solution to the industry's over-capacity problem was judged by the MMC to be anti-competitive. Despite being told by ICI that it would close its plants anyway if the deal did not go through, the MMC took the view that this would be preferable to acquisition, since 'it would enable all other players in the market to compete for ICI's share, with the spoils going to those who competed most effectively' (para 6.89) *Kemira Oy – ICI Report*, 1991.

QUESTIONS

1 What is meant by the term 'supply' in economic analysis? Indicate some of the main determinants of the supply of a product.
2 Distinguish between a change in supply (that is, a shift in the supply curve) and a change in the quantity supplied (that is, a movement along an existing supply curve).
3 What is measured by price-elasticity of supply? Outline the factors which can affect the elasticity of supply of a product.
4 Explain why increasing output in the short run will usually lead to higher unit costs, while increasing output in the long run may not.
5 Analyse the significance of 'returns to the variable-factor input' and 'economies of scale' for firms' cost structures.
6 What is meant by the term 'minimum efficient scale' of operation? What is its significance for supply costs and market structure?
7 Why is it important to maintain some reasonable 'balance' between industry supply and demand over the longer term?

Chapter 4

Market demand and market supply interactions

As noted in Chapter 1, market demand and supply interactions play a fundamental role in allocating scarce economic resources and in determining which goods and services are to be produced, the prices at which they are sold and the quantities of each supplied and consumed. The concept of the 'equilibrium' market price and quantities transacted are at the heart of this process.

4.1 THE EQUILIBRIUM MARKET PRICE

The equilibrium market price is the price at which the quantity demanded of a product by consumers is exactly equal to the quantity supplied by producers. In Figure 4.1 the equilibrium market price, OP, is determined by the intersection of the market demand and market supply curves. At any other price than OP the market is in disequilibrium, and forces operating within the market will be set in motion to move the price to the equilibrium position. For example, at a lower initial price such as OP1 there is excess demand of Q_1Q_2, since the quantity demanded at this price is greater than the quantity supplied. In competitive markets there will be an upward pressure on price in such a seller's market, reflecting a shortage of the product and bidding by buyers to acquire the limited supplies available. As price rises from OP_1 to OP, some consumers will be deterred from buying the product by the higher price, so that demand contracts along the demand curve towards point X. At the same time the price rise from OP_1 to OP encourages suppliers to offer more of the product for sale, so that the supply expands along the supply curve towards X. By contrast, at a higher initial price such as OP_2 there is excess supply of Q_3Q_4, since in this case the quantity supplied at price OP_2 is greater than the quantity demanded. In competitive markets there will be a downward pressure on price in such a buyer's market, as suppliers compete to dispose of surpluses. As price falls from OP_2 to OP some suppliers will be discouraged from offering the product, so that supply contracts along the supply curve towards point X. At the same time the price fall from OP_2 to OP will encourage consumers to buy more of the product so that demand expands along the demand curve towards X. Only at price OP are market demand and market supply fully synchronised at point X, where the quantity demanded (OQ) exactly matches the quantity supplied.

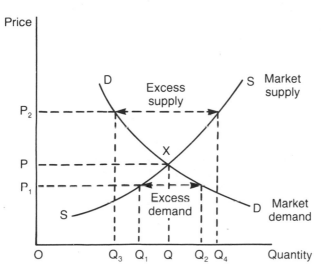

Figure 4.1 Equilibrium market price

4.2 CHANGES IN THE EQUILIBRIUM MARKET PRICE

The equilibrium market price will move to a higher or lower level in response to a change (that is, a shift) in the demand curve or in the supply curve. For example, if market demand increases as a result of, say, an increase in consumers' disposable income, this will cause the market demand curve to shift upwards to the right, leading to an increase in the equilibrium market price. In Figure 4.2(a) the market demand curve shifts from DD to D_1D_1 and, with an unchanged market supply curve, at a price OP the extra demand leads to an excess demand equal to QQ_3. This excess demand causes the equilibrium market price to increase from OP to OP_1, choking off the excess demand. By contrast, if the market demand curve were to shift to the left, reflecting, for example, a change in consumer tastes away from this product, then the equilibrium market price would fall. If market supply were to increase as a result, say, of a fall in production costs, this would cause the market supply curve to shift downwards to the right, leading to a fall in the equilibrium market price. In Figure 4.2(b) the market supply curve shifts from SS to S_1S_1 and, with an unchanged market demand curve, at price OP the extra supply leads to an excess supply equal to QQ_4. This excess supply causes the equilibrium market price to fall from OP to OP$_2$, choking off the excess supply. By contrast, if the market supply curve were to shift to the left as a result, for example, of an increase in production costs, then the equilibrium market price would rise.

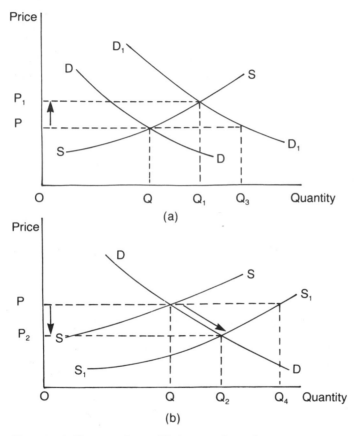

Figure 4.2 Changes in equilibrium market price

In this way changes in market demand and market supply, working through their effect on the equilibrium market price, serve as a 'resource signaller' leading to an increase or decrease in the resources deployed in the market.

The magnitude of the price changes necessary to restore equilibrium in markets will depend upon the price elasticity of supply and demand in these markets. Thus if supply of the product is price-inelastic so that the market supply curve has a steep slope, then an increase in demand will require a large price increase to restore market equilibrium, and a decrease in demand will be associated with a large price decrease. By contrast, if supply of the product is price-elastic so that the market supply curve has a shallow slope, then an increase in demand will need only a small price increase to restore equilibrium and a decrease in demand will be associated with a small price decrease. Figure 4.3(a) shows these two possibilities.

Similarly, if demand for the product is price-inelastic so that the market demand curve has a steep slope, then an increase in supply will require a large price decrease to restore market equilibrium and a decrease in supply will be associated with a large price increase. By contrast, if demand for the product is price-elastic so that the market demand curve has a shallow slope, then an increase in supply will need only a small price decrease to restore equilibrium, and a decrease in supply will be associated with a small price increase. Figure 4.3(b) shows these two possibilities (see Box 4.1).

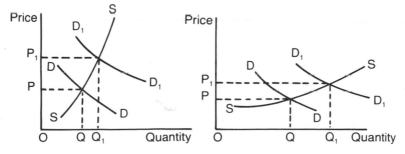

(a) Supply elasticity and changes in demand

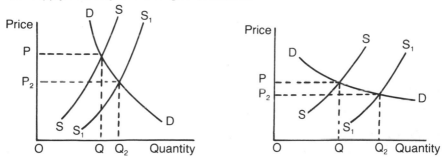

(b) Demand elasticity and changes in supply

Figure 4.3 Size of changes in equilibrium market price

4.3 PRICE MOVEMENTS OVER TIME

Some markets are characterised by a marked degree of price instability around the underlying trend line in price movements, whereas other markets exhibit a much more stable pattern of price changes over time. In some cases the explanation for this lies in changes in demand associated with the business cycle, with certain markets (for example, house building) being more severely affected by such changes than others (for example, cigarettes). In other cases the 'controllability' of supply plays a decisive

Box 4.1   Demand and supply analysis and taxation policy: the incidence of taxation

Demand and supply analysis can be used to indicate the effects of the imposition of indirect taxes on products.

The incidence of an indirect tax (such as excise duty or value added tax) generally depends upon the price-elasticity of demand (and supply) of the products being taxed, with producers bearing most of the burden of the tax where demand is elastic and buyers bearing most of the burden of the tax where demand is inelastic. Figure (a) and (b) contrast the two situations.

In Figures (a) and (b) the imposition of an indirect tax equal to BE_1 shifts the supply curve vertically upward from S to S_1. The effect of the tax is to increase equilibrium price from OP to OP_1 and reduce equilibrium quantity from OQ to OQ_1. Where product demand is price-elastic as in Figure (a), the price increase is small and the reduction in quantity sold is large, with producers bearing most of the burden of the tax in lost sales and reduced profit margins. By contrast, where product demand is price-inelastic as in Figure (b), the price increase is large and the reduction in quantity sold is small, with buyers bearing most of the burden of the tax in the form of a higher price. The relative burden of the tax borne by consumers is CE_1 and that borne by producers is BC in both (a) and (b).

In choosing which products to levy indirect taxes upon, governments usually select products such as cigarettes and alcohol, demand for which is highly price-inelastic, in order to ensure that buyers bear the burden of the tax and that the effects upon suppliers and employment are minimised.

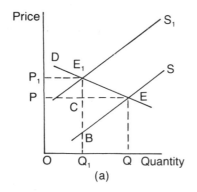

(a)

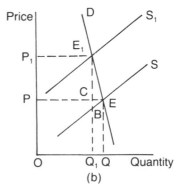

(b)

influence. Typically, price levels in highly concentrated markets supplying manufactured goods tend to be much more stable than in basic commodity markets (coffee beans, wheat), which are usually highly fragmented and where supply 'disruptions' are often precipitated by unpredictable climatic and other production problems (crop disease, pests, etc.). The coffee market provides a good illustration of these two situations.

Since 1983 most of the world coffee beans market has been covered by a primary commodity stabilisation agreement, the International Coffee Agreement (ICA), which sets export quotas for each member country. Despite this, as Figure 4.4 shows, the sterling price of coffee beans has fluctuated markedly, being characterised by a pattern of abrupt increases, principally in reaction to external events, followed by a gradual drift downwards. A severe frost in Brazil, the leading supplier country, led to a sharp fall in output and caused the world price to treble between 1976 and 1977. The price then declined as output levels were restored. In 1979, however, further Brazilian frosts led to another sharp rise. After a short period of decline, the price of coffee beans remained broadly flat. In 1985 supply disruptions in Brazil, this time caused by droughts, caused the world price to take off again. Another period of decline during 1986 and 1987 was then followed by a relatively stable period until 1989 when disagreements within the ICA led to its suspension, and the price fell rapidly to below its nominal 1976 level.

Figure 4.4 also shows the wholesale list price of Nescafé, the UK's leading coffee brand over the period 1976–90. Around 25 per cent of the wholesale price represents the cost of coffee beans, the other main costs being labour and capital charges. Wholesale prices have moved in a 'step-like' fashion broadly in line with changes in the price of coffee beans, apart from 1986–90. (The 'failure' of wholesale prices to respond fully to the fall in coffee bean prices was the reason why the Monopolies and Mergers Commission was asked to investigate the UK coffee market.) The competitive situation also has a bearing on price movements. In many markets a high degree of price parallelism occurs and price changes are

Table 4.1   Change in list prices per case (Nescafé and Maxwell House) for large volume customers

| | £ per case of 24 100–gram jars | | | | |
| | Nescafé | | | Maxwell House | |
Date of change	Price	Amount of change	Date of change	Price	Amount of change
1.1.86	35.78	2.40	3.1.86	35.77	2.40
3.3.86	37.94	2.16	5.3.86	37.93	2.16
9.3.87	35.54	−2.40	9.3.87	35.53	−2.40
6.3.89	37.43	1.89	7.3.89	37.42	1.89
22.1.90	32.63	−4.80	29.1.90	33.10	−4.32

Source: Soluble Coffee Report, Monopolies and Mergers Commission, 1991

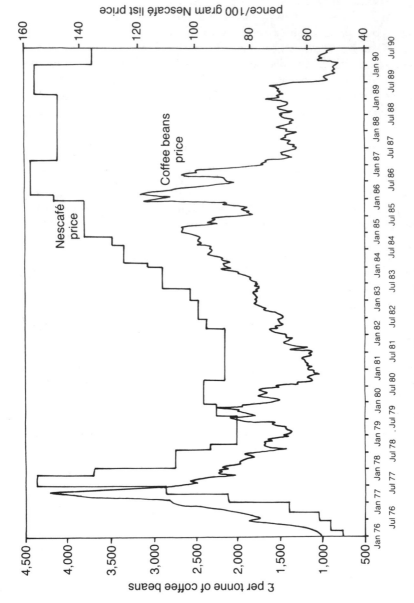

Figure 4.4 The wholesale list price of Nescafé and coffee beans prices, 1976–90
Source: Soluble Coffee Report, Monopolies and Mergers Commission, 1991

activated by a price leader or by collusion between suppliers (see Chapter 5). In the case of coffee, Nestlé (producer of Nescafé) has been 'accepted' as price leader by its chief rival (General Foods, producer of Maxwell House) and other manufacturers – see Table 4.1.

4.4 DEMAND AND SUPPLY INTERACTIONS ILLUSTRATED

The interaction of demand and supply in determining market prices is a key feature of all kinds of markets: agricultural produce, manufactured goods, factor inputs and financial assets. In this section we look briefly at the operation of demand and supply forces in the agricultural, labour, rented housing and foreign currency markets.

4.4.1 Why the prices of some agricultural products remain at depressed levels

For some agricultural products there has been a tendency for their prices to decline over the long-term as a result of a slow rate of growth in demand and increased production. Over recent decades the populations of most advanced industrialised countries have tended to grow only very slowly so that there have been few extra mouths to feed in these countries. In addition, while real incomes in these countries have risen considerably, very little of this extra income has been spent on food, the demand for foodstuffs being very income-inelastic (see Chapter 2). Thus over time the demand curve for agricultural products has tended to shift to the right, but by only a small amount, as indicated in Figure 4.5 by the shift from DD to D_1D_1. At the same time the efficiency and output of agricultural products has improved dramatically. Farm mechanisation, better drainage and irrigation, new seed strains, fertilisers and pesticides have improved yields per acre and farm productivity. Thus the supply of many agricultural products has expanded dramatically in developed countries, as indicated in Figure 4.5 by the shift of the supply curve from SS to S_1S_1.

The combination of small demand growth and large supply growth has led to a long-term decline in the prices of agricultural products, from OP to OP_1 in Figure 4.5, with a parallel fall in farm revenues and incomes, and a tendency for people to migrate from farms to cities in search of better-paid employment.

In order to ameliorate the effects of market forces upon agricultural producers, many governments have sought to intervene in such markets through various support schemes (see Section 4.5.1).

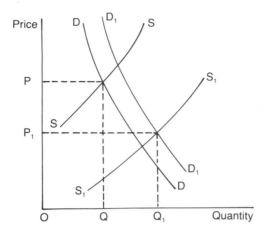

Figure 4.5 Long-term demand and supply for agricultural products

4.4.2 Why are accountants paid more than office cleaners?

The determination of wage rates in labour markets depends upon the supply of, and demand for, labour. The supply of labour in general depends upon the size of the population; school-leaving and retirement ages; skills, training and experience; entry barriers to professions and jobs through qualifications requirements, etc.. The demand for labour is influenced by, for example, the size and strength of demand for the goods and services produced by workers, the proportion of total production costs accounted for by wages and the degree of substitutability of capital for labour in the production process.

As a consequence of these factors, the labour market cannot be regarded as a single homogeneous market but must be seen as a number of separate labour markets, each with its own particular characteristics. For example, as Figure 4.6 shows, a group of workers such as accountants, whose skills are in limited supply and the demand for whose services is high, will receive a high wage rate; office cleaners, by contrast, require little or no training or skills and are usually in plentiful supply in relation to the demand for their services, so their wage rates are comparatively low. The wage differential between these two groups is $W_S - W_O$.

In order to improve the standard of living of low-paid workers, governments may introduce minimum wage legislation (see Section 4.5.2).

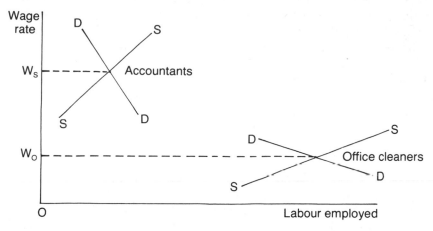

Figure 4.6 The markets for accountants and office cleaners

4.4.3 Why have rents risen?

The market for private rented accommodation (houses, flats, etc.) has been characterised by rising rents in many industrial countries, particularly in densely populated urban areas (such as inner cities). The reason for this can be found in underlying changes in the demand for and supply of private rented accommodation, as illustrated in Figure 4.7. The demand for rented accommodation has risen over the long term in particular because of modest increases in the general population, more dramatic increases in city populations as workers have migrated to urban areas; and as people have tended to spend a larger proportion of their income on housing. The

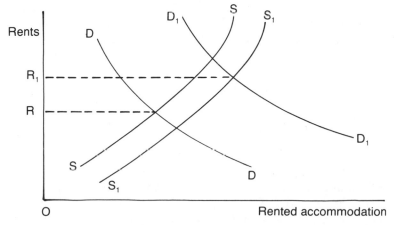

Figure 4.7 Long-term demand and supply for rented accommodation

supply of rented accommodation, by contrast, has grown only slowly, largely because of restrictions on the availability of land in urban areas. In consequence, the increase in demand for rented accommodation has outstripped the increase in supply, leading to an increase in rents from OR to OR_1 in Figure 4.7.

Governments may introduce controls which establish maximum rents for accommodation in order to ensure that people on low incomes can afford to rent housing (see Section 4.5.3).

4.4.4 Why the exchange rates of currencies fluctuate

In currency markets characterised by floating exchange rates, the price of one currency expressed in terms of another tends to vary with changes in the demand and supply of that currency. Thus in Figure 4.8 the price of sterling in terms of US dollars (or exchange rate) is OP_E. Demand for sterling DD comes from US importers seeking to acquire sterling to pay for British exports to the USA and US business people seeking to acquire sterling to invest in the United Kingdom. Supply of sterling comes from UK importers seeking to supply sterling and acquire dollars to pay for US exports to the United Kingdom and UK business people seeking to supply sterling and acquire dollars to invest in the USA.

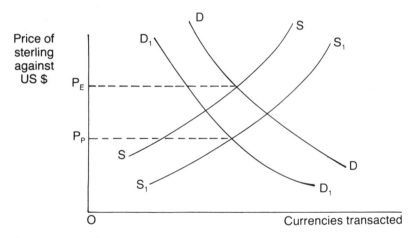

Figure 4.8 Exchange rates

If the UK's international trading performance deteriorates then: (a) with its exports declining this will have the effect of shifting the demand curve for sterling to the left, to D_1D_1 and (b) with its imports increasing, the supply curve for sterling will shift to the right, to S_1S_1. The combined effect of these changes will cause the exchange rate to fall to OP_P. By contrast, an improvement in a country's international trade performance will tend to lead to a rise in its exchange rate.

Governments often seek to establish a fixed exchange rate for their currencies, in order to avoid the uncertainty associated with fluctuations in exchange rates (see Section 4.5.4).

4.5 PRICES AND OUTPUTS : MARKET DISTORTIONS

Distortions to the allocative efficiency of markets leading to 'false' or 'inappropriate' market prices and outputs can occur in a number of ways, principally through the imposition of governmental price and output controls, and monopoly. Examples of the former are discussed below, while the problem of monopoly is examined in detail in Chapter 5.

4.5.1 Agricultural support schemes

In formulating agricultural policy, governments may seek to encourage national self-sufficiency in food production, stabilise food prices and provide extra revenue for farmers to preserve rural employment. These policies can take a variety of forms designed to boost demand for agricultural products or to reduce the supply of such products.

If the government's aim is to raise farm revenues then it could set minimum prices for agricultural products which are above the long-term market clearing prices.

This involves establishing a 'floor', or intervention price, as in Figure 4.9. The free market equilibrium price and output levels are OP_E and OQ_E. If the government 'imposes' a price floor on the market, OP_F, then it creates a situation of excess supply. Producers are encouraged to expand supply, increasing market output from OQ_E to OQ_F. However, at the higher price consumers demand only the quantity OX. To make the price hold, the government itself must buy the surplus output XQ_F at the fixed price of OP_F. Although in this case producers benefit from price controls by receiving higher incomes, consumers are 'penalised' by having to pay a higher price OP_F rather than OP_E, while additional resources are employed in this market which (in opportunity cost terms) could be used more efficiently in other industries. The surplus output has to be stockpiled and may eventually be wasted (foodstuffs in particular are subject to deterioration and may have to be destroyed).

This minimum price floor system lies at the heart of the European Community Common Agricultural Policy (CAP), where each year agriculture ministers of member countries agree floor or intervention prices for a wide range of agricultural products, then act to buy up surpluses to keep market prices at the intervention levels.

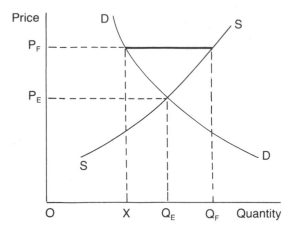

Figure 4.9 Minimum price floor

When governments set a floor or intervention price which is above the world price, then they must act to check inflows of imports attracted by the artificially high prices. This requires some kind of variable import levy which serves to bring the price of imported commodities up to the intervention price so that they cannot undercut the price of domestically supplied commodities. Again where intervention price is above world price it is impossible to export surplus commodities, unless an export subsidy is paid to exporters to enable them to sell at competitive world prices. The European Common Agricultural Policy embodies such a system of import levies and export subsidies.

An alternative means of supporting farmers' incomes involves the use of deficiency payments, as in Figure 4.10 where farmers sell their produce at the market clearing price OP_E, and then receive a subsidy from the government equal to P_EP_F to top up the market price received to the guaranteed price OP_F set by the government.

Government pays deficiency payments of P_EP_FXY to farmers, so the cost of agricultural support is ultimately borne by taxpayers. However, consumers pay only the market price OP_E, which avoids the artificial contraction of demand Q_FQ_E which would be associated with imposing a high, artificial selling price OP_F. Such a deficiency payments system was employed by the UK to support its farmers prior to the UK joining the European Community in 1973.

Guaranteed, high minimum floor prices, supported by intervention buying which adds to demand, encourages farmers to produce yet more unless they are constrained in some way. Thus agricultural support policies often also embody schemes to reduce supply. Supply restrictions can take two main forms:

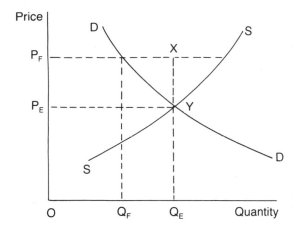

Figure 4.10 Deficiency payments

1 *Production quotas,* whereby farmers are granted the right to produce or sell only a specified quantity of their produce at a guaranteed price. The European Common Agricultural Policy has imposed such production quotas for milk and other products.
2 *Acreage controls,* whereby farmers are restricted to planting only a proportion of their land and are offered financial incentives to leave the rest of their land fallow. The United States has used acreage controls extensively and more recently the European Community have adopted 'set-aside' policies of this type.

Both kinds of supply restriction operate as in Figure 4.11 to restrict supply from SS to S_1S_1, thereby raising price from OP_E to OP_S and reducing the

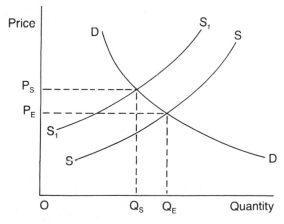

Figure 4.11 Supply restrictions

quantity traded. Such supply restrictions avoid the need for governments to buy up and stockpile surpluses, by reducing production of agricultural products, though this has the effect of reducing supplies to consumers and artificially raising prices.

Any system of agricultural support which seeks to increase farm incomes by artificially raising prices of agricultural products tends to lead to chronic surpluses, as farmers are all encouraged to produce more. Furthermore a guaranteed price which is high enough to generate a modest income for small, less efficient farmers will tend to produce very large revenues for large, more efficient farmers. Such systems also tend to be expensive to operate (see Box 4.2) and may become subject to widespread fraudulent abuse.

Box 4.2 The cost of argricultural protection

In 1992 agricultural subsidies in the European Community totalled £88 billion in the form of national taxation, value added tax, import duties and export subsidies. This represents a payment of £1,020 per year for a family of four within the European Community. The amount of support was equivalent to £10,000 for every full-time farmer in the Community and corresponds to £634 for each hectare of farmland.

English farmers are able to claim subsidies of:

- £124 for every tonne of cereals;
- £142 for every hectare of cereals if they take 15 per cent of their land out of production;
- £3,125 per tonne of beef plus £58 per beef cow or £69 per breeding cow;
- £18 per ewe;
- £2,723 per tonne of butter.

The UK's Intervention Board is responsible for 'intervention' buying in the British market to keep farm prices at pre-set levels, and stock-piles surplus food products. In May 1993 its unsold stocks included:

- 1.3m. tonnes of barley
- 160,000 tonnes of beef
- 11,000 tonnes of butter.

By keeping the prices of agricultural products in the European Community high the Common Agricultural Policy (CAP) penalises consumers by preventing them from buying at lower world price levels.

Other countries also subsidise their agricultural sector. For example, in 1992 agricultural subsidies in the United States were £52 billion.

Source: OECD, reported in *Sunday Times*, 27 June 1993.

4.5.2 Minimum wage rate stipulations

Governments may impose minimum wage rates in some sectors of the labour market so as to ensure that low-paid workers are able to enjoy a basic standard of living.

However, if the government imposes minimum wage rates which are significantly above those obtained through 'free' collective bargaining, the result is likely to be greater unemployment by creating a situation where the demand for labour is lower than its supply at the minimum wage level. This is illustrated in Figure 4.12, where the introduction of a minimum wage rate (OP_W) above the market-clearing wage rate (OP_E) leads to a fall in the number of people employed from OQ_E to OQ_W.

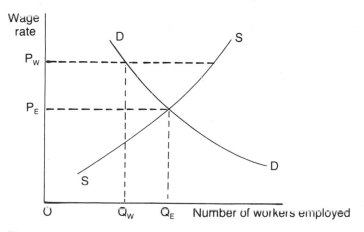

Figure 4.12 Minimum wage rates

An alternative way to improve the wages of low-paid workers might be to help them improve their productivity through better education and training. This would have the effect of shifting the demand curve for such workers to the right, as in Figure 4.13. This would result in both higher wages, OW_1, and more workers being employed, OQ_1.

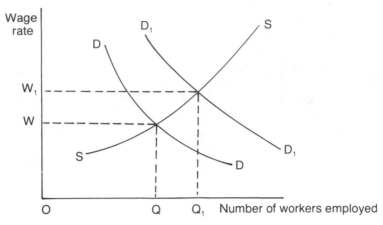

Figure 4.13 Labour demand and productivity

4.5.3 Rent controls

Governments may intervene to set maximum prices in some markets to ensure that products are 'affordable' – for example, they may set maximum rents so that people on low incomes are able to afford housing accommodation. As with prices which are set artificially high, however, price controls which deliberately set prices below market rates can be equally counter-productive when looked at 'in the round'. In Figure 4.14, the free-market equilibrium price and output levels are OP_E and OQ_E. If the government imposes a price ceiling on the market, OP_C, then it creates a situation of excess demand. At this price consumers demand the quantity OQ_C but suppliers are only prepared to offer quantity OY, and thus a proportion of demand remains unsatisfied. To meet the shortfall in supply the government itself may be prepared to supply the extra output. For example, in the case of housing, the government could build publicly owned houses which it could then rent out to tenants at a low subsidised rent. In terms of the workings of the free market, however, the imposition of rent controls makes the situation worse rather than better. Specifically there is no inducement for suppliers to increase the stock of housing, nor, if rents are set so low that the profit return on renting out property is inadequate, do property owners have the resources to ensure that the existing stock of housing is kept in good repair, leading to a qualitative deterioration in average living accommodation. Furthermore, such controls can lead to the development of a 'black market' in housing, with landlords demanding large initial one-off deposits from tenants who are competing for the limited accommodation available, before they are prepared to grant a tenancy agreement.

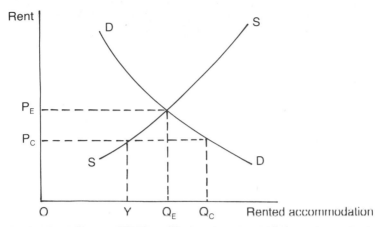

Figure 4.14 Price ceilings

4.5.4 Exchange rates

Governments may seek to fix the external value of their currencies in order to promote orderly currency markets and reduce the degree of uncertainty for firms in concluding trade deals. Fixed exchange rate systems were established on a global basis for over twenty years after the Second World War, under the International Monetary Fund rules; more recently, European Community countries have attempted to operate fixed exchange rates under the terms of the Exchange Rate Mechanism (ERM).

Under a fixed exchange rate system currencies are assigned a central par value in terms of the other currencies in the system. Figure 4.15(a), by way of example, shows the fixed exchange rate of the UK pound sterling against the US\$, OE_E, which corresponds initially to the equilibrium rate of exchange. A small range of fluctuation around the par value is usually permitted both in an upward direction (for example, E_E E_U) and a downward direction (for example, E_E E_D) to reflect day-to-day demand and supply changes. Once the exchange rate is fixed, countries are expected to maintain this rate for fairly long periods of time using 'support' buying and selling to keep the exchange rate within its permitted band. Thus, for example, as in Figure 4.15(a), if the market for sterling were to fall to D_1D_1 (because of a fall in American demand for UK exports – see Section 4.4.4), resulting in the exchange rate falling below its permitted floor price, then the UK authorities must boost demand for sterling from D_1D_1 to, say, D_2D_2 by buying sterling (using its reserves of dollars), thus bringing the exchange rate back within the permitted limits. By contrast, if, as in Figure 4.15(b), the market supply of sterling were to fall to S_1S_1 (because of a drop in UK demand for American exports) resulting in the exchange rate rising above its permitted ceiling price, then the UK authorities must increase the supply of sterling from S_1S_1 to, say, S_2S_2 by selling pounds for dollars, thus bringing the exchange rate back within the permitted limits.

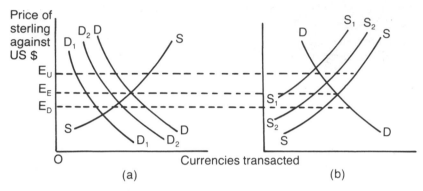

Figure 4.15 Fixed exchange rates

In practice, under a fixed exchange rate region there are limits to the extent to which a government can use support buying to prevent the exchange rate falling. Where currency flows are very large and include much speculative selling of the currency, then the government's foreign currency reserves and borrowings can be insufficient to support the currency, so that the fixed exchange rate has to be abandoned and the currency exchange rate allowed to fall to its market level. This occurred in the case of sterling in 1992, when the United Kingdom left the Exchange Rate Mechanism.

QUESTIONS

1 What is meant by the terms 'equilibrium market price', 'excess demand' and 'excess supply'?
2 Analyse some of the factors which may serve to change the ruling equilibrium market price.
3 The coffee bean market was in equilibrium at a price of £120 per tonne traded in 1991. If all crops harvested during the year are traded, explain what you would expect to happen to the equilibrium market price and quantity traded under the following circumstances:
   (a) in 1992 a drought causes crops to fail, and the price of tea falls;
   (b) in 1993 perfect climatic conditions produce a record crop, and the price of milk rises.

4 Why are the prices of some products more stable over time than other products?

5 Why have governments attempted to control the prices of agricultural products? Examine the possible effects of establishing minimum prices for agricultural products.

6 Examine the rationale for governments setting maximum rents for rented accommodation. Why might rent controls produce perverse economic and social results?

7 Explain the workings of a fixed exchange rate system and indicate some of the difficulties encountered in maintaining fixed exchange rates.

Chapter 5

The theory of markets

The 'theory of markets' is concerned with how scarce factors of production are allocated between the multitude of product markets in the economy. More specifically, the theory of markets is concerned with the determination of the prices and outputs of goods and services and the prices and usage of factors of production.

The theory of markets distinguishes between types of markets by reference to differences in their market structure. The main structural distinction is made according to the degree of seller concentration, that is, the number of suppliers and their relative size distribution. Other structural features emphasised include the character of the product supplied, that is, whether it is a homogeneous product or differentiated, and the condition of entry/exit to the market. Given these structural distinctions, market theory examines the way in which market structure interacts with market conduct to produce particular patterns of market performance.

The main market 'situations' considered by the theory of markets are the two polar extremes of the market spectrum – perfect competition and monopoly – and two 'intermediate' market structures – monopolistic competition and oligopoly. In order to facilitate a comparison of performance results between these four market types the assumption is made that all firms seek to maximise profits. This body of analysis shows perfect competition to yield performance results superior to those of the other market forms. However, the conventional theory of markets is deficient in a number of respects, particularly in regard to its portrayal of firm cost structures and its lack of attention (by definition) to dynamic performance criteria – process and product innovation. Accordingly, it is necessary to take a much broader, more empirically orientated view of market performance and market structure-conduct-performance inter-relationships. This is done in Chapter 8.

5.1 PERFECT COMPETITION

Perfect competition is characterised by:

1 many firms and buyers, that is, a large number of independently acting firms and buyers, each firm and buyer being too small to be able to influence the price of the product transacted;
2 homogeneous products, that is, the products offered by the competing firms are identical not only in physical attributes but are also regarded as identical by buyers who have no preference between the products of various producers;
3 free market entry and exit, that is, there are no barriers to entry (hindrances to the entry of new firms) or impediments to the exit of existing sellers;
4 perfect knowledge of the market by buyers and sellers.

In a perfectly competitive market, individual sellers have no control over the price at which they sell, the price being determined by aggregate market demand and supply conditions. Each firm produces such a small fraction of total industry output that an increase or decrease in its own output will have no perceptible influence upon total supply and, hence, price. Further, given that consumers regard the homogeneous outputs of the competing sellers as perfect substitutes, no firm can increase its price above the ruling market price without losing all of its custom. Thus, the demand curve facing the firm will be a horizontal straight line at the ruling market price. In consequence, marginal revenue, MR (the additional revenue obtained from selling one extra unit of output) equals average revenue, AR (total revenue divided by the number of units sold). The competitive firm is a 'price taker', accepting price as something completely outside its control, and will simply adjust its output independently to the most profitable level at that price. In doing so the firm will need to take into account the cost of producing output, in particular the marginal cost, MC (the additional cost incurred in producing one extra unit of output) and the average cost, AC (total cost divided by the number of units produced): that is, the firm will continue to produce additional units of output so long as price (=MR=AR) exceeds marginal cost. When the additional revenue obtained from selling one extra unit of output is exactly equal to the additional costs incurred in producing that output, then the firm will have achieved a level of output/sales at which it maximises profits. Figure 5.1(a) shows the short-run competitive equilibrium position for a representative firm and the industry. The individual supply schedules (MCs) of 'x' number of identical firms are summed horizontally to obtain the industry supply curve (SS). Given industry demand (DD), the short-run equilibrium price and output are OP_e and OQ_e. Taking the equilibrium price as given, the competitive firm establishes its profit-maximising output at the level OQ_f

($P=MC$). Since the firm's average costs include a 'normal' profit return on capital employed at price level OP_f the firm receives an 'above-normal' profit per unit equal to xy and total above-normal profits of $P_f$xyz.

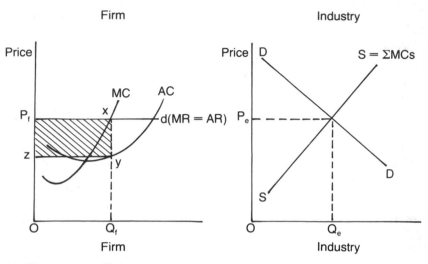

(a) Short-run equilibrium

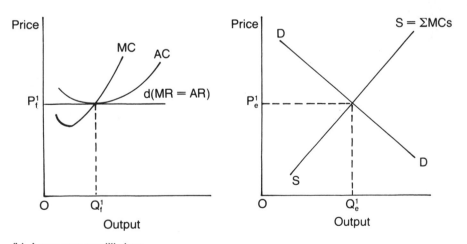

(b) Long-run equilibrium

Figure 5.1 Perfect competition

The long-run equilibrium position can also be ascertained. It is deduced from the assumptions of profit maximisation, perfect knowledge and free entry and exit, that unless the returns to the productive resources employed in this market are at a level that could be derived from their use in an alternative market elsewhere in the economy (that is, they are earning a normal profit), resources will enter or leave this market. In general, outputs will be adjusted to demand until market output is extended (or reduced) and price reduced (or increased) to the point where the average cost of supplying that output is just equal to the price at which that output sells.

If, as in the example above, established sellers are earning above-normal profits then new resources will be attracted into the industry, thereby increasing total market supply and reducing market price. This process will continue until the excess profits have been competed away. Figure 5.1(b) shows the long-run competitive equilibrium position for the representative firm and the industry. Given an unchanged industry demand (DD), the long-run equilibrium price and output for the industry are OP^1_e and OQ^1_e. Given the equilibrium price, the firm establishes its profit maximising output at the point OQ^1_f, where $P = MC$ at the point of minimum long-run average cost.

Static market theory shows perfect competition to result in a more efficient market performance than other forms of market organisation (see especially the comparison with monopoly). Specifically, market output is optimised at a level equal to minimum supply costs; consumers are charged a price just equal to minimum supply costs, with suppliers receiving a normal profit return.

5.2 MONOPOLY

Monopoly is characterised by:

1 one firm and many buyers, that is, a market comprised of a single supplier selling to a multitude of small, independently acting buyers;
2 a lack of substitute products, that is, there are no close substitutes for the monopolist's product;
3 blockaded entry, that is, barriers to entry are so severe that it is impossible for new firms to enter the market.

In static monopoly the monopolist is in a position to set the market price. However, unlike a perfectly competitive producer the monopolist's marginal and average revenue curves are not identical. The monopolist faces a downward-sloping demand curve (DD in Figure 5.2) and the sale of additional units of its product forces down the price at which *all* units must be sold. The objective of the monopolist, like that of the competitive firm, is assumed to be profit maximisation and it operates with complete knowledge of relevant cost and demand data. Accordingly, the monopolist will aim to produce at that price-output combination which equates mar-

ginal cost and marginal revenue. Figure 5.2 indicates the short-run equilibrium position for the monopolist. The monopolist will supply OQ_e output
at a price of OP_e. At the equilibrium price, the monopolist secures above-
normal profits (P_exyz). Unlike the competitive firm situation, where entry
is unfettered, entry barriers in monopoly are assumed to be so great as to
preclude new suppliers. There is thus no possibility of additional productive resources entering the industry and in consequence the monopolist
will continue to earn above-normal profits over the long term (until such
time as supply and demand conditions radically change). Market theory
predicts that given identical cost and demand conditions, monopoly leads
to a higher price and a lower output than does perfect competition.

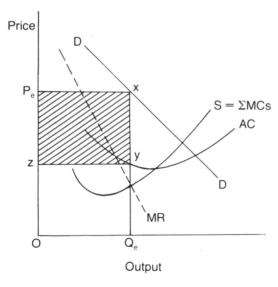

Figure 5.2 Monopoly

5.3 MONOPOLY AND PERFECT COMPETITION COMPARED

Equilibrium under perfect competition occurs where supply equates with
demand. This is illustrated in Figure 5.3 where the competitive supply
curve is MC (the sum of all the individual suppliers' marginal cost curves).
The competitive output is OQ_c and the competitive price is OP_c. Since the
supply curve is the sum of the marginal cost curves, it follows that in
equilibrium, marginal cost equals price. Assume now that this industry is
monopolised as a result, say, of one firm taking over all the other suppliers,
but that there are no economies of scale to be gained from rationalising
production into fewer, larger plants. Thus, the monopolist continues to
supply the market, as before, from the many small plants it has acquired.

It follows that the marginal costs will be the same for the monopolist as for the competitive industry, and, hence, their supply curves will be identical. As noted above, the monopolist seeking to maximise profits will equate marginal cost with marginal revenue, though in the case of monopoly, marginal revenue will be below price. In consequence, in equilibrium, market output falls from OQ_c to OQ_m and the market price rises from OP_c to OP_m.

The conclusion of competitive optimality, however, rests on a number of assumptions, some of which are highly questionable, in particular the assumption that cost structures are identical for small, perfectly competitive firms and large monopoly (and oligopolistic) suppliers, while, given its static framework, it ignores important dynamic influences, such as technological progress.

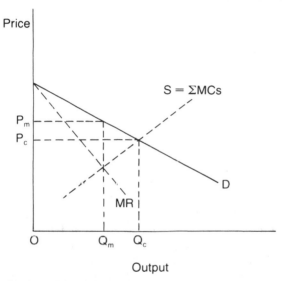

Figure 5.3 Monopoly and competition compared

In a static monopoly, a fundamental assumption is that costs are the same for both small competitive suppliers and a single (multi-plant) monopolist. In practice, however, production in a particular market is often characterised by significant economies of scale. In such cases opportunities exist for monopolists to rationalise production and concentrate output in fewer, larger plants (or even a single plant), with consequent reductions in unit costs. Figure 5.4 illustrates the reduction in unit costs achieved through exploiting economies of scale.

The downward-sloping long-run average cost curve (LRAC) shows the potential for reducing unit costs by producing on a larger scale. The average and marginal costs of a small-scale plant are shown by AC_{pc} and MC_{pc}, whilst the average and marginal costs of a large-scale plant are shown by AC_m and MC_m. The unit cost difference between the two plants $(C_{pc} - C_m)$ shows the potential which a large-scale producer has for lowering prices.

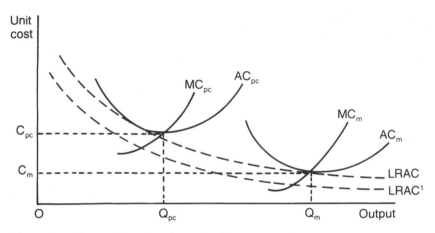

Figure 5.4 Economies of scale and unit cost reductions

The fall in unit costs as a result of the rationalisation of production by the monopolist lowers the short-run marginal cost curve of the monopolist (MC_m) compared to the original short-run marginal cost curves of the smaller competitive suppliers (MC_{pc}). This is shown in Figure 5.5. Because of the fall in unit costs, *more* output is produced by the profit-maximising monopolist (OQ_m) at a *lower* market price (OP_m). There is growing evidence to the effect that the long-run average cost curve (and hence the related MC curve) for many capital-intensive markets is L-shaped, as in Figure 5.4. In these markets total demand and individual market share, not cost considerations, are the factors limiting the size of the firm. The firm may thus grow and find a level of output such that further expansion would be unprofitable. However, in doing so it may become so large relative to the market that it attains a degree of power over price. This is not to deny that the monopolist could further increase output and lower price, were it not trying to maximise its profit. Such a position would not, however, be the result of a return to perfect competition. What has happened is that the firm, seeking its best profit position, has abandoned the status of an insignificant small competitor. It has not necessarily done so through a systematic attempt to dominate the market. On the contrary, it is the underlying cost conditions of the market that have impelled this growth. In such a market it is possible that small 'competitive-sized' firms cannot survive. Moreover, to the extent that the unit costs are lower at higher production levels the large firm is a technically more efficient entity.

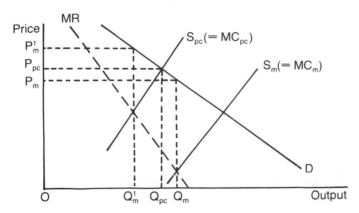

Figure 5.5 Progressive monopoly

The analysis developed above also neglects *dynamic* aspects of the market system. In practice, major improvements in consumer welfare occur largely as a result of technological innovations, that is, the growth of resources and development of new techniques and products over time, rather than adjustments to provide maximum output from a given (static) input; and often monopolistic elements function as a precondition and protection of innovating effort. A monopolist, earning above-normal profits, will have the financial resources to promote technical advance, but its incentive to innovate may be weak given the lack of effective competition. However, technological advance is a means of lowering unit costs and thereby expanding profits; and these profits will not be transitory, given barriers to entry; hence, the monopolist must persist and succeed in the area of technological advance to maintain its dominant position.

Diagrammatically, the proposition that monopoly may lead to a more effective performance can be demonstrated by using Figures 5.4 and 5.5. In Figure 5.5 the competitive market produces OQ_{pc}, where short-run marginal cost equals price. If this industry were monopolised, the conventional expectation would be a price rise to OP^1_m and an output decrease to OQ^1_m. However, if the monopolist in such a market introduces cost-saving innovations, the long-run average cost curve in Figure 5.4 will shift downward from LRAC to LRAC^1, and the marginal cost curve will fall. This fall in the marginal cost curve means that the monopolist may actually produce more (OQ_m) at a lower price (OP_m) than the original competitive industry, as shown in Figure 5.5.

It is, of course, possible that society will remain worse off under monopoly, even if the monopoly innovates; the benefits of innovation may not outweigh the costs of monopolistic exploitation.

Between the extremes of perfect competition and monopoly lie a number of intermediate forms of market which display some characteristics of the two extreme types, in particular 'monopolistically competitive' and 'oligopoly' markets.

5.4 MONOPOLISTIC COMPETITION

Monopolistic competition is characterised by:

1 many firms and buyers, that is, the market is comprised of a large number of independently acting firms and buyers;
2 differentiated products, that is, the products offered by competing firms are differentiated from each other in one or more respects. These differences may be of a physical nature, involving functional features, or may be purely 'imaginary', in the sense that artificial differences are created through advertising and sales promotion;
3 free market entry and exit, that is, there are no barriers to entry preventing new firms entering the market or obstacles in the way of existing firms leaving the market. (No allowance is made in the theory of monopolistic competition for the fact that product differentiation, by establishing strong brand loyalties to established firms' products, may act as a barrier to entry.)

Apart from the product differentiation aspects, monopolistic competition is structurally very similar to perfect competition.

The analysis of individual firm equilibrium in monopolistic competition can be presented in terms of a 'representative' firm – that is, all firms are assumed to face identical cost and demand conditions, and each is a profit maximiser – from which it is then possible to derive a market-equilibrium position.

The significance of product differentiation is that (a) each firm has a market which is partially distinct from its competitors; that is, each firm faces a downward-sloping demand curve (d in Figure 5.6(a)), although the presence of closely competing substitute products will cause this curve to be relatively price sensitive; (b) the firms' cost structures (marginal cost and average costs) are raised as a result of incurring differentiation expenditures (selling costs).

The firm, being a profit maximiser, will aim to produce at that price (OP), output (OQ) combination, shown in Figure 5.6(a), which equates cost (MC) and marginal revenue (MR). In the short run this may result in firms securing above-normal profits of XY per unit or PXYZ in total.

In the long-run, above-normal profits will induce new firms to enter the market and this will affect the demand curve faced by established firms

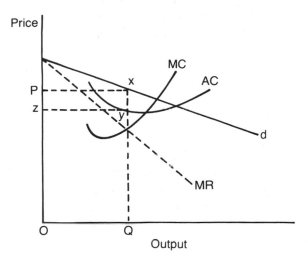

(a) Short-run equilibrium

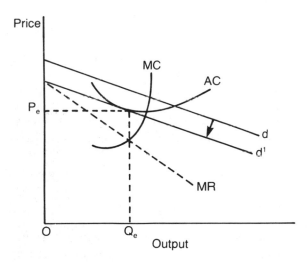

(b) Long-run equilibrium

Figure 5.6 Monopolistic competition

(that is, push the demand curve leftwards from d to d¹, thereby reducing the volume of sales associated with each price level). The process of new entry will continue until the excess profits have been competed away. Figure 5.6(b) shows the long-run equilibrium position of the 'representative' firm. The firm continues to maximise its profits at a price (OP$_e$), output (OQ$_e$) combination where marginal cost equals marginal revenue, but now secures only a normal profit return. This normal profit position for the firm in the long run is similar to the long-run equilibrium position for the firm in perfect competition. However, monopolistic competition results in a less efficient market performance when compared to perfect competition. Specifically, monopolistically competitive firms produce lower rates of output and sell these outputs at higher prices than perfectly competitive firms. Since the demand curve is downwards sloping, it is necessarily tangent to the long-run average cost curve (which is higher than the perfectly competitive firm's cost curve because of the addition of selling costs) to the left of the latter's minimum point. Firms thus operate a less than optimum scale of plant and as a result there is excess capacity in the market.

5.5 OLIGOPOLY

Oligopoly is characterised by:

1 few firms and many buyers, that is, the bulk of market supply is in the hands of a relatively few large firms who sell to many small buyers;
2 homogeneous or differentiated products, that is, the products offered by suppliers may be identical or, more commonly, differentiated from each other in one or more respects. These differences may be of a physical nature, involving functional features, or may be purely 'imaginary', in the sense that artificial differences are created through advertising and sales promotion;
3 difficult market entry, that is, the existence of high barriers to entry which represent obstacles in the way of new firms entering the market.

The primary characteristic associated with the condition of 'fewness' is known as mutual interdependence. Basically, each firm when deciding upon its price and other marketing strategies must explicitly take into account the likely reactions and countermoves of its competitors in response to its own moves. A price cut, for example, may appear to be advantageous to one firm considered in isolation, but if this results in other firms also cutting their prices to protect their sales, then all firms may suffer reduced profits. Accordingly, oligopolists tend to avoid price competition, employing various mechanisms such as price leadership and cartels to coordinate their prices. In some cases, those mechanisms are used in order to maximise the joint profits of the firms concerned, leading to industry output and price levels similar to those of a single firm monopoly.

5.5.1 Price leadership

Price leadership results when one firm establishes itself as the market leader and takes the initiative in setting prices and other firms in the market accept its pricing policy. Such leadership can only work, however, where the firm taking the initiating role can be confident that the other oligopolists will follow its lead. This requires a degree of tacit collusion, with an implicit recognition by all firms in the market that one of them is taking the initiative with group interests in mind.

Price leadership may be exercised by a 'dominant' firm. The dominant firm price leader may well be the largest firm in the group, particularly if it is also the lowest-cost supplier. Such low costs enable the firm to take the initiative in setting price and other sellers have little alternative but to follow because of the power of the dominant firm to punish non-compliance by, for example, subjecting non-following firms to selective price cutting.

Figure 5.7 illustrates price leadership by a low-cost firm. Firm A is the low-cost supplier with the marginal cost curve MC_A; firm B has higher costs, with a marginal cost curve MC_B. The individual demand curve of each firm is dd when they set identical prices (that is, it is assumed that total industry sales at each price are divided equally between the two firms); MR is the associated marginal revenue curve. Firm A is able to

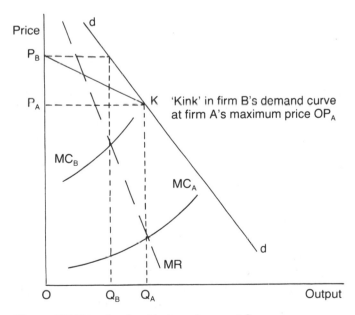

Figure 5.7 Price leadership by a low-cost firm

maximise its profits by producing output OQ_A (where $MC_A = MR$) at a price of OP_A. Firm B would like to charge a higher price (OP_B), but the best it can do is to accept the price set by firm A, although this means less than maximum profit. Given firm B's conjecture about the reactions of firm A to any price change by B, any alternative course of action would mean even less profit. If B were to charge a higher price than OP_A it would lose sales to firm A (whose price is unchanged), moving left along a new 'kinked' demand curve segment KP_B; if B were to cut its price below P_A, this would force firm A to undertake matching price cuts, moving right along the demand-curve segment Kd. Firm B could not hope to win such a 'price war', because of its higher costs. Thus, firm B's best course of action is to charge the same price as that established by firm A.

Alternatively, the low-cost firm might be prepared to accept price leadership by a higher cost rival, since a price which enables the least efficient supplier to cover its costs and make comfortable profits will allow the low-cost firm to make even larger profits. (See Chapter 7, Box 7.6.)

5.5.2 Cartels

The centralised cartel case with all its restraints on individual member firms illustrates collusion in its most complete form. Under the cartel arrangement, a central administration agency determines the price and output of the market, and the output quotas of each of the separate member firms, in such a way as to maximise the joint profits of the group. Price and output will thus tend to approximate those of a profit-maximising monopolist.

Figure 5.8 shows how two firms can get together and set prices so as to maximise total industry profits. The marginal cost curves of each firm (MC_1 and MC_2) are summed horizontally to arrive at an industry marginal cost curve, MC. Equating the cartel's total marginal cost (MC) with the industry marginal revenue curve (MR) determines the profit-maximising output (OQ) and the profit maximising price (OP). Both firms will charge this profit maximising price and each firm will determine its output by equating its own marginal cost to the industry profit-maximising marginal cost level. In this way profits (the shaded areas) are generated between firms on the basis of their individual outputs OQ_1 and OQ_2. It will be noted that firm 1, as the lowest cost producer, receives the largest quota and contributes the most profit to the cartel. However, the profit share-out among cartel members is not necessarily in exact proportion to the profit that each generates, and the lowest-cost producer may contribute some of its profit generated to other cartel members to secure group cohesion, on the grounds that the profits obtained by collaborating with competitors are still greater than from going it alone.

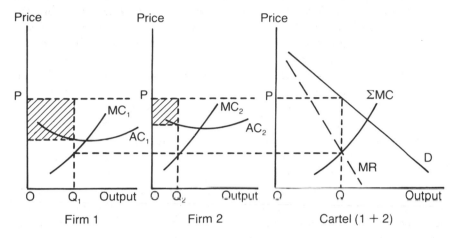

Figure 5.8 Price-output determination for a cartel

Agreement towards a policy of joint profit maximisation is easier the smaller the number of firms, the more homogeneous the product, and the more alike the firms are in terms of cost structure. The break-up of a cartel agreement is most likely to arise from the lowest-cost firms attempting to increase their profits by secretly exceeding their output quotas (see Chapter 7, Box 7.5).

Disagreement over the allocation of quotas and profits is more likely the greater the number of member firms. In practice, full cartels are rarely encountered. Where collusion is practised, this tends to take the form of price-fixing, with firms competing for market share through product differentiation.

5.5.3 Non-price competition in oligopoly

Oligopolists, we have noted, tend to avoid price competition. Instead they prefer to channel most of their competitive efforts into various forms of product-differentiation activity, most notably product variations and sales promotion. Price cuts can be quickly and easily met by a firm's rivals – the likelihood of securing a significant increase in market share through price competition is small, while there is the obvious danger of reduced profits. In consequence, oligopolists are inclined to feel that more permanent advantages can be gained over rivals through non-price competition because product differentiation strategies are often difficult to duplicate so readily and so completely as price reductions.

Advertising is one main form of differentiation activity and may be usefully examined to illustrate the impact of policies in this area. Advertising is aimed at informing prospective buyers of the product's attributes and persuading them that a particular brand is superior to those offered by competitors. The purpose of advertising is to increase the firm's sales and market share by cultivating and maintaining strong brand loyalties.

The extent to which the firm's sales respond to increased advertising depends on the promotional elasticity of demand. A high promotional elasticity of demand will result in a more than proportionate increase in sales. Whether or not it is profitable for the firm to advertise will depend also on production costs. If the firm is operating under conditions of decreasing production costs, its profits will be increased as sales expand. Assuming the firm to be a profit maximiser, selling costs will be increased to the point where the marginal cost of inducing a further shift in the demand curve is just equal to anticipated marginal receipts.

The conventional approach to the analysis of the relationship between advertising and the position of the firm's demand curve is shown in Figure 5.9. It is assumed that the promotional elasticity demand is greater than unity and production costs fall (up to a point) as output expands. It can be seen that advertising produces a beneficial allocative effect insofar as the level of output is higher with advertising (OQ_2) than without advertising (OQ_1) and supply prices have been lowered from OP_1 to OP_2.

If these two conditions are not met, i.e. promotional elasticity of demand is low *and* unit costs do not fall as output expands, the effects of advertising may then be detrimental to the consumer. Specifically the extra costs incurred in advertising may be passed on to consumers in the form of higher prices; and where advertising acts as an important barrier to entry, this can serve to protect excess profits.

Traditional (static) market theory shows oligopoly to result in a 'monopoly-like' suboptimal market performance: output is restricted to levels below cost minimisation; inefficient firms are cushioned by a 'reluctance' to engage in price competition; differentiation competition increases supply costs; prices are set above minimum supply costs, yielding oligopolists above-normal profits which are protected by barriers to entry. As with monopoly, however, this analysis makes no allowance for the contribution that economies of scale may make to the reduction of market costs and prices and the important contribution of oligopolistic competition to innovation and new product development.

5.6 BARRIERS TO ENTRY AND POTENTIAL COMPETITION

It has been indicated that the 'condition of entry' has an important bearing on the long-run rate of profit earned by the suppliers in a market. If new entry to a market can be achieved without impediment (as in perfect competition), the new entrant being at no disadvantage *vis-à-vis* established

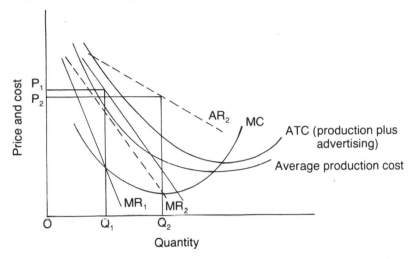

Figure 5.9 Effect of advertising on price and output

producers, there will be a long-run tendency for sellers to earn only normal profits. Where entry barriers are substantial, however, persistent excess profits may be earned by established sellers.

Barriers to entry come in a number of forms. Entrants, for example, may be put at a *relative* cost disadvantage because of their inability (lack of finance, low market share) to operate an optimal-sized plant; entrants may be put at an *absolute* cost disadvantage through the ownership of superior technology, and control of input sources and distribution channels, by established firms; entrants may be unable to establish their products in the market because of customer loyalty to existing brands, built up by cumulative investments in product differentiation.

Whether or not entry into a market will occur depends upon the profits the potential entrant expects to earn. These will depend upon the entrant's own cost position and upon the post-entry price and demand conditions anticipated by it. These factors, in turn, will depend on the anticipated reaction of established producers to entry.

The existing theory of entry is largely based on the assumption that potential entrants anticipate that established firms will *maintain* their outputs at the pre-entry level, following actual entry. This proposition is shown in the context of Figures 5.10 and 5.11, where the barrier to entry is assumed to be one of scale economies. In Figure 5.10, given the above assumption, the potential entrant's demand curve – d entrant – is the segment of the industry demand curve, D, to the right of the pre-entry output OQ₁ produced by established firms. The potential entrant will decide whether or not to enter the market by comparing this demand curve with its own cost position. The potential entrant is assumed to have access to the same average cost curve as that of established firms (i.e. there are no absolute cost advantages accruing to established firms). Economies of scale, however, are important, such that in order to operate a minimum optimal scale of plant, the entrant would need to supply an output of

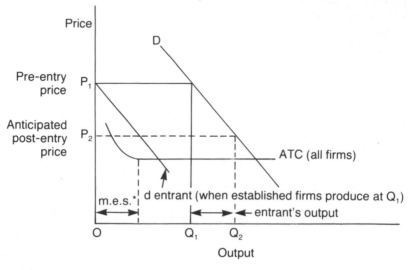

*m.e.s. (minimum efficient scale) = entrant's output

Figure 5.10 Scale economies and new entry

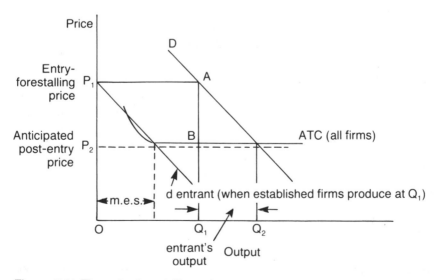

Figure 5.11 The entry-forestalling price

Q_1Q_2. It will be noted that as a result of the addition of this 'extra' output to the existing market supply, the market price is lowered to OP_2. Hence, the price that is relevant to entry decisions is the anticipated post-entry price, not the existing pre-entry price.

The existence of substantial scale economies is not in itself sufficient to prevent entry. Entry will occur despite this factor, provided that the entrant's anticipated cost and demand conditions permit it to make a profit at the new market price. If the potential entrant's average cost curve is below the post-entry price, as in Figure 5.10, entry will occur since the entrant can make a profit; entry will not occur if the anticipated post-entry price is below the entrant's average cost curve, as in Figure 5.11, because losses would then be incurred.

The greater the importance of scale economies, the greater is the amount by which established firms can raise prices above the average cost curve (ie make 'above-normal' profits) without inducing entry.

If the established firms actively seek to prevent the emergence of new competition, then they will aim to produce output OQ_1 in Figure 5.11. The entry-forestalling price is thus OP_1, the height of the scale economies barrier to entry, the size of unit 'excess' profits being measured by the distance AB.

However, there are a number of problems with limit pricing theory. The theory requires established firms to be fully alert to the 'threat' posed by potential entrants. There is no strong empirical evidence that firms do in fact monitor their environments to the extent suggested by the theory, and lack of information makes it difficult in any case to *identify* potential newcomers and the seriousness of their intentions. Moreover, assuming that established firms do actively attempt to prevent entry, there is the problem of agreeing upon the limit price – a particular difficulty when firms have different cost structures. Finally, static theory assumes that a number of market conditions conducive to limit pricing are present, in particular static technology and market demand. In reality, however, such conditions are rarely present. Thus, unless established firms are active innovators and sensitive to changes in consumer demand, opportunities for entry may arise. For example, entrants may install new technology in a new plant, giving them cost advantages over established firms operating older plants, and product innovation may enable entrants to win a viable market share by offering customers products which are superior to those supplied by established firms.

QUESTIONS

1 In what ways does perfect competition result in an 'optimal' market performance?

2 Critically evaluate the proposition that monopoly leads to an 'inefficient' market performance when compared to perfect competition.

3 'The firm under perfect competition can sell as much as it wants at the ruling market price. Should a firm find itself in a monopoly position it would be faced with a downward-sloping demand curve and could only increase sales by reducing price. Therefore, monopolistic control benefits consumers.' Discuss.

4 To what extent does the profit made by a firm depend upon the type of market in which the firm operates?

5 Compare the market performance results of perfect competition with those of monopolistic competition.

6 What is meant by the term 'mutual interdependency'? What are its likely consequences for inter-firm behaviour?

7 Why is price parallelism a feature of oligopolistic markets? Which mechanisms may be used by oligopolists to secure coordinated pricing?

8 Examine the possible effects of advertising on market performance.

Chapter 6

Market structure

Market structure refers to the way in which a market is 'organised'. Market analysis focuses especially on those aspects of market structure which have an important influence on the behaviour of suppliers and buyers and on market performance. Structural features having a major strategic importance in relation to market conduct and performance include:

- the number of suppliers and their relative size distribution, indicating the extent of seller concentration in the market;
- the number of buyers and their relative size distribution, indicating the extent of buyer concentration in the market;
- the nature of the product supplied, whether it is a standardised good or service, or supplied in a variety of differentiated formats;
- the condition of entry to the market (the extent to which established suppliers have advantages over potential new entrants because of barriers to entry) and, likewise;
- barriers to exit (factors encouraging suppliers to remain in the market, even under adverse circumstances);
- the degree of vertical integration, that is, the extent to which suppliers produce their own input requirements, or engage in later processing stages or own distribution outlets;
- the degree to which suppliers are diversified into other markets, giving them 'deep pocket' advantages (cross-subsidisation) over specialised suppliers;
- the extent to which companies operate on an international basis, which gives them options in supplying a market not available to purely national suppliers.

6.1 MARKET CONCENTRATION

Market concentration refers to the extent to which the supply of a good or service is controlled by the leading suppliers of the product (seller concentration), and the extent to which the purchase of a product is controlled by the leading buyers (buyer concentration).

Some markets are characterised by a very high degree of seller concentration. The UK detergents market, for example, is dominated by Procter and Gamble (45 per cent market share in 1992) and Unilever (44 per cent market share); the supply of sugar in the UK is controlled by British Sugar (52 per cent market share) and Tate and Lyle (40 per cent market share), while a single supplier dominates the UK market for household gas (British Gas, 100 per cent market share), matches (Bryant and May, 78 per cent market share) and opium derivatives (a Glaxo subsidiary, 87 per cent market share). Other markets are more fragmented, with the leading suppliers holding smaller market shares. Bird's Eye is the leading supplier of frozen food products in the UK, with a market share of 22 per cent, followed by Ross Young (20 per cent market share) and Findus (5 per cent), the remainder of the market being supplied by a substantial number of smaller manufacturers and a multitude of retailer 'own label' brands (see Box 6.1).

High concentration levels arise for a number of reasons. In many markets, economies of scale in production, marketing and research and development are so important that in order to lower their costs, enhance their marketing effectiveness and be able to develop new products, firms must supply on a large-scale basis. In other cases, a desire to promote more 'orderly' market conditions or an outright desire to 'monopolise' a market have led to an increase in concentration levels. Ultimately, the persistence of high seller concentration over time depends on the exclusion of new competitors from the market. In some markets the level of seller concentration may increase 'organically' as a result of the more successful firms securing bigger market shares at the expense of weaker rivals; in other markets, seller concentration levels may be increased as a result of mergers and takeovers of competitors. The presumption in conventional market analysis is that the former mechanism is preferable, insofar as it occurs *through competition* and brings concomitant beneficial effects on performance (for example, lower prices, better products), whereas takeovers and mergers involve the *elimination of competition*. This distinction, however, is arbitrary. For example, mergers and takeovers may improve market performance by enabling economies of scale to be achieved or by removing excess capacity, while seller concentration achieved through competition is no guarantee of a continuance of beneficial performance results, since once market dominance has been established it may then be 'abused' (see Chapter 9).

On the other hand, a market may become less concentrated over time as the result of public policy (for example, the removal of statutory monopoly protection in the UK gas and telecommunications markets) and the emergence of new competitors. Rank Xerox's share of the UK photocopying

Box 6.1   Market concentration: some UK examples

Market	*Leading suppliers*
Vitamins and dietary supplements	Hanson 27%, Boots 16%, Fisons 9%, Healthcrafts 7%, Holland and Barrett 5%, Britannia Health 4%, Roche 2%, Reckitt and Colman 2%, Warren 2%, others and 'own label' 26%
Portable radios	Sony 32%, Morphy Richards 13%, Philips/Pye 11%, Roberts Radio 7%, Panasonic 6%, Grundig 5%, others 26%
Cakes	RHM 23%, Allied-Lyons 11%, Memory Lane 3%, McVities 3%, other manufacturers 24%, 'own label' 34%
Amplifiers	Pioneer 8%, Rotel 7%, Arcam 6%, Akai 6%, Sony 6%, Technics 6%, Marantz 6%, Audio Lab 5%, Quad 4%, Denon 4%, Mission 3%, AND 3%, Kenwood 3%, Linn 2%, Nalm 2%, others 29%
Tea	Unilever 21%, Allied Lyons 19%, Hillsdown 20%, CWS 10%, others and 'own label' 30%
Shampoos	Procter and Gamble 28%, Elida Gibbs 15%, Smith Kline Beecham 10%, Alberto Culver 5%, others and 'own label' 42%
Processed nuts	United Biscuits 57%, Pepsico 12%, other manufacturers 3%, 'own label' 26%
Insulating firebricks	MPK 39%, Steetley 28%, Morgan 15%, others 17%
Mains cables	DCC 24%, BICC 21%, Pirelli 14%, Sterling 14%, GEC 10%, others 18%
Beer	Bass 22%, Courage 21%, Allied-Carlsberg 16%, Whitbread 12%, S&N 11%, others 18%
Coffee	Nestlé 47%, General Foods 18%, Brooke Bond (Allied Lyons) 6%, other branded 5%, 'own label' 24%

Sources: Retail Business and MMC

market fell from 90 per cent in 1975 to around 30 per cent in 1991 in the face of the entry of powerful international competitors such as Canon (15 per cent market share in 1991) and Kodak (10 per cent market share). Likewise BPB, which was the UK's sole manufacturer of plasterboard until 1988 (1988 market share 97 per cent, imports 3 per cent), saw its market share fall to 76 per cent in 1990 with the entry of three new suppliers, RPL (12 per cent market share) Knauf (6 per cent market share) and Eternit (3 per cent market share).

The significance of seller concentration for market analysis and competitive strategy lies in its effect on the nature and intensity of competition. Structurally, as the level of seller concentration in a market progressively increases, 'competition between the many' becomes 'competition between the few' until, at the extreme, the market is totally monopolised by a single supplier. In terms of market conduct, as supply becomes concentrated in fewer and fewer hands, so that suppliers' fortunes become more and more interdependent, they may seek to avoid certain actions which are potentially ruinous (for example, aggressive price competition), preferring instead to channel their main efforts into advertising and product innovation, activities which offer a more profitable and effective way of establishing competitive advantages over rivals.

Concentration ratios are used by economists to measure the degree of seller concentration in a market. A typical concentration ratio (see Figure 6.1) shows the proportion of total domestic market sales of a product that is accounted for by the largest five *domestic* producers. Such concentration ratios are often used in market analysis and the application of public policy as 'proxies' to indicate the degree of competition or monopolisation present in a market, but their focus is too limited to capture the full nuances of market forces. For example, a concentration ratio may *overstate* the degree of monopolisation of a market because it does not include imports of the product (import penetration may be substantial – as in the UK textile, footwear and car markets) and because it makes no allowance for the effects of high concentration on the buying side of the market (large buyers may pressurise suppliers into discount competition). Moreover, the potency of competition from substitute products may be underestimated because (as discussed in Chapter 1) the concentration ratio may be applied to a market which has been too narrowly 'defined'. By the same token, the degree of monopolisation may be *understated* because although in structural terms the market may exhibit relatively low levels of concentration, suppliers may be parties to a price-fixing and market-sharing cartel. Moreover, a market may be extensively segmented, such that while the overall level of market concentration may be low, particular segments may be dominated by a single supplier. For example, although McCain's accounts for only 2 per cent of the UK frozen food market, it supplies over half the market for frozen chips.

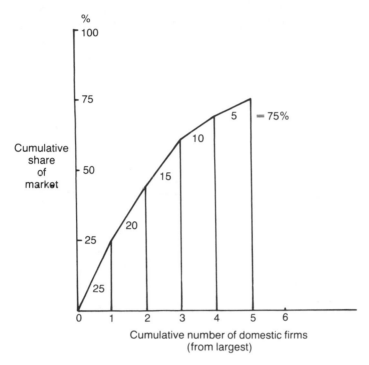

Figure 6.1 Concentration ratio

Buyer concentration is usually negligible or non-existent in most 'final' (that is, consumer good) markets, since purchases by individual consumers are small-scale. Many 'intermediate' (that is, producer good) markets and retailing are, however, themselves heavily concentrated and in a position to exercise buyer power. Thus, for example, the National Health Service accounts for around 90 per cent of UK purchases of ethical pharmaceutical drugs and in recent years has sought to keep drug prices down to keep its own healthcare spending under control; BT is the preponderant buyer of telecommunication equipment in the UK, both as a user itself and as the UK's main distributor of such equipment to other users. The emergence of major multiple retail chains such as Sainsbury and Tesco in the UK has been a particularly potent source of buyer power and these groups have been able to secure favourable bulk-buying discounts from supplying firms.

6.2 PRODUCT CHARACTERISTICS

The products supplied in a market may take the form of broadly standardised items or they may be differentiated in a number of ways: suppliers may offer different *versions* of the 'same' product (for example, 'basic', 'deluxe' and 'super deluxe' models of a small-sized car), may offer a diverse range of the product (for example, small-sized cars, medium-sized cars and large-sized cars), and may attempt to distinguish their particular range and models from rivals' offerings by branding and 'psychological' appeals.

Standardised or homogeneous products are usually found in 'intermediary' goods markets (raw materials, components, etc. – see Box 6.2) and often are supplied according to an industry or government-imposed 'grading' system, as is the case for iron ore, timber, etc. or to a common technical specification, such as the British Standard Specification which covers such things as electric meters, valves, gauges, etc.. Some 'final' products may also be supplied in a standardised format; for example, eggs in the UK are classified by size (Class A, B, C, etc.) and petrol is retailed according to a 'star' code (two star, four star) as well as in unleaded form. Even such products, however, may be subjected to attempts by suppliers to apply branding and other differentiation techniques to reduce their 'sameness'; for example, Esso petrol, it is suggested, 'puts a tiger in your tank', implying a performance superior to rival brands.

Box 6.2   Standard types of plasterboard sold in the United Kingdom

Primary board	*Secondary board*
Baseboard	Duplex
Lath	Vapour barrier
Wallboard	Plastic faced
Fireline	Thermal laminate
Moisture resistant	Paramount dry partition

Source: BPB

Where products are regarded by buyers as homogeneous (that is, virtually identical) and as such closely substitutable one for another, buyers will have no particular 'preferences' for the products of any particular supplier and will be strongly influenced to switch from one supplier's product to another's by a price differential. Thus, in markets where products are highly standardised, market competition is typically price-driven and the prices offered by rival suppliers are likely to be the same (that is, 'parallel') as a result of competitive pressures, rather than because suppliers have deliberately set out to eliminate price competition (that is, to 'rig' the market price through collusion).

In many markets the products supplied are differentiated rather than standardised. Product differentiation takes two main forms:

1 Variations in the physical attributes and properties of the product across

the product range or within a particular model group in terms of, for example, innovatory features, quality, design, functional use and accessories.

2 Products may be differentiated by advertising and promotional techniques aimed at shaping buyers' perceptions of the product.

Product differentiation is an important means of market segmentation, targeting particular products at particular buyer groups, and aims to establish strong customer loyalties to the firm's brands, thereby enabling suppliers to command premium prices while reducing the likelihood of buyers switching to competitors' brands. (These and other aspects of differentiation activity are discussed in more detail below.)

The significance of product differentiation for market analysis is thus that it widens the parameters of competitive action from one based largely on price, to the deployment of various other 'marketing mix' instruments: advertising and sales promotion, new product introductions and variations of existing products, after-sales service, channels of distribution, all of which implies a much more complex and subtle pattern of market behaviour.

Market segmentation, regular new product launches and heavy promotional backing for established brands are a feature, for example, of the paint, coffee and household cleaner markets (see Box 6.3). While product differentiation is often seen as a form of 'market imperfection', this should not be interpreted to mean that heterogeneity as such is bad. Quite the contrary – genuine differences among products, sustained by product innovation, imply greater diversity and more *choices* for consumers.

Box 6.3   Market segmentation and product differentiation in the UK tea market

The table shows a sectoral breakdown of the 'traditional' tea market in the UK which is based largely on differences in product quality. The rest of the market is represented by newly emerging products such as decaffeinated, instant and herb and fruit teas. Every sector includes both bagged and loose teas, except 'in-cup', which is exclusively bagged. Within each of these sectors the leading manufacturers' brands compete against each other and against smaller manufacturers' brands and retailers' 'own-label' brands. Product differentiation is based extensively on tea flavours and packaging, with advertising and promotion being used to emphasise imputed product qualities: 'There's tea, there's tea and there's Typhoo' is a typical advertising 'message'.

Traditional tea types and main brands, 1992

Main brands

Tea type	% market share	Brooke Bond[1]	Premier Teas[2]	Lyons Tetley[3]	Other manufacturers	Retailer 'own label'
Speciality	3.5	• Sir Thomas Lipton	• Melroses • Ridgeways	– –	• Twinings Sp • Jacksons Sp • Taylors Sp	• Sainsbury Speciality • Tesco Speciality • Asda Speciality
Quality	3.0	• Brooke Bond Choicest	• Ridgeways Imperial	• Tetley Gold • Red Label	• Twinings Classic • Taylors Gold	• Sainsbury Gold • Tesco Gold • Asda Gold
Premium	73.3	• Brooke Bond PG Tips • Brooke Bond Scottish Blend	• Typhoo • Glengettie	• Tetley • Quick Brew	• Ringtons • Taylors	• Sainsbury Red • Tesco Premium • Asda Superior
Economy	16.9	• Brooke Bond D	• Fresh Brew • Kardomah	• Silver Label • Orange Label	• Kings Cup	• Sainsbury Brown • Tesco Quality • Asda Fine
In-cup	3.4	• PG Tags	• Typhoo One Cup • Fresh Brew One Cup • Glengettie Tea for one	• Tetley One Cup	–	• Sainsbury Red • Tesco One Cup • Asda Superior

Notes:
[1] Owned by Unilever, 21 per cent market share in 1991
[2] Owned by Hillsdown Holdings, 20 per cent market share in 1991
[3] Owned by Allied-Lyons, 19 per cent market share in 1991

Source: Typhoo Tea Report, 1992

6.3 CONDITION OF ENTRY

Market entry refers to a situation where a new supplier comes into a market. An entrant may be a 'greenfield' (start-up) business which establishes a new supply source, or the entrant could be an existing business which chooses to effect entry by merger with, or takeover of, an established producer in the market. The 'condition of entry' refers to the ease or difficulty new suppliers face in entering a market.

Market entry occurs largely in response to the perceived long-run profit potential of the target market, which in turn is importantly influenced by the size of the market and its perceived growth potential, both with respect to the expansion of total primary demand and particular market segments. Successful new entry requires the firm to overcome any initial *barriers to entry*. In some markets, entry is relatively simple – the establishment of a new hairdressing business, for example, can require little capital outlay (premises can be rented, and second-hand rather than new hair driers, etc. can be purchased) and little training or experience may be required. By contrast, entering the petrochemical market requires the outlay of millions of pounds on complex plant and equipment and specialised know-how. Entry in some markets may be impossible (for example, the government may have established a state monopoly) or temporarily prevented by, for example, exclusive patent rights granted to established firms.

Barriers to entry represent obstacles in the way of firms attempting to enter a market and which operate to give established firms particular advantages over newcomers (see Box 6.4). There are a number of potential barriers to entry, including:

- *Economies of scale*: where unit costs of production, marketing, distribution and research and development, decline with the volume produced, the minimum efficient scale of operation may require entry on a large scale; otherwise entrants would be put at a relative cost disadvantage.
- *Product differentiation:* entrants with 'unknown' and 'untried' products may be unable to win a viable share of the market because of customer loyalty to existing brands built up by established firms through cumulative investment in advertising and sales promotion.
- *Capital requirements*: the cost of financing investment in plant and product differentiation, and meeting initial operating losses, may be prohibitively high.
- *Vertical restrictions*: key raw materials, component sources and distribution channels may be controlled by established firms, thereby limiting access to inputs and market outlets;
- *Absolute cost disadvantages*: entrants, for example, may be denied access to 'best state-of-the-art technology' because of patent rights accruing to established firms, and thus be forced to adopt inferior, higher cost methods of production, etc.

Some potential barriers to entry can be regarded as a 'natural' consequence of the economics of the market (for example, economies of scale); others, however, may be 'artificial' and designed to hamper competition (for example, exclusive dealing contracts). Moreover, entrants must be

Box 6.4   Barriers to entry and market entry: the UK plasterboard market

The UK plasterboard market has been transformed by the entry in 1987 and 1988, respectively of two new businesses, RPL (a joint venture company 51 per cent owned by an established UK building materials group, Redland, and 49 per cent by CSR, an Australian producer of plasterboard) and Knauf, a German producer of plasterboard. Previously, BPB was the sole UK producer of the product, accounting for 96 per cent of market supply (imports accounting for the remainder).

In its evidence to the Monopolies and Mergers Commission (*Plasterboard* report, 1990)) RPL identified a number of barriers to the entry of 'new credible' suppliers to the UK market:

1   Technology represented a major obstacle to a would-be entrant with no existing plasterboard experience. While plasterboard plants could be purchased 'off the shelf', there were often significant technical problems in operation, and, as manufacture was computer-controlled, the ranges of board size increased the complexity of programming.
2   The capital investment required was large and there were additional costs for the entrant not previously involved in plasterboard manufacture.
3   A new entrant had to source its raw materials from outside the United Kingdom because most UK-based supplies (crucially, gypsum) were controlled by BPB.
4   There were significant economies of scale in marketing, distribution, research and development and administration.
5   BPB's strong market presence and its brand 'Gyproc' had been established for many years and would be formidable factors to overcome (para. 7.17).

In the event, these factors were not sufficient in themselves to prevent RPL and Knauf from entering the market. RPL entered the market because it 'believed that, given the existing high margins, unpopular monopoly conditions and prospects for future growth, there would be considerable potential for a second supplier to establish a sound and profitable business in the market' (para. 7.2).

Initially RPL imported plasterboard while it constructed its first (of two) UK plants which came on-stream in September 1989. CSR provided the technology and know-how needed to build the plant, while Redland provided the market expertise and distribution contacts. RPL secured access to supplies of two key raw materials: liner paper by purchasing a 51 per cent interest in a Swedish paper concern, and supplies of gypsum by importing it at competitive prices from

Spain. Knauf's first UK plant came on-stream in April 1989, similarly sourcing inputs from abroad. In 1990 RPL's share of the UK market was 12 per cent and Knauf's 6 per cent. BPB's share had fallen to 76 per cent with imports holding 6 per cent. See Chapter 10.

mindful of the likely reactions of established firms, both to the 'threat' of entry and to actual entry itself. In the former case, established firms may deliberately attempt to forestall entry not only by erecting 'artificial' barriers as noted above, but also by engaging in 'limit-pricing' strategies to reduce the attractiveness of entry (see Chapter 5). In the latter case, established firms may attempt to drive out entrants by various 'spoiling' tactics. According to evidence submitted to the Monopolies and Mergers Commission, BPB (the UK plasterboard group) reacted to the entry of Knauf of Germany in the following manner:

> the principal response of BPB to its entry into the UK market had been the lowering of BPB's plasterboard prices in West Germany very significantly, i.e. by around 30% over a period of one year. Knauf believed that BPB was attempting thereby to cut Knauf's cash flow with a view to preventing it from building a second plant.
>
> (MMC *Plasterboard* report 1990, para. 7.28)

See Chapter 10.

One, or some combination of the above factors may pose particular problems for a small, 'greenfield' (new start-up business) type of entrant. Even here, however, if markets are heavily segmented, opportunities for small 'niche' entrants may arise. For example, although Nestlé dominates the UK coffee market, successful new entry has occurred both at the premium end of the market (Douwe Egberts), and at the economy end where there has been an influx of new firms specialising in the supply of 'own label' brands to the multiple food groups. (See Chapter 10.)

Many of the entry barriers facing newcomers to the main market segments can be circumvented by merger and takeover, with entrants obtaining control of existing production facilities and leading brand names. This kind of entry is a particular feature of firms developing a 'conglomerate' business (see below). For example, BAT, the tobacco concern, entered the insurance market in the UK by acquiring the Eagle Star and Allied Dunbar groups and then entered the USA insurance market by taking over Farmers. Similarly, Nestlé entered the UK chocolate market by acquiring a leading supplier, Rowntree Mackintosh.

Moreover, the whole issue of what is and what is not a 'barrier to entry' has been called into question since much conventional market analysis is based on 'static' market conditions with incumbents invariably being assumed to possess advantages over potential entrants. In a *dynamic* market

situation, however, entrants may be in a position to introduce new technology ahead of established firms, or to develop innovative new products,
thereby giving them cost or product differentiation advantages over established firms. (see Chapter 7.)

The significance of market entry in economic analysis is the role it plays
as a market regulator. Where entry is unimpeded, new firms are able to
enter the market and in the process eliminate any tendency for established
firms to restrict market output and earn 'excessive' profits. (Compare
'perfect competition' and 'monopoly' in Chapter 5.)

6.4 CONDITION OF EXIT

Market exit refers to a situation where an established supplier leaves a
market. Market exit may involve the closure of the firm's plants or their
sale either to other suppliers operating in the market or to an 'outside'
firm wishing to enter the market (see Box 6.5). In the case of the sale of
the firm's capacity to an established supplier, this provides an opportunity
for that firm to increase its market share, and, where appropriate, to
rationalise its own capacity to take advantage of economies of large-scale
production. Market exit often occurs in response to a sustained loss-making
situation or poor profit rate or low perceived growth potential. Spillers, for
example, pulled out of the UK bread-making industry following protracted
losses; Greenall Whitley closed its two breweries because of limited
prospects for its 'real ales' and its beer brands (which it sells through
company-owned public houses) are now produced for it by Allied-
Carlsberg; Hitachi, Sharp and Sanyo have recently exited the UK portable
radio market, again because of poor profit and growth potential. In some
cases, market exit occurs not so much because of poor underlying market
conditions but rather because the firm (specifically, a conglomerate firm)
has undertaken a 'strategic' rethink: the wish to shed 'peripheral' businesses
in order to release cash and management resources, which in opportunity
cost terms could be more effectively redeployed in the firm's other activities, or a retrenchment back to 'core' businesses. Over the years, BAT, for
example, has sold its companies operating in the cosmetics, paper and
packaging, scientific instruments and chain store retailing markets, and is
now focused on the tobacco and financial services markets.

6.4.1 Barriers to exit

Barriers to exit are obstacles in the way of a firm contemplating leaving a
market which serve to keep the firm in the market despite falling sales and
profitability. There are a number of potential exit barriers, including:

Box 6.5 Market exit and barriers to exit in the UK steel castings market

In its 1990 report on the acquisition of three smaller steel casting companies by William Cook, the market leader (market share 30–5 per cent), the Monopolies and Mergers Commission welcomed this development as a further contribution to the rationalisation of an industry in secular decline. Between 1975 and 1981, thirteen plants were closed; in 1981 and 1982 a rationalisation scheme organised by the Department of Industry (which involved cash payments to firms prepared to leave the industry) led to a scrapping of fourteen plants. Taking these two phases together, about one-quarter of the industry's capacity was closed down, primarily by diversified firms with other engineering interests, rather than single-plant operators. Despite these moves, overcapacity has continued to be a problem. The tendency for firms to 'linger on' despite low profitability and losses has been attributed to a number of factors:

> Some of the barriers to exit from the steel castings industry are considerable. The cost of lay-offs and plant closures include both substantial cash payments (which may exceed the cash available to an unprofitable foundry) and management time. Closed plant has to be dismantled (at a cost) and sites cleared up and made safe. For single-plant firms, closure also means the loss of all management jobs too, and in some cases only bankruptcy can force managers to consider closure.
>
> (para 2.58)

In the case of the Cook acquisitions, the MMC noted that after the acquisition of Armadale from another casting firm, Cook intended to close it down (Armadale had been trading at a substantial loss for a number of years) but would transfer certain items of plant and equipment to another of Cook's plants not only to extend its product-range capabilities but also to increase its throughput.

- whether the firm owns the assets used to make the product, or leases them;
- the age of the firm's assets used to serve the particular market and the extent to which they have been depreciated. Where depreciation charges on old assets are low, then operating costs will be lower, and this may encourage the firm to remain in the market despite low prices. On the other hand, with fully depreciated assets the firm would suffer little capital loss in writing off these assets and exiting the market;

- the nature of the firm's assets. Specifically, if the assets are special purpose and so difficult to redeploy to other uses;
- the extent to which the firm's plant and equipment is resaleable in second-hand markets;
- whether the firm needs to make any additional investment in order to remain competitive;
- the extent of market excess capacity, and thus related price and profit levels;
- the extent of shared production and distribution facilities. For example, where a multiproduct firm's plant produces a number of different products rather than just one, then a decision to drop one product could affect the cost and availability of other products;
- the extent of vertical integration. A vertically-integrated petrochemical firm, for example, might find it difficult to drop one product without affecting downstream operations which use that product as a raw material, or upstream operations which rely upon the product as a use for their intermediate material;
- the spread of a firm's product range. A single-product firm would be reluctant to cease making its product, for then the firm would cease trading, whilst a diversified firm would find it easier to exit from one particular market since it has many others available.

As indicated above, it is usually easier for a firm to surmount some of these potential exit barriers if it is able to sell its business as a going concern, as opposed to outright closure.

The significance of market exit in economic analysis, like that of market entry, is the 'regulatory' role it plays. Thus, if there is overcapacity in the market and suppliers are experiencing low profitability or losses, then the departure of some firms (the more inefficient ones especially) from the market will, by reducing supply, enable a closer 'balancing' of supply and demand to be achieved and the establishment of market prices which provide the remaining firms with a 'fair' profit return. However, the 'condition of exit' may not be conducive to the achievement of the desired result.

6.5 VERTICAL INTEGRATION

Some firms operating in a market may be integrated into other vertically related markets, whereas some firms may be single-stage specialists. The coexistence in a particular market of vertically integrated and non-vertically integrated firms can have both favourable and adverse consequences for competition and resource allocation efficiency.

Vertical integration involves the combining in one firm of two or more vertically related activities, as opposed to these activities being performed separately in different firms and then being synchronised through arms'-length market transactions.

Backward integration occurs when a firm begins producing raw materials which were previously supplied to it by other firms (for example, a camera-producer making glass lenses); forward integration occurs when a firm undertakes further finishing of a product, final assembly or distribution (for example, an oil company which sells petrol through its own petrol stations).

From the firm's point of view, vertical integration may be advantageous because it enables the firm to reduce its production and distribution costs, by linking together successive activities, or because it is vital for it to secure reliable supplies of inputs or distribution outlets in order to remain competitive.

In terms of its wider impact on the operation of market processes, vertical integration may lead to various efficiency gains. These include technical economies from combining together successive production processes – for example, the savings made in reheating costs by combining steel furnace operations. Stockholding economies can also arise from the reduction in intermediate contingency and buffer stocks. Vertically integrated firms can eliminate some purchasing and selling expenses in negotiating outside supply and advertising/selling contracts by internalising these transactions within the firm. Managerial economies may accrue by having a single administrative system to handle several production activities, and financial economies may accrue through more advantageous bulk-buying discounts, and by lowering the cost of raising capital. Where firms achieve such efficiency gains through vertical integration, their average costs will tend to fall, thus facilitating a lowering of market prices and an increase in output.

On the other hand, however, where a firm or group of firms already dominate one or more vertical stages, vertical integration may lead to various anti-competitive effects. (See Box 6.6.) Forward integration can secure a market, but it can also foreclose it to competitors; similarly, backward integration can guarantee supply sources but it can also be used to prevent rivals gaining access to those sources. Moreover, if a firm acquires the supplier of a scarce raw material which is used by both itself and by its competitors, then it may be in a position to operate a 'price squeeze', that is, squeeze the profit margins of its competitors by raising their costs by charging them a higher price for the raw material than the price charged for its own use, while setting a relatively low final product price. Such tactics serve not only to discipline existing competitors, but also act as a barrier to entry to potential new competitors. Denied access to markets or materials, or offered access only on disadvantageous terms, potential competitors would need to set up with the same degree of integration as existing firms, and the greater initial capital requirements of such large-scale entry can be prohibitive. Thus, vertical integration may produce, simultaneously, both beneficial or detrimental effects.

Box 6.6   Vertical integration in the UK beer market

In 1989, following the Monopolies and Mergers Commission (MMC) Report on the supply of beer, the Office of Fair Trading ordered the UK's leading brewers (specifically, Bass, Allied, Grand Met., Whitbread, Courage and S&N) to divest a substantial proportion of their public houses[1] and to allow other brewers' products greater freedom of access to their remaining public houses. In the MMC's view the 'tied public house system' had produced few benefits and its main effect had been to limit competition, with various adverse consequences: (a) the price of beer had risen 'too fast' and the high price of lager was not justified by the cost of producing it; (b) there had been a restriction of consumer choice, because a brewer does not usually allow another brewer's beers or other competing products to be sold in outlets which he owns:

> We believe that the complex monopoly has enabled brewers with tied estates to frustrate the growth of brewers without tied estates; to do the same to independent wholesalers and manufacturers of cider and soft drinks; to keep tenants in a poor bargaining position; and to stop a strong independent sector emerging to challenge them at the retail level. We believe also that, over time, the monopoly has served to keep the bigger brewers big and the smaller brewers small.
>
> (para. 1.23)

[1] The MMC recommended that no brewer should own more than a maximum of 2,000 public houses. The OFT, however, implemented a revised formula, allowing brewers to retain a higher number of houses (see Chapter 9).

Leading brewers' ownership of full on-licences (mainly public houses) prior to the MMC report

	Total number of on-licences
Bass	7476
Allied	6858
Whitbread	6628
Grand Met	5266
Courage	5000
S&N	2354
	33582
Other	49518
Total on-licences	83100

6.6 DIVERSIFICATION

Some firms operating in a market may be a division or subsidiary of a 'parent' group which has business interests in a number of other markets, whereas other firms may be single business specialists. As with vertical integration, conglomerates can have both a favourable or an adverse effect on market processes.

A diversified or 'conglomerate' firm is a firm which operates in two or more markets. Diversification may be 'concentric' or 'pure', the former involving some carry-over of production or marketing functions (for example, two firms which utilise a common technological base – razor blades and garden spades, both produced from stainless steel and sold through the same outlets – supermarkets), while in the latter case the products are entirely unrelated (for example, cars and cement).

The main attraction of diversification is the ability to spread risks and broaden the firm's profit-earning potential. Specifically, a one-market firm is vulnerable not only to erratic, cyclical profit returns resulting from the business cycle, but worse still, its very survival may be threatened by a long term decline in market demand. Diversification is thus the main way the firm can reduce its exposure to business risk and fluctuating profitability, while reorientating its activities away from mature and declining markets into new areas offering sustained growth and profit opportunities.

In terms of its wider impact on resource allocation, diversification may, on the one hand, promote greater efficiency and stimulate competition, thereby improving resource allocation, or, on the other hand, by limiting competition, it may lead to a less efficient use of resources.

Diversification may produce synergy (i.e. the two plus two equals more than four effect). Synergy results from complementary activities or from the carry-over of management capabilities. For example, in the case of a diversified merger, one firm may have a strong production organisation, while the other excels in marketing – joining the two renders both firms more effective. Similarly, a high degree of carry-over of management expertise may make it possible to reduce production costs and improve product quality of the combined group.

As noted above, diversification can serve to increase the degree of competition by facilitating entry into industries where entry barriers are too high for smaller, more specialised firms without the financial resources of the conglomerate, i.e., the alternative profit sources to withstand initial losses in new markets whilst getting established. For example, Imperial Tobacco used the profits it generated from its highly profitable tobacco division to enter the UK crisp market, financing the building of three greenfield manufacturing plants and a heavy promotional campaign, and covering a six-year loss-making period. Likewise, BAT has used its tobacco profits to enter the financial services market, acquiring Eagle Star for £968m. in 1984,

Allied Dunbar for £664m. and Canada Trusco Mortgage for £918m. in 1986, and the US Farmers Group for £2.9bn. in 1987.

Diversification can, however, produce various anti-competitive effects. For example, diversified firms are in a position to cross-subsidise temporary losses in a particular market with profits earned elsewhere. This allows the diversified firm to practise predatory pricing in a market, to drive out competitors or discipline them, so raising prices to monopoly levels in the long run. The same financial power and cross-subsidising capabilities of the diversified firm can be used to bear the short-run costs of deterring new entrants into one of its markets, thereby raising entry barriers.

Where diversified firms face each other in a number of markets then they may adopt a less competitive stance, each firm avoiding taking competitive action in markets where it is strong, for fear of risking retaliatory action by diversified rivals in other markets where it is weak. Here firms may develop 'spheres of influence', adopting live-and-let-live policies by dominating in certain of their markets and recognising the dominance of rivals in other markets. The result of such behaviour is a lack of vigorous competition, with higher prices, to the detriment of consumers.

The interdependence of diversified firms as buyers and sellers may also distort competition. Where firm A is both an important supplier to firm B for one product, and an important customer of firm B for another product, they may engage in reciprocal dealing, buying from firms that are good customers rather than alternative suppliers. The practice allows diversified firms to increase their market shares and increase obstacles to new entry.

Thus, diversification may produce, simultaneously, both beneficial or detrimental results (see Box 6.7).

Box 6.7 Diversified firms, competition and efficiency

The matter of diversification has never been a strong 'up-front' issue in the application of UK competition policy: diversification has been looked at, *inter alia*, in the context of horizontal dominance and only *very* occasionally has a conglomerate merger/takeover been investigated. Some interesting light on diversification seen from a 'market perspective' is provided by the proposed takeover in 1977 of Herbert Morris, a crane-maker, by Babcock and Wilcox, a power station supplier, which was opposed by the Monopolies Commission.

Babcock was looking to reduce its dependency upon the power station market and saw the acquisition of Morris as 'being in keeping with its strategic diversification plan' (para. 47). The Commission considered the likely effects of the acquisition in three areas.

1   *Competition*: although there would be no *direct* reduction in competition, since Babcock did not produce cranes (it had done

so until 1972) various intra-divisional trading arrangements might pose problems, for example: Morris bought chains from Parsons, a subsidiary of Babcock, and thus might be 'at an advantage over other crane and hoist makers in the supply of components'. However, the business involved was small and given that no other crane manufacturer voiced objections to the Commisssion on this matter it concluded 'that the effect of the merger on competition would be insignificant' (para. 70).

2 *Production and R & D*: Babcock proposed no changes in Morris products or methods of production, and claimed no advantages in a merger resulting from economies of scale or improved efficiency. The Commission did, however, concur with Babcock's suggestion that Morris 'would benefit from access to the technological expertise of the other Babcock companies and its research and develpoment capability' (para. 72).

3 *Effects on management*: the Commission took the view that the 'imposition' of Babcock's system of corporate management involving strict 'Head Office scrutiny of operational budgets, capital spending programmes. . .' would be 'inappropriate' in the case of Morris and would lead to a loss of efficiency and competitive vigour:

> In our view Morris' success thus far has to a considerable extent depended on the company's independent and quick reacting style of management. Morris believes that such a method of operation requires a small organisation and that the need to work through the chain of command in a large organisation would inhibit its methods and enervate its performance. We see a substantial risk in this case that these fears would prove correct.

This would be compounded by the likely defection of some key Morris executives (paras 73 and 74).

6.7 MULTINATIONAL COMPANIES

The extent to which a particular market is exposed to international influences, particularly competition from imports and the activities of multinational companies (MNCs), can have an important impact on market processes. With the increasing 'openness' of the world economy (for example, the removal of tariffs and quotas under the auspices of GATT) as well as the formation of various regional free trade blocs such as the European Community, international markets have become more accessible to foreign companies. Import penetration (the proportion of domestic sales accounted for by imports) across the UK manufacturing sector taken as a whole is currently around 35 per cent and some particular markets are heavily dominated by imports (for example, printing machinery, motor cars and washing machines).

Furthermore, MNCs (defined as companies which own income-generating assets – plants, sales subsidiaries – in two or more countries) have become more prominent in many markets. MNCs typically use a combination of exporting, strategic alliances with foreign partners based either on contractual arrangements (licensing, co-marketing, etc.) or on joint ownership (equity-based joint ventures, in particular), and wholly-owned direct investment in production, selling and research operations (see Box 6.8).

Each of these strategies has specific attractions (and drawbacks) in enhancing the firm's competitiveness and its ability to successfully enter and develop a profitable position in targeted foreign markets. Exporting, for example, from an established 'home' production plant is a relatively inexpensive and low-risk way of servicing a foreign market (i.e. it obviates the need to invest in overseas plants) and maximum advantage can be taken of centralised production to secure economies of scale and thus lower unit costs. On the other hand, the firm could be put at a competitive disadvantage if host governments were to impose import restrictions, if exchange rates became unfavourable, or if the firm should lose touch with changing host country market conditions. Strategic alliances may be attractive as a means of foreign market entry if they allow partners to achieve synergistic effects through contributing particular mixes of resources and skills to a degree unavailable to each partner separately – for example, enabling foreign firms to take advantage of host country firms' local market knowledge and distribution channels. Strategic alliances, however, need careful handling to optimise results – lack of commitment, disagreements over operational matters and strategic direction may blunt the seizing of competitive opportunities. Wholly-owned foreign direct investment can be expensive and risky, but in many cases the 'presence' effects of operating locally (familiarity with local market conditions, the cultivation of contacts with local suppliers, distributors and government agencies, the ability to supply 'just-in-time' from in-market plants and the provision of back-up services such as maintenance and repair) may be important factors in building profitable market share over the long run. Moreover, direct investment by internalising various aspects of a firm's market servicing operation may enable it both to avoid the transaction costs of using market intermediaries and to increase its production and marketing effectiveness through a greater control of key operational functions.

Multinationality can confer certain advantages to a firm which are not

Box 6.8 Glaxo's international operations

Glaxo is a leading global supplier of pharmaceuticals, with production, sales subsidiaries and R & D facilities in the major markets of the USA, Japan and Europe. The company's foreign market servicing strategy in its main markets is based on a distinction between 'primary' and 'secondary' production and the advantages of having a 'local' presence. Primary manufacture consists of the production of the patented active ingredients of its drugs, which for competitive reasons are produced exclusively in the UK and Singapore and then exported to secondary manufacturing plants where they are incorporated into final products and marketed through sales subsidiaries. Given local preferences, packaging adaptations are necessary in most markets (design, size and instructions, colours and capsules v. tablets etc.). A comprehensive sales force 'on the ground' is also considered to be an important competitive advantage, as marketing pharmaceuticals is critically a business of 'selling quality to doctors'.

In the 1980s, the launch of Zantac, an anti-ulcer drug, propelled Glaxo into the big league. In the USA, the company's most important market, Zantac was co-marketed (from July 1983) with a European pharmaceutical firm which had its own established sales subsidiary in the States. This, however, was only a spring-board into the market, and was soon followed, in late 1984, by the establishment of a combined greenfield manufacturing, sales and R & D operation. Having an FDI presence has helped the company with the USA authorities over drug registration as well as giving the company an American 'persona', which has been important in cultivating contacts at the general practitioner level. All in all, FDI has had a significant impact on the company's market share and profitability and its competitive potential has been enhanced further by its USA R & D facility. (Buckley, Pass and Prescott, 1992).

open to a purely domestic firm and thus improve its ability to compete against domestic suppliers in the local market. First, an MNC can take advantage of differences in country-specific circumstances. Given a world economy that consists of a spectrum of countries at different stages of economic evolution, certain general country advantages may have knock-on effects in terms of creating or augmenting firm-level competitive advantages, which the MNC can exploit on a global basis. For example, the MNC may locate its R & D establishments in a more technologically advanced country in order to draw on that country's embodied scientific and technological infrastructure and skills to develop innovative new processes and products. This has been an important consideration influencing Japanese pharmaceutical companies to set up research facilities in the USA and UK. Similarly, MNCs may locate their production plants in a less developed country, in order to take advantage of lower input costs, in particular the availability of cheap labour. Thus, for example, Thomson, the leading French maker of audio and video equipment, has shifted the production of its cheapest video-cassette recorders from Berlin to Singapore, to reduce supply costs. Second, MNCs enjoy the flexibility of being able to choose an appropriate mode of servicing a particular market to maintain its competitiveness. Thus, Nissan reduced its exports to Europe, switching to a UK-based manufacturing plant in order to enhance its market penetration in the face of the appreciation of the yen, but more particularly the protectionist stance of the European Community which has limited Japanese car imports. Third, like conglomerates, MNCs can 'subsidise' horizontal entry and expansion in foreign markets from profits generated from other overseas companies. Nissan, for example, incurred cumulative losses on its UK manufacturing operation of £130m. between 1986 and 1991, before moving into profits. Additionally, MNCs may use transfer pricing to 'squeeze' local competitors or to shift profits from high to low-tax countries in order to maximise corporate revenues.

QUESTIONS

1 What does a concentration ratio measure? Indicate how a concentration ratio may overstate or understate the degree of competition/monopolisation present in a market.
2 The products supplied in a market may be standardised or differentiated. Discuss the nature and significance of this distinction for competitive behaviour.
3 Indicate the nature of barriers to entry. Examine the circumstances in which new entrants may be able to overcome them.
4 What are barriers to exit? How might they affect the performance of a market?
5 Examine some of the possible benefits and disadvantages of vertical integration for market processes.
6 How might the fact that some firms in a market are part of a diversified group affect the operation of market processes?
7 Discuss how the foreign market servicing modes available to a multi-national company may give it a competitive advantage over firms which produce and sell only in their domestic markets.

Chapter 7

Market conduct

The second major influence on market performance is market conduct, which itself, as we have noted in the previous chapter, is significantly affected by various structural variables. Market conduct refers to the behavioural characteristics of suppliers and buyers as they interact in the market. Key elements of market conduct emphasised in market analysis include:

- the objectives of suppliers (for example, their profit and sales growth targets) and the product requirements of buyers (for example, low prices, product performance and sophistication);
- the marketing instruments and strategies available to firms which can be used to establish competitive advantage over rival suppliers. These include various pricing tactics and marketing-mix combinations such as advertising and sales promotion, quality variations, packaging and design, etc. The choice of appropriate marketing strategies will, of course, vary from market to market, depending on product characteristics and, critically, on an understanding of those product attributes which command buyer satisfaction;
- the mutual interdependency of suppliers, which serves to constrain individual freedom of action and often leads, particularly in markets characterised by high seller concentration, to coordinated behaviour patterns, for example, price leadership and collusion;
- the relationship between suppliers and buyers, in particular the impact of bulk-buying policies.

In sum, most markets exhibit both competitive and cooperative tendencies, and firms must be mindful of these forces in formulating appropriate competitive strategies. The significance of market conduct in terms of its impact on wider resource allocation issues lies in the contribution of 'competition' to an effective market performance; specifically if competitive forces are 'working' effectively, then benefits to society accrue in the form of low-cost supply, 'fair' prices, and process and product innovation.

7.1 FIRM OBJECTIVES

A firm's objectives are the goals which it sets for itself in respect of profit returns, sales and assets growth, etc., which in turn determine the strategic and operational policies it adopts.

The firm may pursue a single objective or multiple objectives; objectives may be operationalised in 'maximisation' or 'satisfactory' target-level terms; the time-frame in which objectives are pursued may be short-term or long-term. Thus, it can be seen that objective-setting can be a complex matter. Critical factors affecting the setting of objectives include who controls decision-making in the firm, and the various constraints -institutional, financial and environmental, etc. – impinging upon this process.

Economic theories of the firm emphasise that firms which are owner-controlled will tend to pursue single-period profit maximisation or multi-period profit maximisation (see Chapter 5); likewise, theories of finance suggest that the operational goal of the firm will be to maximise the value of the firm (shareholders' wealth) over the long term. Firms which are management-controlled will tend to pursue objectives such as multi-period sales-revenue maximisation and asset-growth maximisation (see Box 7.1). In this latter case, although shareholders are the owners of the firm, there is a *de facto* divorce of ownership from control, enabling the appointed representatives of the shareholders, namely members of the board of directors, to make the key decisions affecting the firm's business. In general, shareholdings are too fragmented and shareholders, as 'outsiders', are too remote from the seat of power to be able to exercise control over the business, thus leaving the incumbent managers relatively free to run the company as they see fit. Obviously shareholders' interests cannot be ignored (i.e. directors can be removed at the annual general meeting (AGM) if the firm is badly managed and dividends are not paid). However, within this constraint managers will be able to set objectives which enhance their own interests; sales-revenue maximisation and asset-growth maximisation objectives, it is argued, result in 'bigger' firms – big firms pay higher salaries to managers and accord them greater power and status.

An alternative framework to the largely normative maximisation view of objective-setting is provided by the 'organisational' or 'behavioural' schools, which argue that the decision-making process at work in most firms tends to produce objectives couched in 'satisfactory' terms – objectives tend to reflect organisational bargaining between the various divisions of the firm (marketing, production, finance, etc.), resulting in the specification of objectives which are generally 'acceptable' (i.e. satisfactory) to all participants, rather than optimal for one group alone. Maximisation is ruled out in any case by the organisational school as being unattainable in a business environment which is highly uncertain, so that the degree of

Box 7.1   Sales-revenue and asset-growth maximisation

Baumol's (1967) 'sales-revenue' and Marris's (1964) 'asset-growth' models offer alternative assumptions with regard to firms' objectives to that of the traditional assumption of profit maximisation (see Chapter 5).

Sales-revenue maximisation

The firm is assumed to seek to maximise sales revenue, subject to a minimum profit constraint (determined by the need to pay dividends to shareholders and to finance expansion). In Figure (i) sales revenue is maximised at output level OQ_s. If the firm's minimum profit constraint is at level A, then the sales-revenue maximising output level of OQ_s will provide sufficient profits. If the firm's required profit level is B, however, the sales-revenue maximising output OQ_s is clearly inadequate. The firm's output would then be lowered to level OQ_s^*, which is just compatible with the profit constraint. Clearly, the higher the minimum profit figure required, the more important the constraint becomes and the profit-maximising (OQ_m) and sales-revenue maximising output levels will be closer together.

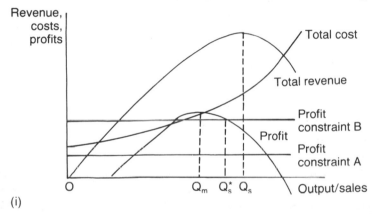

(i)

Asset-growth maximisation

Salaried managers of larger joint-stock companies are assumed to seek to maximise the rate of growth of net assets as a means of increasing their salaries, power, etc., subject to maintaining a minimum share-value, so as to avoid the company being taken over, with the possible loss of jobs. In Figure (ii) the rate of growth of assets is shown on the horizontal axis, and the ratio of the market value of company shares to the book value of company net assets (the share-valuation ratio) on the vertical axis. The valuation curve rises at first as increasing asset growth increases share value, but beyond growth rate (G) excessive retention of profits to finance growth will reduce dividend payments to shareholders and depress share values. Managers will tend to choose the fastest growth rate (G*) which does not depress the share valuation below the level (V¹) at which the company risks being taken over.

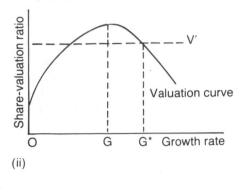

(ii)

precision and 'perfect knowledge' that is required to achieve optimisation is simply not to be found.

In recent years, many firms have issued a 'mission statement'. This sets out in general terms the firm's business aims, designed to give substance to the perceived purposes of the firm to the outside world and to provide the firm's own employees with an indication of what they are attempting to achieve through their collective endeavours. For example, the tobacco company, Gallaher: 'Built on a strong tobacco base, the group's philosophy is to concentrate on a strictly limited number of business areas for diversification. By this means the company aims to ensure secure and consistently growing profits' (Annual Report, 1988). In practice, firms resort to more *explicit* criteria, such as earnings per share and rate of return on capital/ investment, to 'benchmark' corporate achievements. Gallaher for instance (like its parent company, American Brands) typically requires its business divisions (tobacco, optics, housewares, office products, etc.) to achieve at least a 20 per cent rate of return on capital employed.

In sum, profit, sales and asset growth are inextricably linked, and although firms may accord priority to one of these, the reality is that they must be pursued simultaneously: asset growth requires the generation of profits to finance it, while profit growth itself, as Gallaher indicates, may be sustained only if the firm is able to expand its asset base over time.

7.2 COMPETITIVE STRATEGY/ADVANTAGE

A useful framework for analysing the forces driving competition in a market and the formulation of appropriate competitive strategies is provided by the work of Michael Porter (1980, 1985). The Porter 'schema' is briefly summarised below as a prelude to a more detailed look at key elements of market conduct.

Competitive strategy involves the formulation of strategic plans by a firm aimed at ensuring that the firm is able to meet and beat its competitors in supplying a particular product market. Competitive strategy constitutes an integral part of overall business strategy (deciding which markets to operate in), since no matter how many or how few product markets the firm chooses to be in, its corporate prosperity depends fundamentally on how well it succeeds in the individual product markets making up its business portfolio. A main concern of competitive strategy is to identify:

1 the competitive strengths and weaknesses of one's own firm and of rival firms;
2 the nature and strength of the various forces driving competition in a market (see Figure 7.1). The key to a successful competitive strategy is then:
3 to understand fully what product attributes are demanded by buyers (whether it be low prices or product sophistication), with a view to:
4 establishing, operationally, a position of *competitive advantage* which makes the firm less vulnerable to attack from established competitors and potential new entrants, and to erosion from the direction of buyers, suppliers and substitute products.

Competitive advantage refers to the possession by a firm of various assets and attributes (low-cost plants, innovative brands, ownership of raw materials, etc.) which give it a competitive edge over rival suppliers. To succeed against competitors in winning customers on a *viable* (profitable) and *sustainable* (long-run) basis, a firm must, depending on the nature of the market, be cost-effective and/or able to offer products which customers regard as preferable to the products offered by rivals. The former enables a firm to meet and beat competitors on price, while the latter reflects the firm's ability to establish product differentiation advantages over competitors.

Cost advantages over competitors are of two major types:

1 absolute cost advantages, that is, lower costs than competitors at *all* levels of output deriving from, for example, the use of superior production technology or from vertical integration of input supply and assembly operations;
2 relative cost advantages, that is, cost advantages related to the scale of output accruing through the exploitation of economies of scale in production, marketing and research and development and through cumulative experience/learning curve effects.

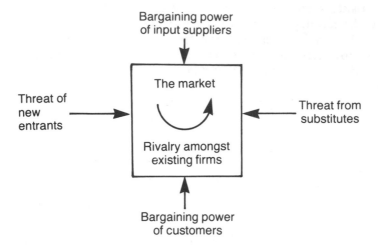

Figure 7.1 Forces driving competition in a market

Over time, investment in plant renewal, modernisation and process innovation (either through in-house R & D or the early adoption of new technology developed elsewhere) is essential to maintain cost advantages.

Product differentiation advantages derive from:

- a variety of physical properties and attributes, notably the ability to offer products which are regarded by customers as having 'unique' qualities or as being functionally superior to competitors' products;
- the particular nuances and psychological images built into the firm's products by associated advertising and sales promotion techniques.

Again, given the dynamic nature of markets, particularly product life cycle considerations, competitive advantage in this area needs to be sustained by an active programme of new product innovation and upgrading of existing lines, together with novel advertising campaigns to continue to stimulate customer interest in the firm's products.

Building on these competitive advantages, Porter suggests there are three main strategies for competitive success: cost leadership, differentiation and 'focus' (see Figure 7.2). Low costs, particularly in commodity-type markets, help the firm not only to survive a 'price war', should one break out, but, importantly, enable it to assume the role of market leader in establishing price levels which ensure high and stable levels of market profitability. By adopting a differentiation strategy, a firm seeks to be 'unique' in its market in a way that is valued by its customers, thus reducing the likelihood of 'defections' to rival brands and often enabling the firm to establish premium prices over competitors' offerings. General cost leadership and differentiation strategies seek to establish a competitive advantage over rival suppliers across the whole market or a substantial part of it. By contrast, 'focus' strategies aim to build competitive advantages in narrow segments of a market, but again either in terms of cost or, more usually, differentiation characteristics, with 'niche' suppliers catering for speciality product demands.

Strategic advantage

Strategic target	Uniqueness as perceived by customers	Low-cost position
Industry-wide	Differentiation: General Motors	Cost leadership: Nissan
Particular segment only	Differentiation focus: Mercedes-Benz	Cost focus: Skoda

Figure 7.2 Competitive strategy in the global car industry

7.3 COMPETITION

Competition refers to the process of active rivalry between the firms operating in a market as they seek to win and retain buyer demand for their brands. Competition can take a number of forms, and three of these methods of competition are discussed in detail below – price competition, advertising and promotional competition, and new product competition. A fourth, related, aspect of competition, cost-effectiveness, represents an essential way of strengthening the market position of a supplier. The ability to reduce costs is a vital means of underpinning price competition, or, alternatively, because it increases profit margins at existing prices it provides extra financial resources for the firm to increase its advertising expenditure or spend more on the development of new products. The nature and intensity of competitive relationships in a market, in turn, depends on various factors such as product and buyer characteristics, the extent of market concentration, and cost and demand considerations.

7.3.1 Price competition

Of all the marketing mix variables, price is particularly significant to the firm, in that it is fundamentally related to the generation of corporate income (price × quantity = total revenue minus total cost = profit). Other marketing mix variables represent a cost to the firm and need to be 'recouped' by increasing the quantity sold of the product (or by increasing its price).

There are three basic methods which firms use to set the prices of their products:

1 Cost-based pricing, which relates the price of a product to the costs involved in producing and distributing it. A number of formulas may be used for this purpose, including 'full-cost mark-up', 'cost-plus' or 'breakeven' ('marginal cost') pricing;
2 Demand-based pricing, which relates the price of a product to the intensity of total demand for it and acknowledges differences in demand intensities between sub-groups of buyers which facilitates the use of 'price discrimination' techniques.
3 Competition-based pricing, which relates the price of a product to the prices charged by rivals. In practice, firms use a combination of these methods in setting their prices.

Over time, a firm's prices will need to be adjusted to reflect changing market conditions:

- A general increase in industry costs (a wage increase, for example) will require firms to increase their prices, although the more efficient firms may be able to absorb the increase by increases in productivity.
- Falling demand may lead to price cuts as firms strive to maintain volume (particularly where fixed costs constitute a high proportion of a firm's total costs) or 'charge what the traffic will bear' at times of peak demand.
- Increases in competitive pressures may also require a firm to re-align its prices or bring out cheaper variants of its product (see below). In general, however, suppliers (particularly oligopolistic firms operating in concentrated markets) will try to avoid aggressive price competition because 'price wars' are mutually ruinous. Instead, 'orderly' price levels tend to be preferred, with firms adhering to price leadership conventions or collusion to control prices (see section 7.4). Moreover, in many markets segmentation and product differentiation have blurred the traditional notion of price competition, since they involve firms selecting a price structure which reflects differences, for example, in product type and qualities (see Box 7.2). Thus, firms compete by offering customers various 'value for money' combinations across a broad product range. By contrast, in the case of 'standardised' products their commodity-like nature tends to result in a heavy emphasis on price as a selling feature, but again the intensity of this is often tempered by a desire to avoid destructive discounting.

In terms of its wider impact on market processes, price competition is seen by market analysis as being particularly conducive to the promotion of economic efficiency. Specifically, price competition serves to eliminate inefficient, high-cost producers, removes any tendency for firms to secure 'excess' profits, thereby ensuring that consumers are charged 'fair' prices (that is, a market price which is consistent with the real economic costs of supplying the product, including a so-called 'normal' profit return to suppliers – contrast 'perfect competition' and 'monopoly', Chapter 5).

Some examples of price competition

- *Motor cars*: Ford was forced to cut the price of versions of its new 'world' car, the Mondeo, in the United Kingdom less than a month after its launch in March 1993, reducing prices by £200–£1200. The launch price was described by Ford as 'provisional', but the company's decision to reduce the price was largely in response to a backlash from the powerful fleet buyer sector, which considered the Mondeo to be overpriced, despite all the extras. More broadly, Ford was forced to follow Vauxhall, Rover, Peugeot and some other makers in cutting dealers' margins from 17 per cent to 10 per cent to 'pay' for price cuts. Prices of the Granada and Scorpio were cut by an average of 10 per cent. The list price of the Granada 2-litre LX four-door, previously £19,155, was reduced (April 1993) to £16,995, while the Fiesta 1.1 LX three-door was reduced from £8,375 to £7,990.

  In January 1993 Mercedes-Benz announced that it had come to recognise that it would 'no longer be able to demand premium prices for its products based on an image of effortless superiority and a content of the ultimate in automotive engineering' (press statement). The company was going to take the radical step of moving to 'target pricing'. This involves finding out 'what the customer is willing to pay in a particular product category – priced against its competitors – it will add its profit margin and then the real work will begin to cost every part and component to bring in the vehicle at the target price.'

- *Grocery retailing*: Tesco cut the prices of around 500 grocery products in March 1993 in its battle against the food discount groups: 'there is price competition and there's no doubt in our mind that it will become more severe' (Tesco press interview). The UK discount sector (where prices are typically 10–20 per cent below Tesco prices on a limited line of products) currently accounts for around 10 per cent of UK grocery sales. Previously it was dominated by Kwik-Save, but it has been given added competitive bite by the arrival of Aldi from Germany and Netto from Denmark. New retailing concepts, in particular the USA-style 'club warehouse' format (where club members are typically given discounts of 33 per cent), currently operated in the UK by Nurdin and Peacock and Westco (the US Group) will intensify competitive pressures further.

- *Cigarettes*: In April 1993 Philip Morris cut the price of Marlboro, its

Box 7.2   Retail prices of selected tea brands in leading supermarket stores, 1992

(£ per 250g/80 bags) *Main sectors*	
Speciality	*Average*
Own label	1.55
Jacksons Piccadilly	1.93
Twinings	2.49
Quality	
Own label	1.25
Twinings Classic	1.79
Ridgways Imperial	1.85
Tetley Gold	1.89
Brooke Bond Choicest	1.89
Premium	
Own label	1.16
Typhoo	1.56
PG Tips	1.56
Tetley	1.56
Lyons Quick Brew	1.57
Economy	
Own label	0.67
Own label	0.92
Lyons Silver Label	1.37
Typhoo Fresh Brew	1.45
Brooke Bond D	1.29
In-cup	
Own label	1.05
Fresh Brew One Cup	1.59
Typhoo One Cup	1.69
Tetley One Cup	1.69
PG Tags	1.79

Source: Retail Business

dominant USA brand, from $2.15 to $1.75 in order to stem the loss of market share to cut-price brands. In the early 1980s Marlboro had accounted for around one-third of the US market, but its share in 1992 was down to 22 per cent. This move was seen to be controversial, one tobacco analyst suggesting: "This strategy has got to work because the Marlboro product is vastly superior in terms of image, packaging and quality of tobacco than the lower-priced products', while another was more sceptical: 'All that investment in the brand, then you tell people that you can now buy for less than $2 what was worth $2.15 until yesterday. The buyer is never going to believe you again' (*Sunday Times*, 11 April 1993).

- *Personal computers*: In 1992 IBM moved into the low-price segment, introducing a range of new models under the Ambra brand name to compete head-to-head with the cheap 'clones' which had taken a substantial share of the market away from the company's main up-market brands. In Europe the low-price segment now accounts for around 45 per cent of the personal computer market and is increasing rapidly: 'IBM saw a market place segment that had grown to significance in which they did not participate' (company spokesman). IBM is addressing this market on a country-by-country basis, as PC prices, distribution channels and buying patterns vary widely in different parts of the world.

7.3.2 Product differentiation

Product differentiation is used by suppliers to distinguish their own products from those offered by competitors. There are two basic ways in which products can be differentiated:

1 by variations in the physical appearance and attributes of the product based on differences in design, styling, colouring and packaging and differences in quality, composition, accessories, innovatory features and performance results;
2 broadly similar products may be differentiated in the minds of buyers by the use of advertising and sales promotion techniques which emphasise imputed or subjective aspects of the product, for example, 'better than', 'washes cleaner and whiter than'.

The purpose of product differentiation is to create and sustain a demand for the firm's products by nurturing consumer brand loyalty. Product differentiation is an important means of establishing competitive advantage over rival suppliers, and in some markets, most notably those characterised by high levels of seller concentration, it is often regarded as constituting a more effective competitive strategy than price competition. The attraction of product differentiation competition over price competition lies in the fact that whereas price cuts, for example, can be quickly and completely matched by competitors, a successful advertising campaign or the introduction of an innovatory product is less easily imitated. Moreover, whereas price competition lowers firm's profitability, product differentiation tends to preserve and even enhance profit returns. In particular, the establishment of product uniqueness may allow firms to command premium prices over competitor's offerings (as is the case with Nescafé coffee – see Chapter 10). Moreover, in some cases the costs of advertising and R & D expenses can be built into the final prices paid by customers, so it is they rather than the supplier who finances this form of competition. Finally, product differentiation may serve as a barrier to entry, thereby protecting existing market shares against competitive encroachment.

Advertising and sales promotion competition

Advertising is used to both *inform* prospective buyers of a product's existence and attributes and to *persuade* them that the product is superior to similar products offered by competitors.

Although some advertising is generic and aimed at promoting 'the product' in general (for example, the UK Tea Council has for some years advertised the merits of tea, to stem a loss of sales to coffee), most advertising is brand-specific and is used to improve the market share of a particular supplier's brand at the expense of competitors.

Advertisements and advertising campaigns typically carry a 'message' designed to influence and reinforce buyer behaviour. Studies have indicated that advertising of established brands is essentially one of 'competitive maintenance', ensuring that a brand is constantly at the forefront of people's minds, and by 'reassuring' customers of the brand's value to them, advertising serves to establish strong brand loyalty, thereby encouraging repeat purchases:

> the general aim is to inform, remind and reassure the housewife, in language which she can understand and with a careful highlighting of the particular attributes which consumer research shows are likely to appeal to her, of the quality of the product being advertised, and so create a strong distinctive and attractive brand image.
>
> (para. 46, *Household Detergents Report*, Monopolies Commission)

Thus, advertising can serve to reduce the degree of cross-elasticity of demand between brands and to reduce the likelihood of customers switching to alternative brands in the face of price cuts by competitors. More proactively, advertising may reinforce buyers' perceptions of the product as being sophisticated and 'up-market' (as is the case, for example, of exotic perfumes), thereby enabling premium prices to be charged.

While advertising seeks to develop and sustain sales by creating brand loyalty over the long run, sales promotions are largely used in short, sharp bursts to support, for example, the introduction of a new brand, to renew interest in a brand whose sales have fallen and, periodically, to stimulate extra demand for a well-established brand. A variety of techniques are used for this purpose, including free trial samples, money-off packs, 'two-for-the price-of-one' offers, extra quantities for the same price, product competitions offering prizes, coupons offering gifts, trading stamps, in-store demonstrations, point-of-sale displays, etc.

A key point to emphasise is that the ultimate 'success' of advertising and sales promotion in stimulating demand cannot be divorced from the intrinsic qualities and properties of the brand itself. It is these factors which are of crucial importance in determining customers' satisfaction with the brand and hence their willingness to repeat purchase it. Thus, slick advertising may induce some buyers to purchase a brand once, but if the brand fails to live up to expectations because, for example, its quality or performance is poor, then existing buyers will defect and adverse word-of-mouth publicity will further kill off sales. The same considerations apply in respect of new product launches. Although conventional economic analysis suggests that advertising acts as a barrier to entry, in that entrants with unknown brands are at a disadvantage compared to established brands (and entrants are thus forced to spend more on advertising for each sale gained) the *real* barrier to entry to entrants (possessing adequate financial resources to finance advertising spend) is the need to come up with an innovative product. Studies have shown that successful new brands are typically 'more distinctive/novel/superior' in comparison to established brands, i.e. product uniqueness is a critical factor. In this context, advertising is an important adjunct to a brand's launch, serving to act as an 'entry facilitator' by bringing the brand to the attention of the buying public and encouraging retailers to stock the product.

Advertising intensity (the proportion of advertising expenditure to sales turnover) varies from market to market depending upon, for example, the nature of the product, the extent of market segmentation and the degree of seller concentration. Fast-moving consumer goods markets which are characterised by a high frequency of repeat purchases tend to exhibit high advertising intensity ratios (Table 7.1), as do certain consumer durable goods markets (for example, motor cars, washing machines, televisions); even some commodity-type products, for example petrol, may be

Table 7.1 Advertising sales ratios: selected markets, 1990

	%
Toothpaste	15.2
Shampoo	14.1
Washing powder	11.0
Breakfast cereal	10.3
Cough medicines	9.2
Margarine	8.5
Sauces and pickles	8.2
Soluble coffee	7.6
Soup	7.0

Source: Advertising Statistics Yearbook, 1991

extensively advertised, emphasising imputed rather than provable product qualities ('Esso puts a tiger in your tank').

In many markets, advertising and sales promotion expenditures run into many millions of pounds and often suppliers in more concentrated markets become locked into a competitive advertising and sales promotion battle (see Box 7.3). In 1992, for example, the three leading suppliers of tea in the UK spent collectively £24m. on advertising. Individual brand spend can vary enormously, with brand leaders tending to absorb the bulk of these expenditures, although major spending will also be undertaken to launch new brands.

Box 7.3   Advertising expenditure by major tea suppliers, 1988–92 (£000)

	1988	*1989*	*1990*	*1991*	*1992*
Brooke Bond	12409	6949	6675	10377	9865
Lyons Tetley	5613	6709	9253	8238	9390
Premier Teas	5455	3479	3744	6676	5378
Total (including others)	25129	19449	21884	27657	27745

Source: MEAL

In terms of its impact on resource allocation processes in a market, advertising has been variously criticised on the grounds that it increases supply costs, raises market entry barriers and distorts 'rational' decision-making by buyers. Equally, however, by facilitating mass-production and distribution of a product, advertising may lower supply costs through scale economies and may facilitate new product launches (see Chapter 8, Section 8.2).

Product competition

The ability of a firm to offer a brand which is distinctively 'superior' to competitors' brands is a key means of establishing brand leadership in a market. Nestlé, for example, has achieved just such a position in the UK coffee market, where its main Nescafé brand and segmented derivatives command a 56 per cent market share in the face of strong competition from upwards of 200 other manufacturers' brands and retailers' own-labels. As indicated previously, while good physical distribution and advertising can help sell a brand (interestingly, surveys have shown that consumers regard Nescafé advertisements as 'ordinary'), customer satisfaction with a brands' intrinsic qualities and performance remains paramount in securing and maintaining brand leadership. Continuous upgrading of established brands (Nescafé was introduced to the UK market in 1939) is usually necessary to secure longevity and to 'buck' or spin-out the typical product life cycle configuration of eventual maturity and decline. Nescafé's reputation has been preserved and enhanced by meticulous attention to product detail and quality improvements. Moreover, Nestlé has been able to capitalise on established customer goodwill to the Nescafé 'name' as a guarantor of quality by introducing a range of new variants of the brand into other market segments (see Box 7.4 and Chapter 10). Such 'brand transference' possibilities can considerably reduce the expense of a new product launch and achieve rapid market penetration.

In many markets, regular new product launches are necessary to replace 'tired' brands and to stimulate renewed buyer interest in the supplier's product range. The motor car market is a case in point, where manufacturers bring out new models, incorporating improved engine performance, accessories and design features, to replace older lines; Nissan, for example, replaced its ageing Bluebird model with the Primera in 1991, while, as noted in the previous section, in 1993 Ford launched its new 'world' car, the Mondeo, to replace the Sierra.

New product development requires firms to commit resources both to scientific research aimed at inventing new products and to *innovation*, that is, the refinement and modification of research ideas and prototypes aimed at the ultimate development of commercially viable products. Research and development is usually very resource-intensive and the substantial capital outlays required to pursue development work, coupled with a high risk of failing to come up with a marketable product, tend to favour the larger business which is able to cross-subsidise R & D out of profits from existing products and also to pool risks. For example, in the pharmaceutical industry, where stringent safety and efficacy standards are required by governments, the cost of developing a marketable new drug is typically £100m. plus. A very high proportion of development work is aborted – in 1993, for example, Fisons abandoned the development of Tipredane, an asthma drug, writing-off an investment of £21m. Nonetheless, in many industries small innovative firms continue to coexist alongside large firms – as in, for example, computer software and electronics.

In technologically dynamic markets the ability to develop new innovative products is often a critical factor in establishing competitive advantage over rival suppliers. Although it may be possible to buy in research ideas and products from other firms through licensing deals, this may represent a poor substitute in competitive terms for the establishment of a firm's own internal pool of R & D skills and competencies; that is, it is the difference between the firm being able to assume the position of market leader and it becoming a 'me-too' follower. New products can be used to enhance the firm's position in established market sectors, or they can be used to develop new market segments, thereby securing 'first-mover' advantages.

Box 7.4   Nestlé brand development, 1939–89

Date		
1939	L	Nescafé Powder
1955	L	Nescafé Blend 37
1965	L	Nescafé Gold Blend
1970	R	Nescafé granulated
1973	L	Nescafé Fine Blend
1975	L	Nescafé Nescore
1977	L	Nescafé Elevenses
1978	L	Nescafé Gold Blend decaffeinated
1981	R	Nescafé granulated
1982	L	Nescafé Good Day
1984	L	Nescafé Gold Blend roast and ground
1985	W	Nescafé Good Day
	L	Nescafé Alta Rica
	L	Nescafé Cap Colombie
1986	L	Nescafé decaffeinated
	R	Nescafé Blend 37
	R	Nescafé Gold Blend
1987	L	Nescafé Blend 37 roast and ground
1989	R	Nescafé Nescore becomes decaffeinated

Code L = Launch, R = Relaunch, W = Withdrawal

Source: Monopolies and Mergers Commission, *Soluble Coffee* Report, 1991

How permanent or transient these advantages are will depend on the degree of product uniqueness, whether the product can be 'protected' by patents (twenty years in the United Kingdom, 17 in the United States) and marketing back-up. For example, Polaroid was able to develop and maintain its dominance of the 'instant camera' segment of the US photography market against the competition of Kodak as a result of patent protection (Kodak's instant camera was found to have infringed Polaroid's patent and it was forced to withdraw it from the market). By contrast, Full Moon's non-patented Ecover brand, which initially pioneered a sizeable niche segment for 'green' detergents in the United Kingdom was quickly undermined by Procter and Gamble which used a brand transfer strategy to introduce a new competitive product (Ariel Ultra) into this segment.

In strategic terms, firms in most markets need to pursue a *sustained* new product development programme in order to maintain competitive advantage. Ideally, given product life cycle tendencies and new product competition, firms need to possess a product portfolio consisting of mature, growth and new products, together with embryonic products in the R & D pipeline. From a wider resource allocation perspective, new product competition is beneficial insofar as it widens consumer choice and leads to the introduction of superior products, although the proliferation of 'me-too' copy-cats may make this spurious. The contribution that new products can make to improving market performance is explicitly recognised in many countries where patent protection can be granted to inventors.

7.4 'CONTROLLING' COMPETITION

While firms may seek to advance their market positions by various competitive means, as discussed above, competition at times may be 'inconvenient' and 'unprofitable'. Firms may wish to avoid competition (particularly price competition) as a defensive response to poor trading conditions and a desire to promote 'orderly' markets. More predatorily, firms may seek to monopolise a market either by *structural* means (building up positions of market dominance by mergers and takeovers) or by various collusive *conduct* arrangements (cartels, restrictive trade agreements and price leadership systems) which eliminate inter-firm competition. In addition, powerful suppliers may use a variety of trade practices (exclusive dealing, tie-in sales, full-line forcing, etc.) which put smaller competitors and potential entrants at a disadvantage.

7.4.1 Collusion

Collusion involves the deliberate suppression of competition between themselves by a group of rival suppliers. Collusion may be confined to a single area of business activity, for example prices, or may cover a wider range of limitations, including coordinated marketing, production and capacity adjustments. Collusion may be practised through formalised arrangements for coordinating inter-firm behaviour, as in cartel or restrictive trade agreements, or operated by more informal means through, for example, an information agreement, concerted practice or price leadership convention.

Cartels/restrictive trade agreements

Cartels and restrictive trade agreements can take a number of forms. For example, suppliers may set up a sole selling agency which buys up their individual output at an agreed price and arranges for the marketing of these products on a coordinated basis. Another form is where suppliers operate an agreement which, for example, sets uniform selling prices for their products, thereby suppressing price competition, but with suppliers then competing for market share through product differentiation strategies. A more comprehensive version of a cartel (see Box 7.5) is the application not only of common selling prices and joint marketing, but also of restric-

Box 7.5 The European plastic cartels

In 1989, twenty-three European chemical producers were fined a total of ECU 60m. (£92m.) for operating illegal cartels in the supply of low-density polyethylene (LdPE) and PVC – two kinds of widely used plastic materials. The companies concerned accounted for 90 per cent and 80 per cent, respectively, of the European Community market for these materials. The LdPE cartel was established in 1976 in response to the onset of the recessionary conditions following the oil price increases of 1973. Falling demand and over-investment had left the industry burdened with overcapacity, and price competition was rife. Initially, the cartel sought only to fix prices (see figure) but later introduced production quotas to limit output. This collusion was orchestrated by senior executives of the firms at a series of meetings held in Zurich and operationalised through regular meetings of divisional managers.

Evidence provided to the European Commission by one of the firms involved in the cartel showed that there had been more than twenty attempted joint price increases between 1976 and 1985. However, the cartel worked somewhat imperfectly, with some members undercutting agreed prices (by giving customers 'secret' discounts) and exceeding their quota limits. The PVC cartel was set up in late 1980 aiming, like the LdPE cartel, to set common prices (fifteen coordinated price increases were attempted between 1980 and 1985) and to limit production through a quota system. Again, however, 'cheating' served to limit the effectiveness of the cartel.

Although described as 'crisis cartels', established to ameliorate poor trading conditions rather than to secure monopoly returns (as per the OPEC cartel in oil) executives of the firms concerned knowingly entered into clandestine collusion of the kind specifically prohibited by Article 85 of the Treaty of Rome.

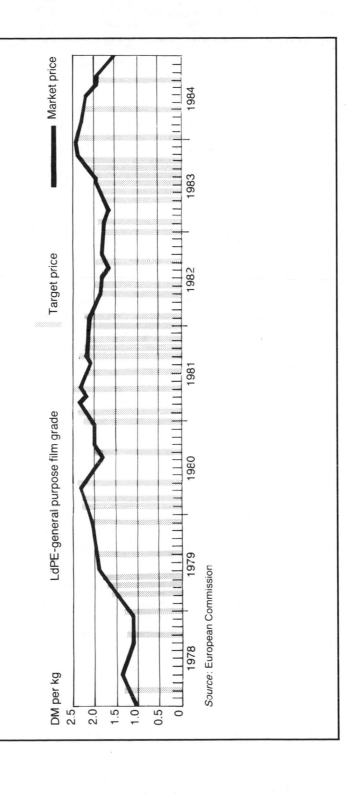

Source: European Commission

tions on production involving the assignment of specific output quotas to individual participants (see Chapter 5) and the coordination of capacity adjustments to ensure that market supply is kept broadly in line with market demand.

A number of factors are crucial to the successful operation of a cartel, in particular the participation of all significant suppliers of the product and their full compliance with the policies of the cartel. In practice, non-participation of some key suppliers and 'cheating' by cartel members, together with the ability of buyers to switch to substitute products, may well serve to undermine the viability of the cartel. In many countries, most notably the US and European Community, cartels concerned with price-fixing, market-sharing and restrictions on production and capacity are prohibited under competition law (see Chapter 9).

Information agreements

An information agreement is an informal arrangement between rival suppliers which involves them in furnishing each other with details of their prices, discount terms, output and sales figures etc. Although some of the information exchanged may be innocuous and could be obtained from normal trade sources (for example, rivals' prices) some data are of a highly confidential nature, prompting the question of why firms are prepared to disclose such information to competitors. In the UK, concern that information exchanges between competitors might well be used as a cloak for collusion between firms has led to the requirement that certain agreements must be registered with the Office of Fair Trading.

Price leadership

In some markets, firms employ price leadership conventions to 'coordinate' their prices, accepting one of their number as the 'lead' firm in changing market prices. Price leadership takes two main forms:

1 *Dominant firm price leadership*: where the largest firm in terms of market share (and/or the lowest cost producer) leads off price changes (usually price increases) which other firms are prepared to follow because the price established yields them adequate profits (see Chapter 5) or, occasionally, because of the power of the dominant firm to 'punish' non-compliance (by, for example, subjecting non-following firms to selective price cutting). A variant on this theme is price leadership by a high cost firm which more efficient firms are prepared to follow because this enables them to secure even higher levels of profitability (see Box 7.6).

2 *Barometric price leadership*: where a particular firm is 'adopted' as the

price leader because it has proved adept at reading changing market conditions.

Price leadership systems are often seen by suppliers as a useful means of coordinating their price policies so as to limit price competition and avoid ruinous price wars. They may, however, act as a cloak for informal collusion, and as with the arrangements discussed above, operate in a way detrimental to resource allocation efficiency.

Box 7.6   Price leadership in the UK salt market

In its 1986 *Report on the UK Salt Market*, the Monopolies and Mergers Commission (MMC) condemned the lack of price competition between the two major suppliers, British Salt (50 per cent market share) and ICI (45 per cent market share). It was particularly critical of BS, identified as the most efficient supplier (costs per tonne, £22.89 compared to ICI, costs per tonne £29.32) for 'accepting' ICI's price leadership, which had resulted in its securing a very high level of profitability (56 per cent rate of return on capital employed, compared to ICI's 24 per cent). The figure shows a high degree of price parallelism, with ICI taking the lead in raising prices in the 1980s. The market had previously been characterised by formal price collusion which had been outlawed by the UK competition authorities, but the Commission was concerned that this 'spirit of cooperation' and the avoidance of price competition had lingered on:

> The evidence that we have found leads us to the conclusion that price competition ... has been extremely limited. British Salt, as the low cost producer, could have put more competitive pressure on ICI, and still have achieved a good return on capital. Instead in recent years it has chosen to follow the price increases of ICI ....
>
> This has resulted in domestic price increases made by the two companies being significantly greater than they would have been in effective competition.
>
> (para. 9.30)

To remedy this situation the MMC recommended the imposition of price controls on British Salt, thus limiting its ability to increase prices.

Prices for bulk pure dried vacuum salt			
British Salt		ICI	
Date of price increase	Price (£/tonne)	Date of price increase	Price (£/tonne)
20. 5.76	11.14	10. 5.76*	11.15
22.11.76*	12.24	1.12.76	12.25
25. 4.77	13.59	4. 4.77*	13.60
26. 7.77	14.19	14. 7.77*	14.20
24. 7.78*	15.47	21. 8.78	15.50
19. 3.79	16.68	1. 3.79	16.66
3. 7.79*	18.29	23. 7.79	18.33
31.12.79*	20.67	4. 2.80	20.69
30. 6.80*	24.67	14. 7.80	24.59
19. 1.81	26.51	5. 1.81*	26.43
18. 1.82	30.20	4. 1.82*	30.13
24. 1.83	32.60	10. 1.83*	32.54
23. 1.84	34.20	9. 1.84*	34.17

* Price Leader

Source: MMC

7.4.2 Anti-competitive practices

Firms may employ various trade practices which, while in some cases yielding economic benefits, serve to reduce their exposure to competition. The practices referred to below, when operated by *an established dominant firm*, can be severely anti-competitive:

1 *Aggregated rebates*: the supplier offers distributors/retailers a discount which is based on their total purchases over a specified time period (usually one year), rather than on smaller individual orders. Aggregated rebates can help the supplier increase his sales, but at the same time may serve to limit competition by discouraging distributors from handling the products of rival suppliers.
2 *Exclusive dealing*: the supplier contracts distributors/retailers to sell his products on an exclusive basis, thereby depriving rival suppliers access to these distribution outlets.
3 *Full-line forcing*: the supplier requires distributors/retailers to stock not only his principal products but additionally other products from his range. For example, an oil company might require a filling station contracted to sell its petrol, to sell its brand of lubricants, anti-freeze and other motoring accessories, thereby squeezing out rivals' products.

4 *Tie-in sales*: the supplier encourages a dealer/customer not only to buy the product of primary interest to him but also, as part of the same transaction, some other related product. For example, a supplier of colour film might attempt to tie the processing of that film to themself by including an inclusive processing charge in the price paid for the colour film.
5 *Selective price-cutting*: suppliers may use selective price cuts to oust competitors. This can be particularly effective when employed by a full-range supplier against suppliers who operate in niche segments or in limited geographic areas. For example, the dominant UK supplier of plasterboard, BPB, was found by the Monopolies and Mergers Commission to have attempted to limit competition from the Germany-based Knauf group by cutting its plasterboard prices in the German market. Additionally, BPB had 'increased the net prices on products not sold by the new entrants [Knauf, Redland and Eternit] ... and reduced the net prices on products readily available from the new entrants' (para. 7.9 *Plasterboard* Report). See Chapter 10.

QUESTIONS

1 Discuss the various firm objectives which have been suggested as alternatives to the profit-maximisation assumptions employed in conventional market analysis.
2 Outline Porter's 'forces driving competition' framework and discuss his three 'generic strategies' for achieving corporate success.
3 What are the possible advantages and disadvantages of price competition for (a) the firm and (b) market performance.
4 Examine the role of advertising and sales promotion as means of establishing competitive advantage over rivals.
5 Discuss new product development in the context of the product life cycle and the need to maintain a firm's competitive advantage over rivals.
6 Discuss the possible advantages and disadvantages of product differentiation for market performance.
7 Distinguish between 'formal' and 'informal/tacit' mechanisms for limiting competition between firms.

Chapter 8

Market performance

Market structure and market conduct interact to produce certain patterns of market performance. As noted in Chapter 5, in conventional market analysis, markets which are competitive are shown to yield performance results which are superior to those characterised by varying degrees of market imperfections. However, this analysis is limited in scope and needs to be augmented by a broader-based, more empirical view of market processes and performance.

Essentially, market performance refers to the effectiveness of suppliers in a market in utilising scarce economic resources to their maximum efficiency and to the ultimate benefit of consumers. Important elements of market performance include:

- *production costs*: the production of the market's output at the lowest possible cost;
- *advertising and promotional costs*: the utilisation of cost-effective distribution and selling techniques;
- *prices and profits*: the setting of 'fair' prices so that buyers are charged prices which are fully consistent with the production and distribution costs of supplying the product, including a reasonable (that is, non-monopolistic) profit return to suppliers;
- *product performance*: the satisfaction of consumer demands for product variety and sophistication, that is, the maximisation of consumer choice and value-for-money attributes;
- *technological progressiveness*: the introduction of process and product innovations which enable supply costs and prices to be reduced in real terms and which provide consumers with new, technically superior products.

In practice, evaluating market performance is difficult since there are no 'absolutes' to indicate an optimal position. What is a 'fair' price or a 'normal' profit return? If market profit levels are on the low side, this might suggest that firms have charged consumers reasonable prices. Equally, however, it may reflect the fact that firms have dissipated profit potential because they are grossly inefficient, and although prices appear to be fair they are in fact 'inflated' because of higher costs. Similarly, how does one judge whether or not advertising expenditures in an industry are 'reasonable'? In some markets (brand differentiated markets) advertising plays a significant role in the competitive process and advertising expenses may contribute a relatively high proportion of total supply costs – but when does it become 'excessive'?

8.1 PRODUCTION COSTS

An important dimension of market performance is the ability to produce the market's output at the lowest possible cost. A number of factors affect the level of costs. First, as discussed in Chapter 3, the extent to which firms are able to exploit available economics of large-scale production is one important consideration. Ideally, firms should produce their outputs in plants of optimal scale (see Box 8.1). In Figure 8.1(a) the minimum efficient scale of operation is OA. At this level of output economies of scale are fully exploited and production costs are minimised. If plant sizes are sub-optimal (for example, OB) then actual supply costs will be higher than attainable costs. The balance of market supply and demand is also a significant factor (see Box 8.1). If a market is beset by over-capacity, either because firms have been over-optimistic in forecasting the growth of demand and invested in too much new plant, or because demand has gone into secular decline, then capacity utilisation rates may be insufficient to achieve full efficiency. This can be an acute problem in industries which are highly capital-intensive and where fixed costs represent a significant proportion of total costs. Thus, if optimal-sized plants (OA) are under-utilised because of a shortfall in demand (OC) then, again, supply costs will be higher than attainable costs.

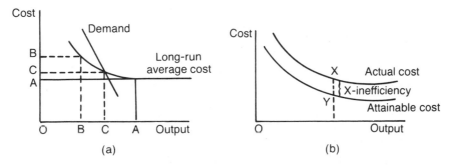

Figure 8.1 Productive efficiency

Monopolies and Mergers Commission, para. 4.51:

> Estimates of the minimum efficient scale varied. BPB considered that it would be 10 million square metres, while RPL said 25 million square metres and Knauf 20 million square metres. BPB considered that costs per square metre of plasterboard produced would continue to fall as scale increased (as lower running costs offset higher capital costs). Above the capacity range of 20 to 30 million square metres, further falls in cost per square metre were modest.

A comparison of these estimates with BPB's, RPL's and Knauf's actual installed capacity are given below and indicate the market is serviced by plants of minimum efficient scale. However, because of an over-capacity problem, some of these plants were barely breaking even ('the minimum economic output lies in the range of 60–70% of plant capacity', MMC para. 9.48). *Industry* capacity-utilisation rates were estimated at 58–63% in 1989–90 (nominal capacity = 314 million square metres, compared to sales in 1990 of 193 million square metres and 182 million square metres in 1989.

UK plasterboard capacity 1990

		million square metres (9.5mm basis)
BPB	East Leake plant	63
	Kirkby Thore plant	54
	Robertsbridge plant	36
	Sharpness plant	26
	Sherburn plant	51
		230
RPL	Bristol plant	38
Knauf	Sittingbourne plant	46
		314

A further factor affecting cost levels is the incidence of 'X-inefficiency' which may serve to negate the lower costs achieved through exploiting economies of scale. X-inefficiency represents various internal inefficiencies in a firm (that is, the poor deployment and management of resources within the firm arising from, for example, bureaucratic rigidities and restrictive labour practices), which increase costs at all levels of output, as shown by the distance XY in Figure 8.1(b). X-inefficiency is likely to be present in large dominant firms which lack effective competition 'to keep them on their toes'.

As noted earlier, a substantial degree of market concentration may be necessary if firms are fully to exploit available economies of large-scale operations. Where unit costs are minimised only at higher rates of output, plants and firms may have to be large relative to the markets in which they operate in order that optimal technical efficiency is attained. Evidence produced by Pratten (1971) for a sample of UK industries indicated that economies of scale are substantial in many industries. In most cases market concentration levels were found by Pratten to be consistent with, or greater than, the estimated minimum efficient scale of operation. However, in most industries sub-optimal sized plants survive for reasons such as barriers to exit or because they cater for specialist market niches (for example, in the UK brewing market there are upwards of 100 small 'mini'-breweries, specialising in the production of distinctive real ales, which operate with minimal overheads and low distribution and marketing expenses). Moreover, the use of flexible manufacturing technologies facilitates the coexistence of cost-effective small-scale plants alongside larger plants in some markets, for example 'mini' mills in the production of steel products.

In addition to static scale economies which serve to reduce unit costs, there are also the *dynamic* influences of 'learning effects' and technical innovation to be considered. Learning effects refer to the process whereby managers and operators learn from experience how to operate new technologies more effectively over time, such that a growing familiarity with, and the repetitive operation of, a new technology enables unit costs of production to be progressively reduced (see Table 8.1).

Table 8.1   Silicon transistors: cost reduction, 1954–67

	Industry total accumulated volume (million units)	Unit costs ($ constant)
1954	0.02	23.95
1956	0.53	19.94
1958	3.60	15.57
1960	17.20	11.27
1962	56.80	4.39
1964	224.00	1.35
1966	977.80	0.58
1967	1,456.90	0.52

Source: Boston Consulting Group (1968)

The combination of scale economies and cumulative experience may well indicate a decisive cost advantage in favour of the large, dominant firm. It is argued that experience is 'firm-specific' in the early stages of an industry's development, so that the firm which secures the market leadership also obtains a cost advantage over its less experienced competitors. In this way, early leaders are able to consolidate their position and ultimately emerge as quasi-monopolists. Concentration achieved through *cost effectiveness*, the Boston Consulting Group argues, is reflective of competitive forces rather than their suppression; the realisation of cost reductions through experience is not automatic but depends crucially on a competent management's sensitivity to competitive pressures, actual and anticipated. In their view, the interaction of competitors over time provides a guarantee that superior cost improvements by one competitor will result eventually in the displacement of the less effective competitors. On this interpretation, therefore, unless firms constantly aim to minimise costs, they will be vulnerable to competition.

A similar argument to the one above is often used in connection with the propensity of large firms to innovate. Where technological change is rapid, a firm must develop and exploit new processes, techniques and products to stay at the forefront of the market; not even the strongest monopolist can insulate itself from dynamic changes in the long run (see section 8.5).

The X-inefficiency phenomenon has attracted attention because, as noted above, it may serve to negate cost reductions associated with exploiting economies of scale. The X-inefficiency proposition suggests that while oligopolists and quasi-monopolists may have initially secured their dominant position in a market because of their superior efficiency, the subsequent lack of competitive pressures may cause them to become complacent, bureaucratic and cost-ineffective. Measuring X-inefficiency is intrinsically difficult, so that studies in this area tend to rely on circumstantial evidence. For example, typically where firms encounter commercial setbacks due to increased competition, falling demand, etc., they react by 'trimming' 'surplus' expenditures which have grown in more prosperous times, 'tighten-up' on routine and repetitive tasks and removing 'dead wood'. *A priori*, there are good grounds for suggesting that competition, by ensuring that only the efficient survive, will act to reduce the incidence of X-inefficiency. From a strategic perspective, attention to cost-cutting is an important facet of achieving and maintaining cost leadership in a market.

8.2 ADVERTISING AND PROMOTIONAL COSTS

A second important element of market performance is the level of advertising and promotional expenditure. If these are 'excessive' then market costs and prices may be raised and new entry prevented, thus enabling established firms to secure above-normal profits (see section 8.3).

In many markets, particularly those characterised by high levels of seller concentration and differentiated (branded) products, advertising and sales promotion are used extensively to maintain and expand firms' market shares. Thus, as seen by the firms operating in a market, advertising and sales promotion are key ways in which they compete against each other. In this sense advertising and sales promotion are pro-competitive and fundamental to firms' corporate success. Conventional market analysis, however, views this issue differently, typically portraying advertising and promotional competition as a 'bad' thing, insofar as it is engaged in as a *substitute* for price competition, such activity being seen by firms as a 'safer' and more profitable form of rivalry than price competition (see Box 8.2). From a *static* resource allocation perspective this distinction is crucial – price competition serves to *lower* market prices and profit rates, whereas advertising and promotional competition tend to increase supply costs and prices. Conventional market analysis assumes that selling activities raise producer prices, since the extra costs incurred in such activity are simply passed on to customers. In static analysis advertising is shown as being solely concerned with brand-switching between competitors within an *unchanged* overall market demand. Figure 8.2(a) depicts the effects of this on market costs and prices.

The profit-maximising price-output combination (PQ) without advertising is shown by the intersection of the marginal revenue curve (MR) and the marginal cost curve (MC). With advertising, the addition of selling costs serves to raise the marginal cost curve to MC_1 so that the PQ combination (shown by the intersection of MR and MC_1) now results in a higher price (P_A) and lower quantity supplied (Q_A). This 'negative' view of advertising, however, needs to be tempered by the role advertising plays in maintaining firms' market shares and, in particular, ensuring that firms' sales volumes continue to remain at levels which enable them to fully exploit economies of large-scale production and distribution. From a

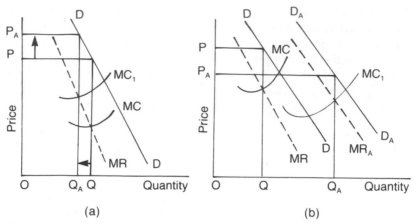

Figure 8.2 Advertising and its effect on market costs, output and prices

Box 8.2   Advertising competition in the UK breakfast cereal market

The controversial issue of price competition versus differentiation competition was to the fore in the Monopolies Commission's investigation of the UK breakfast cereal market. The market is seen by those in it as one in which there is intense competition. Appeal and quality of product are regarded as essential prerequisites of success, while advertising and promotion are regarded as a necessary means of securing and retaining sufficient public acceptance of the branded products to ensure profitable and growing sales. Kelloggs, the market leader, argued that the industry's products were substantially differentiated from one another, each offering to the consumer different product attributes comprising product type, product base, taste and presentation, as well as price. Consumers often had individual preferences for particular brands and were strongly influenced in their choice of product by factors other than price. Demand for breakfast cereals was, therefore, not highly sensitive to price and in consequence price competition was not likely to be very effective. The limited nature of price competition and its relative unimportance was thus seen by Kelloggs as resulting from the nature of the industry's products and not from the structure of the industry. The Commission, however, took the opposite view of the matter, considering the extent of concentration in the industry to be the decisive influence:

We consider that fear of price competition, and the recognition that it is dangerous to embark on, arise from the fact that supply to so large a proportion of the market is concentrated in so small a number of manufacturers. We believe that this fear is a major factor leading manufacturers to find ways

> of competing otherwise than in price. We do not, therefore, accept Kelloggs' assertion that the nature and extent of competititon in the industry would be unaltered if there were a larger number of manufacturers.
>
> (para. 79)

dynamic perspective, advertising and sales promotion, far from increasing supply costs, may contribute to the achievement of lower overall market supply costs and prices. This is depicted in Figure 8.2(b). The initial profit-maximising price-output combination (PQ) without advertising is shown by the intersection of the marginal revenue curve (MR) and the marginal cost curve (MC). The effect of combined firm advertising is to expand total market demand from DD to $D_A D_A$, with a new marginal revenue curve (MR_A). This expansion of market demand enables firms to achieve economies of scale in production which more than offset the additional advertising cost. Hence, the marginal cost curve in the expanded market (MC_1) is lower than the original marginal cost curve MC. The new profit-maximising price-output combination (determined by the intersection of MR_A and MC_1) results in a lower price (P_A) than before and a larger quantity supplied (Q_A). Where the leading firms in an industry *already* have market shares which enable them to operate at sales volumes beyond the point of minimum efficient scale, further heavy advertising expenditures, it is argued, will tend to raise supply costs. (This was the substance of the Monopolies Commission's objection to the high levels of advertising in its report on the household detergents market, where advertising and promotional expenditure was found to account for around one-quarter of the retail price of the leading suppliers' brands.)

Conventional market theory also suggests that advertising by established firms acts as a barrier to entry. Thus, established firms are able to secure high profits while forestalling entry. The potential new entrant is depicted as being at a disadvantage because it has an 'unknown', 'untried' product. In order to penetrate the market the entrant must 'buy' itself market share (in static analysis, at the expense of established firms) by breaking down customer loyalty to existing brands. In terms of Figure 8.3, this involves the entrant incurring initial penetration costs (I) over and above the unit advertising expenditures (A) necessary to maintain any given sales volume of an already established brand. Entrants may face higher penetration costs either because they are unable to match the economies of scale in advertising enjoyed by established firms (OM), or even though they may have the financial resources to reach the minimum efficient scale of advertising, 'extra' expenditures are still required to break down customer loyalty to existing brands.

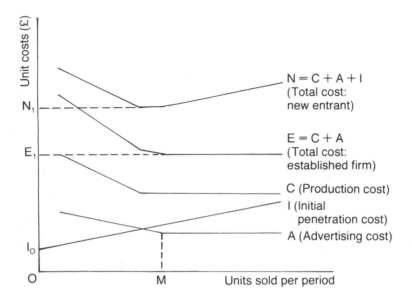

Figure 8.3 Market penetration costs
Source: Comanor and Wilson, 1967

An alternative view of advertising, however, emphasises its supportive role in underpinning entry. Studies show that successful new entry by greenfield suppliers is fundamentally linked to their ability to offer consumers a new innovative brand that performs better or is in some way more distinctive than established brands (see Box 8.3 and Chapter 10). Advertising is an adjunct to this process; advertising is an 'entry facilitator', playing an essential role in launching, building and maintaining demand for the new brand.

8.3 PRICE AND PROFIT LEVELS

Production, advertising and promotional costs are important factors affecting the supply-side efficiency of a market. Ideally, supply costs should be minimised. Price and profit levels provide the bridgehead into the demand side of the market. Ideally, market prices and profits should be consistent with the real economic costs of supplying the product, including a 'normal' profit return to suppliers. In practice, the concept of 'normal' profits is somewhat elusive, since what might be considered an adequate profit return in the provision of one product might represent a totally inadequate reward in providing some other product. Insofar as markets differ, for

Box 8.3 Advertising and entry barriers in the UK coffee market

In 1991 the Monopolies and Mergers Commission reported on the UK coffee market. Nestlé ('Nescafé') held a 56 per cent market share by value in 1989 and had successfully maintained its market leadership in the face of strong new entry competition from General Foods ('Maxwell House' etc. – 18 per cent market share), Brooke Bond ('Red Mountain' etc. – 6 per cent market share) and a multitude of retailers' 'own label' brands (combined market share 24 per cent). Nestlé was commended by the MMC for its superior efficiency and innovativeness in a highly competitive market place. It was these factors which underpinned its strong market position and made entry more difficult. While it cannot be denied that advertising costs (national launches typically cost upwards of £5 million) might act as some deterrent to entry, a more formidable obstacle is the need to offer innovative products. Both the entry of General Foods and Brooke Bond into the mass market (other entrants have chosen limited market niches) were facilitated by their 'deep pocket' ability to finance initial entry expenses, including advertising. However, their subsequent failure to undermine Nestlé's market position despite higher advertising-sales ratios indicates that it is product quality and consumers' perceptions of the 'value for money' provided by a brand which represents the core competitive advantage in this market (see Chapter 10).

example in their risk profiles, capital investment requirement and R & D propensities, this implies that profit rates need to be looked at on a case-by-case basis to determine the reasonableness or otherwise of observed price and profit levels. This in itself can be problematic, as indicated later. If, for example, profits are on the low side, this may suggest that firms are pursuing conservative pricing policies, or it may reflect the fact that firms are grossly inefficient, or low profitability may result from recessionary demand conditions. On the other hand, high profits need not result from superior efficiency and buoyant demand conditions, but instead may be due to monopolistic exploitation.

Price and profit levels need to be looked at *dynamically*. We may accept as justifiable:

1 short-term losses to firms and markets resulting from a transitory imbalance of supply and demand (that is, business cycle tendencies);
2 losses to firms and markets which are sufficiently prolonged as to eliminate inefficient firms and to induce a reduction of surplus industry capacity;

3 short-term excess profits which induce an industry to enlarge a capacity which is low relative to demand;

4 temporary excess profits to firms for being especially innovative or efficient or for taking high risks.

Persistent, prolonged or chronic excess profits, sustained over a long period, must be judged somewhat differently. In general, such a situation reflects a monopolistic 'abuse' of market power, a lack of effective competition, and impediments to new entry – consumers are 'exploited' by having to pay a price for the product over and above the real economic cost of supplying it.

Conventional market analysis focuses particularly on this aspect of market performance and emphasises the critical role of seller concentration as a determinant of differences in price and profit levels between markets. According to static analysis, consumer welfare is optimised when consumers are charged prices that are equal to the lowest real resource cost of producing that product, including a normal profit reward to suppliers. This is achieved only under conditions of perfect competition, as was depicted in Chapter 5. Oligopoly and monopoly markets are shown to yield suppliers above-normal profits.

In static theory, the presumption is that this excess profit is 'taken out' of the market by enterprise owners. If market processes, however, are viewed *dynamically*, this presumption may prove to be unduly myopic. In practice, it is suggested that enterprise owners usually plough back a proportion of current profits as a means of expanding the business, to finance plant modernisation and to fund expensive and risky R & D. Failure to do this, it is argued, will cause firms to stagnate and increase their vulnerability to the emergence of new competition. Thus, to reiterate a point made earlier, the issue of profitability (and lack of it) needs to be looked at in the context of risk-taking, efficiency and the development of new technologies and products, and profits (and losses) need to be judged 'reasonable' or otherwise in relation to these factors and prevailing competitive conditions in the market (see Box 8.4).

Box 8.4 Profits and losses: selected Monopolies and Mergers Commission (MMC) cases

- BPB   (plasterboard) – market share 76 per cent – rate of return on capital employed 37 per cent (1985–9)

MMC comment: BPB's high level of profitability was due in part to 'improved efficiency, coupled with high and rapidly expanding demand' but was also due in part to the fact that 'BPB was able to charge its customers prices for plasterboard higher than would have been the case in conditions of more normal competition and this, we find, was a step taken by BPB to exploit the monopoly situation' (para. 9.105).

- Nestlé (coffee) – market share 56 per cent – rate of return on capital employed 42 per cent (1985–9)

MMC comment:

> It may be regretted that no other firm has to date proved as effective a competitor as Nestlé, but this is no reason, we feel, to conclude that Nestlé's performance is against the public interest. Nestlé is, in our view, a highly effective and successful competitor in this market: its high profitability need not lead us to penalise that success in a market character-ised by a wide degree of choice. Its high profitability should indeed be seen as an incentive for other firms to compete in this lucrative market.
>
> (para. 7.79)

- InterMed (artificial lower limbs) – market share 70 per cent – rate of return on capital employed 53 per cent (1985–7)

MMC comment:

> We have considered whether these rates of return were higher than would normally be expected in a low-risk business of this nature, conducted as it is with completely creditworthy customers [mainly the National Health Service]. We consider that the prices obtained are higher than would have been achieved in the absence of the monopoly situation.
>
> (para. 8.12)

- ICI (fertilisers) – market share 29 per cent (1990)

In recent years ICI had made losses on its fertiliser business and proposed to sell it to Kemira Oy, a Finnish fertiliser producer which was a major competitor to ICI in the UK market (19 per cent market share). The MMC recommended that the acquisition be vetoed, even though ICI told the Commission that in the event of the divestment not going through it intended to close its fertiliser plants anyway. Although the Commission considered that closure was a 'real possi-bility', this was preferable to acqustion since 'it would enable all other players in the market to compete for ICI's share with the spoils going to those who competed most effectively' (para. 6.89).

Market theory predicts that markets which are highly concentrated will achieve profit rates greater than the normal profit return achieved under conditions of perfect competition. Little empirical support has been found for the proposition that there may be a continuous relationship between profitability and concentration levels, but studies show that high concentration markets, particularly those characterised by dominant firms and difficult entry conditions, tend to earn higher rates of profit than markets with moderate-to-low levels of seller concentration (see Hay and Morris 1991, George, Joll and Lynx 1992).

However, a number of qualifications must be borne in mind when considering the association between profit rates and concentration. In the first place, it cannot be inferred that concentration levels and entry barriers in any sense *completely* explain profit performance. There are other factors, for example the degree of risk and capacity utilisation levels that influence profit rates. Firm efficiencies are also an important factor, since studies also reveal wide variations in firms' profitability as between firms comprising the same core group of oligopolists in a market. Second, the fact that there may be statistically significant associations between concentration and profit rates tells us little about the economic significance of such relationships. As emphasised above, it may be that high profitability is compensated for by innovation and superior efficiency. Third, caution needs to be exercised in imputing causality. A causal relationship running from concentration to profitability can operate through an effect on price and/or on *cost*. The usual interpretation of the relationship as one affecting only price is based on acceptance of the 'collusive' theory of oligopolistic behaviour; that is, high concentration facilitates formal and informal collusion on price, and hence profits are likely to approximate monopoly levels. The alternative explanation that high profits are associated with cost effectiveness has received less attention, but nevertheless merits careful consideration. It must be recognised that the combined effects of scale, learning and technology may well result in significant cost advantages accruing to leading producers and it is this real cost advantage, rather than abusive behaviour, which maintains their superior profitability.

8.4 PRODUCT PERFORMANCE

Product performance refers to the variety and quality of existing products and firms' efforts to improve existing products and innovate new products over time. Conventional market analysis emphasises the important role played by choice in the enhancement of consumer welfare. Product diversity which offers buyers a product line of brands incorporating different mixes of product attributes and sophistication, rather than a single homogeneous 'no frills' item, enables consumers to select a product which best accords with their own individual preferences. The extent of choice in a market is a function of the number of suppliers, the comprehensiveness of their product lines and the degree of market segmentation. *A priori*, the greater the number of suppliers in a market, the greater the number of alternative supply sources available for buyers to turn to. However, even if suppliers are few, they may each offer a wide variety of brands, both within particular market segments and across market segments. Again, *a priori* the more a market is segmented, the greater the degree of perceived product variety. In some cases suppliers may offer a variety of brands in all segments of the market, while in other cases they may choose to adopt a more focused approach, confining their offers to one or a limited number of market niches. In the UK coffee market, for example, there are currently over 200 different brands on offer, ranging upwards from cheap retailers' own label brands to exotic coffee blends sold at premium prices. Nestlé, the market leader, offers brands in all market segments whereas Douwe

Box 8.5   Choice and value for money: the UK coffee market

> The Monopolies and Mergers Commission concluded that brand competition in the coffee market had worked to the advantage of consumers:
>
> - 'The great extent of choice of product available to the consumer meant that her or his interests were amply safeguarded.' It was evident from the actual extent of choice available (over 200 brands) that Nestlé's market share (56 per cent) 'was the result of the exercise of choice by consumers and in no way the result of limited choice' (para. 5.4).
> - Given the wide variety of brands at different prices, 'consumers had great freedom to choose what price to pay'. The fact that a high proportion of consumers had freely chosen Nescafé in preference to other brands was reflective of their satisfaction with the brand: 'If Nestlé's brands had not represented good value for money at those prices they would have lost market share' (para. 5.6).
> - The market research studies we have seen confirm that:
>
>   > quality has improved over time, and that most participants in the market are continuing to improve the quality of their products. Given the continuing choice available to consumers, with a wide spectrum of price and quality alternatives, these improvements in quality would appear to accord with consumer preferences. Nestlé has indeed increased its market share at the expense of own label by offering higher quality and better value for money.
>   >
>   > (para. 7.66)

Egberts sells only in the premium segment (see Box 8.5 and Chapter 10). Likewise, Ford offers a number of models (Granada, Mondeo, Escort and Fiesta, etc.) in different segments of the car market and different versions of each of these models (differentiated by engine size, trim, accessories, etc.). Rolls-Royce, by contrast, operates only in the top end of the luxury car segment.

There can be a number of drawbacks to product diversity. Choice spectrums may be superficial, with the brands on offer being largely 'me-too' copy-cats rather than representing substantive product differences. 'Product proliferation' is a characteristic feature of many markets, and while the availability of a wider choice of brands may indicate that competition is strong, the *overall* effect of such activity may well be perverse. In particular, small production runs and the fact that each brand requires its own marketing effort to support it may well serve to increase supply costs.

A second aspect of product performance relates to the extent to which the introduction of new products and the qualitative improvement of existing products serves to enhance consumer welfare by providing consumers with better value for money in terms of price/quality trade-offs. In Figure 8.4 an improvement in product quality from OQ_1 to OQ_2 can allow the firm to charge a higher price to reflect this improvement. If price is raised less than proportionately with the increase in product quality as shown in the Figure (price increasing from OP_1 to OP_2) then the consumer receives a net benefit from product improvement.

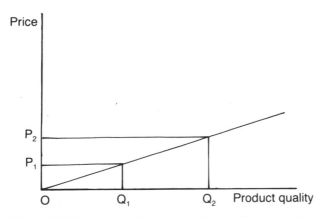

Figure 8.4 Product performance: price/quality trade-offs

In practice, quality improvements are difficult to measure. In evidence to the Monopolies and Mergers Commission in the coffee investigation, Nestlé claimed that consumers had benefited materially from the fact that it had been able to reduce the real price of its main brand, Nescafé, as a result of productivity gains, while at the same time upgrading the quality of the product.

The impact of new product development on consumer welfare is discussed in the next section.

8.5 TECHNOLOGICAL PROGRESSIVENESS

Technological progressiveness is an important dynamic element of market performance, technical advance enabling market supply costs and prices to be reduced in real terms and consumers to be provided with superior products. The scope for process and product inventions and innovations varies considerably between industries, depending upon their technological profiles and the nature of the product supplied. In some markets, for example computers and consumer electronics, the pace of technical change has been rapid. The storage capacity of mainframe computers has increased enormously, while a host of related technologies and products have been spawned – work stations, word processors, personal computers and note-pad computers. In consumer electronics new product development has led to improvements in sound reproduction, with cassettes and, latterly, compact discs largely displacing the vinyl LP. This has been underpinned by related advances in delivery systems, cassette and CD recorders and, increasingly, multi-deck systems incorporating all the main formats as well as providing tape-to-tape and tape-to-radio recording facilities. Likewise, in the television market, black and white TV sets have been largely superseded by ever-improving colour TV formats capable of receiving cable as well as conventional programme transmissions and augmented by video recorder facilities.

Advances in computer technology in turn have spawned many technological and product improvements elsewhere. Conventional telecommunication networks have been upgraded and made more comprehensive and efficient by the use of computer-operated digital control systems and satellite links, while the industry has developed a range of new products, including cordless (mobile) telephones, voicemail and voiceprint. In the motor car market, new product development and assembly operations have been enhanced by the use of computer-aided design (CAD) and computer-aided manufacturing (CAM) techniques. Even 'traditional' industries such as brewing have been transformed by the introduction of computer-controlled production systems which have improved quality control and operating efficiencies.

In some cases technical advance can be dramatic and can significantly lower supply costs, leading to 'breakthrough' products. The cost of producing flat glass, for example, was radically reduced by the invention of Pilkington's revolutionary float-glass process, while the cost-structure and product performance of the UK crisp market was transformed with the introduction by Imperial Tobacco of new mass production and plastic packaging technology which displaced established batch production and paper packaging methods. Mostly, however, technical advance is incremental and gradual, as technologies and products are improved by familiarisation and experimentation. Even so, the long-term effect on supply costs and product performance can be pronounced (see Box 8.6).

Box 8.6   Advances in computer technology

The figure shows the time and cost for a computer to process 1,700 typical operations. Early electric computers based upon vacuum tubes and valves were slow and expensive to operate, though the speed and cost of data processing fell with the introduction of transistor circuits. Solid-state circuits and silicon microchips have continued to accelerate cost reductions in computing and continuing improvements in the capacity and cost of microchips are likely to offer further scope for cost improvements in computing. However, future developments in computers cannot be expected to rely on electronics alone as the technological base, since there are physical limits to the number of components per chip, and because the speed with which electronic signals can be transmitted places limits on computer speed of operation. The next generation of computers are therefore likely to rely on the merging of electronics, optical fibre and laser technologies in order to overcome the speed-restricting resistance of silicon chips.

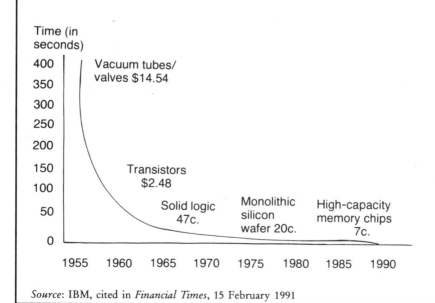

Source: IBM, cited in *Financial Times*, 15 February 1991

In a *dynamic* market environment, where changes in technology and short product life cycles can rapidly make a firm's costs uncompetitive and its products obsolete, suppliers are under considerable pressure to invest in R & D and to improve operational efficiencies. The competitive strategy/advantage framework developed by Porter (1980, 1985) highlights the importance of 'first-mover' advantages in introducing new technologies ahead of competitors to establish and maintain cost leadership and product innovation to nurture product differentiation advantages over rivals. Conventional static market analysis, by definition, ignores this important feature of market performance. However, various attempts have been made to integrate technological dynamics into mainstream market analysis (see Hay and Morris 1991, George, Joll and Lynx 1992).

According to Schumpeter (1965) and Galbraith (1967), it is competition based on dynamic technologies that ultimately results in substantial welfare gains to society, more so than the kind of price competition which produces static optimality. In Galbraith's view, large firms and concentrated markets are especially conducive to promoting inventive and innovative efforts. Significant inventions and innovations in a world of complex technology require considerable capital outlays, which only large firms can provide; the riskiness of researching and developing new innovations is such that only large firms, with the ability to sustain initial losses or to pursue so many inventive efforts that risk is effectively pooled, can undertake major programmes; the primary motive for inventive and innovative activity is the profits that may eventually accrue through successful efforts – the market position of the firm must be sufficiently strong that it can indeed reap the rewards of its initiative. The first two arguments imply that firms must be large in an absolute sense to become active inventors and innovators, whereas the third implies that firms must be relatively large in their markets, or alternatively are accorded temporary 'monopoly power' by patent protection.

8.5.1 Firm size

With regard to the act of invention, large firms appear to be no more prominent than the individual inventor or the small firm. Jewkes, Saward amd Stillerman (1969), for instance, in a study of 61 major inventions, found that most of these had emanated from outside the R & D departments of large firms. Regarding innovation, which on average is much more highly resource-intensive, the large firm is more advantageously placed. Most of the inventions listed by Jewkes were in fact subsequently developed commercially by larger firms. Evidence on the extent of innovation in UK firms of different sizes is provided by Pavitt, Robson and Townsend (1987). As Table 8.2 shows, although in 'input' terms (R & D spending) the largest firms in the sample accounted for four-fifths of the total, in 'output' terms (number of significant innovations), smaller firms made a substantial contribution to the innovation process.

Table 8.2   R & D expenditure and significant innovations by firm size, 1970–9

Firm size (no. of employees)	Gross R & D spending (%)	No. of innovations (%)
1– 499	1.5	28.2
500– 999	1.8	6.7
1,000–4,999	7.5	12.0
5,000–9,999	8.9	6.0
10,000+	80.3	47.1

Source: Pavitt, Robson and Townsend, 1987

8.5.2 Market structure

Is a competitive or monopolistic environment a better breeding ground for innovations?

The resource argument

Perfectly competitive firms earn only 'normal' profits – oligopolistic firms and monopolists are in a position to sustain 'above-normal' profits: ergo the latter have more resources to finance expensive R & D and to tackle a wider range of likely projects.

The incentive argument

Competitive markets, by their very nature, demand that a firm keeps pace with its rivals in all areas of competition. If it fails in this task, it can quickly lose market share or even be forced to exit the market altogether. Monopolists, by contrast, do not have to innovate to survive, given the lack of effective competition. They may delay the introduction of new innovations even after they have been developed in order to 'milk' their existing technologies and products.

However, this is a somewhat myopic view of monopoly. On the contrary, it may be argued that dominant firms have strong incentives to innovate: process innovation, for example, is a means of lowering unit costs and thereby expanding profits; and these profits will not be of a transitory nature, given the existence of barriers to entry; hence the monopolist must persist and succeed in the area of technological advance to maintain its dominant position: what is the point of being a monopoly supplier of candles when the candle has been displaced by the incandescent light bulb?

The fact that some form of monopolistic protection may be necessary to stimulate invention and innovation has been recognised by governments which have established patent systems. In the UK, for example, the Patent Office can grant a patentee exclusive rights over an invention for a maximum of twenty years from the date on which the patent was first filed. The patent system has the twin objectives of encouraging inventors to undertake the risks and expenses of breaking new ground by offering them temporary monopoly control to profit from their work, and of providing for the eventual dissemination of advances in technology to the benefit of society as a whole.

The empirical evidence on the relationship between high market concentration and innovation using cross- sectional data has proved inconclusive. Scherer (1990) sums up the research literature in this area thus:

> We emerge again with a threshold concept of the most favourable industrial climate for rapid technological change. A little bit of monopoly power, in the form of structural concentration, is conducive to invention and innovation, particularly when advances in the relevant knowledge base occur slowly. But very high concentration has a favourable effect only in rare cases, and more often it is apt to retard progress by restricting the number of independent sources of initiative and by dampening firms' incentive to gain market position through accelerated research and development. Likewise, it is vital that barriers to new entry be kept at modest levels, and that established industry members be exposed continually to the threat of entry by technically audacious newcomers.

Thus, on balance, moderate degrees of market concentration seem preferable to high concentration levels, especially those containing a single dominant firm. In the former case, it is argued, the leading firms are sufficiently large as to generate the *resources* required to fund R & D while at the same time having strong *incentives* to introduce innovations for competitive advantage reasons.

QUESTIONS

1 Examine how economies of scale, learning effects and technical innovation can lower market supply costs.
2 What is 'X-inefficiency'? How does it arise and what is its significance for industry supply costs?
3 Examine the possible impact of advertising expenditures on market supply costs.
4 Critically evaluate the theoretical proposition that advertising can act as a barrier to entry.
5 Indicate what is meant by 'normal' profit in market theory. In practice, what problems arise in trying to judge whether profits are 'reasonable' or 'excessive'?

6 'Product diversity can be beneficial for consumers, but "product proliferation" can be wasteful and inefficient.' Discuss.

7 Examine the 'resources' and 'incentive' arguments relating to invention/
innovation in respect of (a) firm size and (b) market structure.

8 Discuss the pros and cons of the patent system in stimulating the invention of new processes and products.

Chapter 9

Industrial and competition policy in the United Kingdom and European Community (European Union)

As the discussion so far indicates, in general terms it is not possible to specify an 'optimal' industrial structure which is applicable to all market situations. For example, in simple technology industries a large number of small producers may be compatible with supply efficiency; by contrast, in industries characterised by complex technologies and economies of scale, low-cost supply may require the bulk of industry output to be produced by only a few large suppliers. Moreover, given the dynamic nature of market forces (changing technologies, products, the level and pattern of demand, etc.) a continuous 'restructuring' process may be required in order:

- to eliminate instances of 'market failure', such as unnecessarily high supply costs due to the operation of sub-optimal sized plants, or unnecessarily high price and profit levels due to monopolisation;
- to enable firms to take advantage of new opportunities, such as the need to adjust to the greater scale and competitiveness required to succeed in a newly established common market or a general reduction in world tariff levels.

Thus, restructuring initiatives can be wide-ranging, involving, for example, both increased seller concentration in 'sunset' and 'sunrise' industries (the former to rationalise supply capacities and the latter to attain 'critical mass' in respect of economies of scale); and deconcentration to reduce the market power of dominant suppliers.

In some cases, market forces themselves may be sufficiently strong to elicit appropriate structural responses; for example, loss-making firms may exit the market, thus removing a problem of excess capacity, or new firms may enter a market, thus removing a problem of excess profits. However, if markets are unable to respond fully to eliminate such inefficiencies, either due to inertia or structural rigidities (high exit and entry costs), then some outside agency may be required to act as a catalyst for change, intervening directly or indirectly in the industry's affairs. Examples here would include government-sponsored rationalisation schemes, including plant closures, mergers and takeovers, on the one hand, and the creation of more competitive market structures by deconcentration measures and the prohibition of price-fixing cartels. Thus, depending on the circumstances, restructuring can be seen to be an aspect of both industrial policy and competition policy; that is, both policies are directed towards improving industrial performance.

9.1 INDUSTRIAL POLICY

Industrial policies are concerned with promoting industrial growth and efficiency and adapting industry to conditions of economic and technological change. Whilst it is widely recognised that in 'enterprise' economies, market forces are the basic factor shaping the development of industry, in many cases market mechanisms have failed to bring about the required degree of structural adaptation. Thus, industrial policy is seen as an adjunct to a government's general desire to promote the optimum use of economic resources.

9.1.1 Approaches to industrial policy

The implementation of industrial policy can take several forms, ranging from the use of general environmental measures and *ad hoc* intervention in selected areas, to a deeper involvement in the functioning of industry. In the latter case emphasis is placed on planning-type techniques and on efforts directed to the medium-term or long-term organisation of a country's economy. This approach focuses on the strategic development of industry as an interrelated whole, and the need to 'direct' or encourage the movement of resources into key areas. In the former case, where there is no predetermined view of future development, emphasis is placed on the operation of fiscal, monetary, trade and other policies conducive to industrial advancement, augmented by more specific types of policy action in such areas as technology policy, regional policy, government procurement, and financial assistance and restructuring initiatives in industrial sectors and industries. (See Box 9.1.)

UK and EC industrial policy has tended to be piecemeal and *ad hoc*. Currently, UK and EC industrial policy is largely concerned with promoting enterprise and innovation within the framework of competitive markets, rather than overt interventionism aimed at replacing market forces.

9.1.2 Industrial policy in the United Kingdom

Industrial restructuring initiatives were first introduced in the United Kingdom in the 1920s and 1930s. Various rationalisation schemes were applied to industries such as textiles, coal-mining, shipbuilding and iron and steel,

Box 9.1   Industrial policy mechanisms employed by different types of economy

	Economy type		Broad category of mechanisms employed	Implementation procedures
A	Centrally planned economy	1	National plan	Resources directed as part of an interlocking system; implementation of directives by specific organisations and enterprises
B	'Mixed economy'	2	State/parastatal ownership of key infrastructural and strategic industries	Operation of industries in accordance with national industrial policy
		3	Macroeconomic measures	Manipulation of overall tax rates, interest rates, etc.
		4	Indicative planning mechanisms	Investment incentives; competition policy; 'targeted' intervention, such as industry reorganisation schemes; loans and grants for R & D etc.
C	Private enterprise economy		As 3 and 4 above	As above

which were suffering from problems of declining demand and chronic excess capacity. In the second half of the 1940s a number of industries were nationalised, in the main public utilities – gas, electricity, postal services and railways, together with the iron and steel industry (denationalised in 1953). Since that time, interest in industrial policy has blown hot and cold and there has been a lack of consistency in approach, reflecting in large measure different views on interventionism as between Conservative and Labour governments. Growing concern with the UK's poor economic performance and international competitiveness in the late 1950s and early 1960s led a Conservative government to establish the National Economic Development Council (see below) in 1962 to tackle this problem on an economy-wide basis. More specifically, a Labour government established the Industrial Reorganization Corporation (IRC) in 1966 to encourage and give financial support to mergers and other rationalisation initiatives. Amalgamations facilitated by the IRC at this time included the merger of GEC and English Electric, the merger of the computer interests of English Electric, Plessey and ICT to form International Computers, and the merger of British Motor Holdings and Leyland Motors to form British Leyland. The IRC was abolished by a Conservative government in 1971, but which nonetheless was forced to bail out a number of failing companies by taking them into public ownership. These included British Leyland, Ferranti and Rolls-Royce. In 1975 a Labour government established the National Enterprise Board (NEB); the main work of this body centred on providing support for the development of small and medium-sized companies. In 1981 the NEB was merged by a Conservative government with the National Research and Development Corporation (a body established in 1949 to foster inventions) to form the British Technology Group (see below).

Between 1962 and 1992 the main thrust of UK industrial policy was centred on improving the efficiency and competitiveness of the industrial base of the economy through the work of the National Economic Development Council (NEDC), together with ongoing general support for innovation and enterprise.

The identification of the threats and opportunities facing British industry and the formulation of strategic programmes for improving efficiency and competitiveness constituted the remit of the National Economic Development Council and its satellite agencies, the Economic Development Committees (EDCs) and the National Economic Development Office (NEDO). NEDC was organised on a tripartite basis, consisting of six members each from the government, the employers (nominated by the Confederation of British Industries) and the trade unions (nominated by the Trades Union Congress) and a small number of other members, including the Director General of NEDC. NEDC met monthly to discuss issues of general concern to the economy and industry in particular. In essence, the approach of NEDC was a form of 'indicative planning', that is, it had no formal mechanism for planning the economy or directing resources into specific industries etc., but instead worked informally to secure a collective commitment to particular courses of action.

While the NEDC took a general view of the economy, the EDCs operated at the grass-roots level, covering various industrial sectors, for example the Food and Drink Manufacturing EDC, the Footwear EDC, and Office Systems EDC, etc., each comprising, like the NEDC, members drawn from government, the unions and management. Their primary task was to assess the performance of their sectors and to agree on steps to overcome problems and develop opportunities. The EDCs published periodic reports on their sectors, giving guidance on ways to improve performance and competitiveness in functional areas like marketing, production and R & D, which were designed to act as catalysts for change. The NEDC was abolished in 1992, reflecting the Conservative view that free competition would force through whatever structural changes were necessary to adapt industries to take advantage of new market opportunities.

The encouragement of innovation and the adoption of new techniques is currently undertaken through DTI-sponsored 'collaborative research' between industry and government/university research departments and various technology transfer programmes. The DTI operates Regional Technology Centres to disseminate information on new technology and to assist in its application at local level, while the DTI's Overseas Technical Information Service provides details of developments elsewhere which may be relevant to UK industries. Running in tandem to these initiatives is the work of the British Technology Group. This agency continues the tradition of one of its parents – the National Research and Development Corporation – in promoting and financially assisting the development and industrial application of specific inventions. More general encouragement is given to inventions by the UK's patent system under the Copyright, Designs and Patents Act, 1988. Under this Act the Patent Office can grant a patentee a monopoly to make, use or sell an invention, for a maximum of twenty years from the date on which the patent was first filed. Finally, the DTI's SMART scheme (Small Firms Merit Award for Research and Technology) provides individuals and small firms (with under fifty employees) with financial assistance to offset in part the development costs of new techniques.

In recent years particular emphasis has been placed on the small-firms sector of the economy. In addition to the SMART scheme, the DTI has various arrangements for encouraging business start-ups and helping firms with initial development problems. The Loan Guarantee Scheme underwrites loans made by the commercial banks to small firms against default, while the Business Expansion Scheme provides tax relief incentives to firm owners and other investors who subscribe equity finance.

9.1.3. Industrial policy in the European Community (Union)

Industrial policy in the EC has developed in a piecemeal fashion, reflecting in the main fundamental political differences between member states as to the scope and depth of interventionist measures (see below). The EC has rejected calls for massive restructuring to create 'EC industrial champions', preferring instead to strengthen the technological and industrial base of the Community by funding collaborative R & D projects, by ensuring that governments operate in keeping with the spirit of the common market by avoiding, for example, bias in their procurement policies favouring local suppliers and 'unfair' subsidisation of local firms and industries.

Research and development programmes

The EC spends about half of its large research budget on programmes aimed at developing commercial applications for new technology, including:

- ESPRIT (European Strategic Programme for Research in Information Technology), which supports projects in key areas of information technology – microelectronics and peripherals, information processing systems and application technologies such as CIM. Esprit's rules of operation require that each project has a minimum of two firms located in at least two different EC countries;
- RACE (Research in Advanced Communications in Europe), which was formed to standardise telecommunications systems and to enable EC countries to develop integrated broadband communications. Applications include cable and pay television, telephones and videophones, data transmission and electronic mail. The EC Commission and industrial participants in projects (of which there must be at least two from two different EC countries) each put up half the cost of projects;
- DELTA (Development of European learning through Technological Advance), which promotes the adaptation of equipment and systems devised for other uses into tools for advanced learning. DELTA projects are mainly in the areas of personal and business computers, artificial intelligence and communications;
- DRIVE (Dedicated Road Infrastructure for Vehicle Safety in Europe), which assists R & D in computer aids for road traffic (route guidance, navigation systems, etc.);
- BRITE/EURAM (Basic Research in Industrial Technology For Europe and European Research in Advanced Materials) funds R & D consortia in advanced materials technologies, design methodology and quality assurance for products and processes, and the application of advanced conventional manufacturing technologies;
- EUREKA, which is an intergovernmental programme linking nineteen EC and EFTA countries plus Turkey, which is designed to coordinate intra-European development projects. Its funds are contributed by national governments, industry participants and the European Commission. Projects are approved at national level and then sent to a Eureka

council meeting for final approval. Most Eureka projects are focused on robotics, information technologies, environment and biotechnologies.

Through these and other related programmes, the EC aims to establish its industries at the vanguard of technological advances and thus enhance its competitive advantages as a trading bloc.

State subsidies

Under Article 92 of the Treaty of Rome, all industrial projects involving government subsidies must be submitted to the European Commission for prior approval. In practice, governments often go ahead with aid schemes, only submitting them for approval after the money has been paid out. Aid projects stand a better chance of approval if they help the economic development of a backward region, promote R & D in a key industry, or reduce over-capacity in an ailing sector (for example, the Commission authorised a large amount of state aid to the steel industry in the mid 1980s to reduce capacity). The Commission dislikes general investment and export aids, and is particularly concerned to limit government grants to 'national champions'. In the case of the car industry, the Commission has been concerned at the high level of subsidies given and now insists on its right of prior approval for all investments in the industry worth more than ECU 12 million that involve any public money. Thus, for example, the Commission has approved the French government's subsidy to state-owned Renault to write-off its debt on two provisos: that Renault, which had benefited from special privileges including various forms of cheap financing, would be subject to normal commercial terms like any private sector company, and that Renault would cut its production capacity by 15 per cent. In other instances the Commission has reduced the amount of state subsidies paid – for example, the Commission reduced the British government's subsidy to the Rover Group by £250 million at the time of its takeover by British Aerospace in 1988. State subsidies have been extensively employed by EC countries to help national firms and industries. (A study by the EC for the period 1981–6, published in 1989, revealed that state subsidies in Luxembourg averaged 6.0 per cent of GDP, Italy 5.7 per cent, Ireland 5.3 per cent, Belgium 4.1 per cent, France 2.7 per cent, West Germany 2.5 per cent, Greece 2.5 per cent, United Kingdom 1.8 per cent, Netherlands 1.5 per cent and Denmark 1.3 per cent.) Clearly, subsidies of this magnitude represent a major obstacle to the creation of the single market.

Public procurement

Public procurement policies are also a problem in the way of establishing a common market. Purchases of products by governments, utilities and state-owned industries represent around 10 per cent of EC output. Traditionally, many governments have refused to purchase products from suppliers outside their own countries, in some cases to promote 'national champions' at the expense of foreign rivals. The European Commission has repeatedly attempted to break down procurement bias, but with little success. A recent study by the Commission (1990) indicated that fewer than 5 per cent of all central, regional and local public orders in the EC went to bidders from other countries, and that many were awarded on a non-competitive, single-tender basis. The Commission has now issued new directives under the Single European Market initiative aimed at making public procurement contracts more open to tenders by foreign companies and more transparent (e.g. by advance advertising and publication of bid details). In 1989, the Commission intervened in support of Bouygues, a French construction group, which had led a consortium which had failed to secure a contract to build a bridge in Denmark, when it was discovered that the contract terms broke EC law by specifying the use of Danish materials and labour. Although EC officials failed to get the contract suspended in this case, it is indicative of a more determined onslaught on parochial favouritism. Under the new rules, procedures are to be established to monitor compliance and review infringements. The Commission has power to correct violations, to set aside unlawful decisions and to award damages.

Treatment of non-EC firms

Industrial policy (in its widest interpretation) can also be applied to non-EC companies with varying degrees of involvement in the EC market through exports and foreign direct investment. Treatment of foreign companies has caused a number of problems. The case of a number of Japanese photocopier companies illustrates some of the issues of concern. In 1986 the Anti-Dumping Office of the European Commission applied countervailing duties averaging 20 per cent on imported Japanese photocopiers, after receiving complaints from domestic producers of unfair competition. To prevent the circumvention of these duties by the companies concerned setting up 'screwdriver plants' in the EC, various anti-circumvention measures were activated, requiring high levels of local sourcing of inputs. One company, Canon, already had a number of EC plants, and the others were forced to follow suit to remain competitive. However, in the anti-dumping case, Canon's EC subsidiaries were treated as foreign companies, whereas the EC subsidiaries of one of the complainants (the US company, Xerox) were considered as EC companies. In the anti-circumvention action, Canon's plants have been investigated for their local content, whereas Xerox's plants have not. There thus appears to be a real danger that EC policy in this area could be used as a protectionist device, pandering to local interests, rather than as an instrument encouraging efficiency and allowing customers to benefit from lower prices etc.

9.2 COMPETITION POLICY

Current policy is aimed at promoting an efficient market performance and in protecting the economic interests of consumers. Since 1948 the UK has developed a comprehensive regulatory framework for controlling dominant firms, restrictive trade agreements, mergers and takeovers and anti-competitive practices (including the Fair Trading Act 1973, Competition Act 1980, Restrictive Trade Practices Act 1976, and Resale Prices Act 1976). In the EC, Articles 85 and 86 of the Treaty of Rome, together with the 1990 Merger Regulation, provide for the control of dominant firms, cartels and mergers and takeovers.

9.2.1 Approaches to competition policy

Competition policy is implemented through the control of market structure and market conduct but also, on occasions, through the direct control of market performance (by, for example, the use of price controls to limit industry profit rates).

There are two basic approaches to the control of market structure and conduct: the non-discretionary approach and the discretionary approach. The non-discretionary approach lays down 'acceptable' standards of structure and conduct and prohibits outright any transgression of these standards. Typical ingredients of this latter approach include:

- the stipulation of maximum permitted market shares (say, no more than 20 per cent of the market) in order to limit the extent of monopolisation of a market by a single supplier;
- the outright prohibition of mergers and takeovers taking firms over the prescribed market share;
- the outright prohibition of cartels and other arrangements involving price-fixing, market-sharing, coordinated capacity adjustments, etc. However, cartels covering joint research and development, technical exchanges and specialisation may be permitted. Additionally, the establishment of temporary 'crisis' cartels may be allowed, to facilitate the removal of excess capacity and eliminate ruinous competition;
- the outright prohibition of specific practices designed to limit competi-

tion, for example, exclusive dealing, resale price maintenance, full-line forcing, etc.

Thus, the non-discretionary approach attempts to promote competitive conditions by a direct attack on the possession and exercise of monopoly power.

By contrast, the discretionary approach takes a more pragmatic line, recognising that often high levels of market concentration and certain agreements between firms may serve to improve economic efficiency rather than impair it. It is the essence of the discretionary approach that each situation should be judged on its own merits, rather than automatically condemned. Thus, under the discretionary approach, mergers, restrictive agreements and practices of the kind noted above are evaluated in terms of their possible benefits and detriments, and only prohibited if they are found to be, on balance, detrimental.

The Williamson (1968) trade-off model illustrates the essence of the discretionary approach, providing a framework for the evaluation of the possible benefits (lower costs) and detriments (higher prices) of a proposed merger.

Figure 9.1 depicts the case of a proposed merger which would introduce market power into a previously competitive market situation. In the pre-merger market, firms are assumed to produce on identical and constant average-cost curves which are represented in aggregate by AC_1. The competitive price OP_1 is identical with AC_1 (a normal profit equilibrium) and the competitive output rate is OQ_1. By contrast, the post-merger combine is shown to produce on a lower constant average-cost curve, depicted by AC_2, but to establish a price not merely in excess of AC_2 but in excess of AC_1 (that is, a price higher than in the competitive case, despite the availability of economies of scale). In such circumstances, a welfare trade-off is required between the loss of consumers' surplus due to the higher price (the shaded area A_1) and the cost savings gain to the producer (the shaded area A_2). In simple terms, if A_1 exceeds A_2, the merger should be disallowed; if A_2 exceeds A_1, the merger should be allowed to proceed. However, even in the latter case there are problems. Any benefits arising from a merger through cost savings accrue initially to producers. For there to be a benefit to consumers, these gains must be passed on in lower prices – but because of the increase in monopoly power there is no guarantee that they will be.

9.2.2. Competition policy in the United Kingdom

UK competition policy is mainly of the discretionary variety, and is administered by the Office of Fair Trading (OFT) operating in tandem with the Monopolies and Mergers Commission (MMC) and the Restrictive Practices

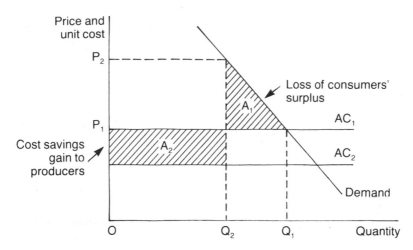

Figure 9.1 Williamson trade-off model

Court (RPC) and, in the case of mergers, the Secretary of State for Industry. The work of the OFT covers six main areas of application:

1 monopolies;
2 mergers and taekovers;
3 restrictive trade agreements;
4 anti-competitive practices;
5 resale price maintenance;
6 consumer protection.

Monopolies

The OFT is responsible for the referral of selected goods and service monopolies (both private and public sector) to the MMC for investigation and report, and for the implementation (where appropriate) of the MMC's recommendations. A monopoly position is defined as a situation where one firm supplies at least one-quarter of the reference good or service (a so-called 'monopoly of scale') or where two or more suppliers who together supply more than one-quarter of a reference good or service restrict competition between themselves (a so-called 'complex monopoly' situation). The criterion of 'the public interest' is used to evaluate monopolies. The term 'public interest' is not specifically defined in competition law, so it has been left to the MMC itself to determine what constitutes offence to the public interest in the particular cases before it. In monopoly cases, the MMC scrutinises the 'things done' by suppliers for evidence of the 'abuse' of market power (see Box 9.2). Two areas are of particular concern:

1 *Predatory pricing policies*, which can result in monopoly profits being earned. The Commission's general position on abusive pricing was clearly stated in one of its earlier reports (*Colour Film*, 1966): 'The public interest appears to us to require . . . that the monopoly supplier should use his position to ensure that the consumer obtains good quality and efficient service at the lowest price consistent with a fair reward to the supplier' (para. 259). This, in the Commission's judgement, Kodak had failed to do and the Commission recommended substantial cuts in Kodak's prices. Box 9.2 indicates more recent instances of price and profit levels considered by the MMC to be excessively high: pest control services, gas, opium derivatives, artificial lower limbs, credit cards and matches. The remedies recommended by the MMC ranged from price freezes (opium derivatives and matches); the removal of offending pricing practices such as price discrimination (gas) and selective price-cutting (pest control services); and arrangements to create a more competitive market situation (artificial lower limbs, gas and credit cards).

2 The use of various *anti-competitive practices*, such as restrictions on distribution which put smaller rivals at a competitive disadvantage and create barriers to entry. These are invariably condemned by the MMC when practised by a dominant firm. As Box 9.2 shows, the MMC was concerned at the anti-competitive effects of vertical integration and loan-tie arrangements in the beer industry; exclusive dealing arrangements in soft drinks; and various restrictions on franchised dealers in the supply of new cars. In addition, the MMC condemned the predatory acquisition of smaller competitors in pest control services and soft drinks.

The approach to the control of monopoly is thus pragmatic, each case being judged on its own particular merits. For the most part the OFT has accepted and implemented the recommendations of the MMC, although on occasions alternative arrangements have been made. In the beer case, for example, the original ceiling of 2,000 public houses per brewer recommended by the MMC was dropped in favour of an arrangement which requires brewers owning more than 2,000 public houses to lease or sell 50 per cent of the additional houses to 'free' tenants (that is, tenants free of a brewer-tie).

Mergers and takeovers

Mergers and takeovers fall within the ambit of UK competition law if they create or intensify a monopoly position (defined by the one-quarter market share rule) or where the value of assets taken over exceeds £70 million. Thus, the legislation can be used to investigate horizontal, vertical and

Box 9.2 Selected reports of the Monopolies and Mergers Commission on monopolies

Monopoly reports	Main offence to the public interest	Main recommendations
Pest control services (1988)	Rentokil 60 per cent market share • excessive price and profit levels; • selective price-cutting; • acquisition of smaller competitors.	• customers should be provided with more information about the calculation of charges; • OFT to be informed about future proposed acquisitions.
Gas (1988)	British Gas 100 per cent market share • policy of price discrimination imposed higher prices on customer less well placed to use alternative fuels, or to obtain them on favourable terms; • additionally, policy of relating prices to those of the alternatives available to each customer placed it in a position to undercut potential gas suppliers.	• deconcentration – BG to contract initially for no more than 90 per cent of any new gas field; • publish a general price schedule for gas and not discriminate in price or supply; • not to refuse to supply gas on the basis of the use made of the gas, or the alternative fuels available.
Beer (1989)	Complex monopoly 'tied' public house system had led to: • excessive increases in price of lager not	• reduce vertical integration – no brewer to be allowed to own more than 2,000 public houses

	justified by costs of producing it; • excessive variation in wholesale prices between regions of the country; • consumer choice limited because brewer-owned outlets limit stocking of other brewers' beers, wines and spirits; • many 'free' tenants were in fact 'tied' to particular brewers because of loans.	(this was not implemented – see text); • 'tied' outlets must sell one or more 'guest' beers supplied by other brewers; • 'tied' tenants to be allowed to buy some beers plus wines and spirits from other suppliers; • no new loan ties which tie free houses to selling one brewer's products.
Opium derivatives (1989)	MSL (subsidiary of Glaxo) 87 per cent market share • excessive price and profits.	• price freeze for three years; • relaxation of import licensing controls, giving European Community suppliers access to UK market.
Artificial lower limbs (1989)	Intermed 70 per cent market share • prices and profits 'higher than to be expected under a stronger competitive situation'; • unreasonable pressure put on public sector purchasers.	• divestment of one of Intermed's subsidiaries to reduce its market share – *not* to be sold to Blatchford, the second largest supplier, with a market share of 26 per cent.

Credit card services (1989)	Complex monopoly • profits of the leading five credit card issuers higher than to be expected under a stronger competitive situation; • 'no discrimination' rule, under which traders are required to charge the same price for purchases made with credit cards as those paid by cash.	• freedom of traders to charge lower prices for cash transactions than credit card purchases.
Petrol (1990)	Complex monopoly • *none* – price and profit levels reflected effective competition.	• situation to be kept under review.
Electrical contracting services at exhibition halls in London	Complex monopoly • 'tying' and preferential financial arrangements limited competition.	• discontinue these practices.
Plasterboard (1990)	BPB 76 per cent market share • *none* – since Commission's previous report (1974), new entry had occurred, resulting in 'vigorous price competition'.	• situation to be kept under review.

Soluble coffee (1991)	Nestlé 56 per cent market share • *none* – 'vigorous price competition' and extensive consumer choice.	
Soft drinks (1991)	• scale and complex monopolies – CCSB (43 per cent) and Britvic (22 per cent); • exclusive dealing restrictions on distributors; • CCSB's policy of acquiring smaller competitors.	• removal of exclusive dealing restrictions; • OFT to be notified of proposed acquisitions.
Photocopiers (1991)	Rank Xerox's share of the market (31 per cent) had fallen substantially (down from 90 per cent in 1970s) since Commission's previous report (1976); • *none* – Rank faced major international competitors.	
New cars (1992)	Complex monopoly • restrictions on distribution imposed by manufacturers on franchised dealers had limited scope for price competition.	• removal of restrictions on distribution, including limiting a dealer's freedom to hold or acquire dealerships and advertise outside his designated territory; limit the total number of the suppliers'

		cars that any dealer may sell during any given period.
Matches (1992)	Bryant and May 78 per cent market share • excessive price and profits; • restrictions on distribution adversely affecting competitors.	• two-year price freeze; • discontinue offending restrictions; • situation to be reviewed before end of freeze period.

conglomerate mergers. The OFT is responsible, in conjunction with the Secretary of State for Industry, for the referral of selected mergers to the MMC for investigation and report and the implementation (where appropriate) of the MMC's recommendations. The criterion of the 'public interest' is again used to judge mergers. Table 9.1 indicates the number

Table 9.1   Mergers/takeovers qualifying under the Fair Trading Act

		Horizontal		Conglomerate		Vertical		Number referred to MMC[b]		Number found against public interest by MMC
	Number[a]	By number %	By value %	By number %	By value %	By number %	By value %	Gross	Net[c]	
1979	257	51	08	42	28	7	4	3	3	0
1980	182	65	68	31	31	4	1	5	4	1
1981	164	62	71	32	27	6	2	8	7	4
1982	190	65	64	30	32	5	4	10	8	2
1983	192	71	73	25	26	4	1	9	7	4
1984	259	63	79	33	20	4	1	4	3	2
1985	192	58	42	38	54	4	4	6	6	0
1986	313	69	74	29	25	2	1	14	10	1
1987	321	67	80	30	19	3	1	8	6	3
1988	306	58	45	41	54	1	1	10	8	3
1989	281	60	44	37	53	2	3	14	12	1
1990	261	75	81	20	16	5	3	20	17	2
1991	183	88	89	7	6	5	5	7	6	7
1992	125	93	97	6	3	1	0	10	6	5

[a] Twenty-five per cent market share rule and asset size criteria. The asset size criterion was increased from £5m. to £15m. in April 1980 and from £15m. to £30m. in July 1984. (In 1994 it was increased to £70m.)
[b] Publication of MMC report not always in same year as referral.
[c] Some mergers/takeovers were 'dropped' after referral.
Source: Office of Fair Trading

and type of mergers falling within the scope of the legislation in recent years. It will be noted that only a very small proportion of these were referred to MMC for investigation, some of which were 'dropped' after referral.

Box 9.3 lists the MMC's findings in some recent merger cases. Since

Box 9.3   Selected reports of the Monopolies and Mergers Commission on mergers/takeovers

Merger reports companies concerned	*Recommendation*	*Reasons for recommendation*
British Airways → British Caledonian (H) (1987)	Permitted, subject to undertakings.	Increased concentration, but BA agreed to release a number of landing slots at UK airports and operating routes to competitors. Further releases were demanded by the European Commission, concerned at the wider effects of the takeover on European routes.
Elders → Scottish & Newcastle (H & V) (1989)	Refused.	Undue concentration – combined group would have had 20 per cent of UK beer market in a market where the MMC was concerned about the operation of the 'tied public house system'. See *Beer Report* (Box 9.2)
Grand Metropolitan → William Hill (H) (1989)	Permitted, subject to divestments.	Disposals of some betting offices, to remove danger of local monopolies.

Coats Viyella → Tootal (**H**) (1989)	Permitted, subject to divestments.	Disposal of Coats domestic thread business and share stake in rival supplier, to maintain effective competition.
Yalé and Valor → Myson (**H**) (1989)	Permitted.	Yale-Myson 35 per cent of gas fire market, but countervailed by major buyer (British Gas).
Kingfisher → Dixon (**H**) (1990)	Refused.	Undue concentration – the two firms are the largest and second largest retailers of electrical goods (combined market share 21–6 per cent) and price compe-tition between the two groups was strong.
BICC → Sterling Cable (**H**) (1990)	Permitted.	Increased concentration in some sectors of cables market (35 per cent of mains cables) but countervailed by strong local competitors, imports and buyer power.
Elders and Grand Metropolitan 'Inntrepreneur' joint venture pub retailing chain, and acquisition of Grand Mets breweries by Elders (**H & V**) (1990)	Permitted, subject to undertakings (see *Beer Report*, 1989) (Box 9.2).	Increased horizontal concentration of beer production: • Elders market share should be reduced from 20 per cent to 17 per cent (two of the four breweries

		acquired have now been sold); • vertical – supply 'tie' proposed for ten years – Commission recommended maximum of five years (OFT agreed seven years).
Trelleborg (Sweden) → McKechnie (**H**) (1990)	Permitted.	Increased concentration of brass market (combined group 52 per cent market share), but countervailed by strong local competitors and imports.
Stagecoach → Formia (**H**) (1990)	Permitted, subject to divestments and undertakings.	Divestment of parts of the combined business to remove local monopoly, undertakings on fares and services.
Kemira (state-owned – Finland) → ICI Fertilizer division (**H**) (1991)	Refused.	Undue concentration – would reduce number of UK-based suppliers from three to two, leaving Kemira with market share of 47 per cent and Norsk (state-owned – Norway) 19 per cent.
Tate & Lyle → British Sugar (**H**) (1991)	Refused.	Undue concentration – would have led to a combined UK market share of 92 per cent

		(Tate – 40 per cent, British Sugar – 52 per cent).
Gillette (USA) financial stake (22 per cent) in Swedish Match (Netherlands), parent of UK-based Wilkinson Sword (H) (1991)	Refused – divestment recommended.	Reduction in competitive vigour – Gillette (60 per cent of UK shaving market) would be in position 'to influence' Wilkinson Sword's (20 per cent market share) policies.
Morgan Crucible → Manville (H) (1991)	Permitted.	Increased concentration. Morgan's share of refractory ceramic fibres increased from 22 per cent to 41 per cent enabling it to compete more effectively against market leader (43 per cent); powerful buyers provided competitive check.
Unichem → Macarthy (H & V) (1992)	Permitted.	Limited impact on retail pharmacy market (combined market share of only 2–3 per cent); vertical links likewise would have little impact, given the small scale of horizontal concentration involved.

H = horizontal; V = vertical

1984, the likely effect of a merger or takeover on *competition* has been the main test of the 'public interest' although due regard is paid to the likely benefits of the merger in securing cost savings, improving R & D effectiveness, etc. Increased seller concentration which results in cost savings etc. may be permitted, provided competitive checks in the form of imports or powerful buyers act to restrain prices etc.

Broadly, the mergers considered by the MMC can be divided into three categories:

1 Those where the MMC recommended that the merger be allowed to proceed unconditionally. These included situations where the merger involved only a minor reduction in competition (Unichem → Macarthy), or put a combined group in a stronger competitive position (Morgan → Manville). Mergers which increased concentration levels significantly were also permitted where the MMC considered powerful buyers, imports or strong local competitors provided an adequate countervailing force (Yale → Myson, BICC → Sterling and Trelleborg → McKechnie).

2 Those where mergers were recommended to proceed but subject to appropriate undertakings and divestments to prevent possible abuse and to create a more competitive market situation (British Airways → British Caledonian, Coats Viyella → Tootal, Grand Metropolitan → William Hill, Elders → Grand Metropolitan and Stagecoach → Formia).

3 Those mergers where the Commission recommended that the merger be refused. These include situations where the merger would have led to a very high level of market concentration (Tate and Lyle → British Sugar, Kemira →ICI fertiliser division); or a more moderate level of market concentration which could lead to a loss of competitive vigour (Kingfisher → Dixon, Elders → Scottish and Newcastle). Additionally, the MMC has ruled against situations where a firm has taken a financial stake in a competitor (Gillette → Wilkinson Sword).

Apart from formal investigation by the MMC, potential threats to the public interest in a number of cases have been resolved by the companies involved negotiating with the OFT an 'acceptable' basis for the merger to proceed without reference to the MMC. For example, Guinness's takeover of Distillers was not referred to the MMC because Guinness undertook to sell off various Distillers brands to competitors. On the other hand, some mergers given the go-ahead by the MMC have been refused (exceptionally) by the OFT, or more frequently, have not subsequently taken place because of shareholder opposition, changes in share prices, etc. For example, Elders dropped its bid for Allied Lyons and instead purchased Courage from Hanson as a means of entering the UK beer market.

Restrictive trade agreements

Restrictive trade agreements are illegal unless they are specifically exempted by the OFT. Parties to restrictive trade agreements are compulsorily required to register such agreements with the OFT. This applies to:

1 all goods and services agreements which contain restrictions (that is, anti-competitive provisions) relating to prices charged, terms and conditions, qualities and descriptions, processes, areas and persons to be supplied; and
2 'information' agreements (goods only) relating to the exchange of information on prices and terms and conditions.

The OFT is responsible for the referral of agreements to the Restrictive Practices Court (RPC) for investigation and report, and the implementation of the recommendations of the Court.

Restrictive trade agreements are presumed to operate *against* the public interest, and the onus is on the parties to them to prove otherwise, to the satisfaction of the RPC. In order to be permitted to continue, parties to a restrictive trade agreement must satisfy the court that not only do the restrictions contained in the agreement contain benefits in one or more of eight ways specified in the legislation (for example, by reducing costs and prices through greater specialisation, or by helping exports and reducing unemployment) but also, crucially, that such benefits, on balance, must outweigh any detriments (for example, higher prices resulting from the elimination of price competition or the protection of high-cost, inefficient producers). Agreements found by the RPC to operate against the public interest are automatically illegal.

Over the years, only fifteen of those agreements defended before the Court have been upheld (books, cement, floor tiles, sulphuric acid, water-tube boilers, black nuts and bolts, iron and steel scrap etc.), while the vast majority of agreements registered with the OFT (over 9,300) have been abandoned voluntarily without a Court trial. Thus, outwardly the attack on collusion has been highly successful. However, in many cases such arrangements have been driven underground and have continued to be operated in secret. In recent years the OFT has unearthed a number of such cartels (see Box 9.4). In 1990, for example, the RPC instigated proceedings against unregistered (and hence, illegal) cartels in ready-mixed concrete, glass manufacturing and distribution and steel reinforcing bars. The RPC found four ready-made concrete suppliers guilty of contempt of court for continuing to operate price-fixing and market-sharing agreements (previously prohibited by the Court in 1979) and fined them £81,000. In the glass industry, forty-one companies were found guilty of operating twelve price-fixing agreements and the RPC required them to give 'assurances' about their future conduct. In the case of steel reinforcing bars, the

Box 9.4   Cases decided by the Restrictive Practices Court

1990	
Ready-mixed concrete	Four suppliers found guilty of operating unlawful price-fixing and market-sharing agreements, in breach of court orders previously made against them. Fines totally £81,000 imposed (see text).
Glass manufacturing and distribution	Forty-one companies found guilty of operating twelve local and nationwide unregistered price-fixing agreements. The companies had agreed to apply common price increases at similar times and had also exchanged information on prices. Undertakings were obtained from the companies that they would cease such arrangements.
The Institute of Insurance Brokers (IIB)	The IIB was found guilty of 'recommending' to members that they boycott placing insurance business with General Accident because that company had refused to deal only with IIB members. Orders were issued requiring the recommendation to boycott to be withdrawn and prohibiting IIB members from giving effect to it.
Steel reinforcing bars	Eight major suppliers were found guilty of operating an unregistered price-fixing agreement. The manufacturers held discussions about raising list prices and an 'understanding' developed that one of them would raise its list prices first, and that the others would then increase their list prices by similar amounts. Undertakings were obtained from the companies that they would cease such arrangements.
1991	
Fuel oil	Seventeen suppliers of fuel oil in north-east England were found guilty of operating an unregistered price-fixing agreement. The companies had agreed on formulas to fix

minimum prices for Kerosene, gas oil and derv. Undertakings were obtained from the companies that they would cease such arrangements.

Buses

Two bus operators in Leicestershire were found guilty of agreeing to fix fares, routes and timetables. Undertakings were obtained from the companies that they would cease such arrangements.

Steel roofing purlins

Three leading suppliers were found guilty of operating unregistered market-sharing and price-fixing agreements. The companies met regularly to share out business from big customers, and had an 'understanding' on price increases necessitated by increases in raw material costs. Undertakings were obtained from the companies that they would cease such arrangements.

Thermal insulation

Eighteen major suppliers were found guilty of operating unregistered price-fixing agreement. The companies undertook to quote discounts from a price list agreed between themselves and to limit the maximum level of discounts available to customers. Undertakings were obtained from the companies that they would cease such arrangements.

Sugar

The two leading suppliers of sugar in the UK (British Sugar, 52 per cent market share, and Tate & Lyle, 40 per cent market share) were found guilty of price-fixing and market-sharing. The companies were parties to 'unwritten' agreements to end a price war in the early 1980s and to keep market shares roughly at the levels prevailing at that time. To ensure this, they had agreed that British Sugar would inform Tate of changes to list prices and discount policy before any announcement to its customers. There was also an 'understanding' that neither company would set its prices aggressively with a view

> to increasing market share beyond a
> certain 'band of tolerance'. Undertakings
> were obtained from the companies that
> they would cease such agreements.

Source: Office of Fair Trading

RPC obtained undertakings from eight manufacturers to abandon price-fixing agreements.

Breaches of orders made by the Court against illegal agreements are a contempt of court and may lead to a fine or, possibly, imprisonment of company officials. The OFT's powers of deterrence and detection under present law are considered to be limited and it has been proposed that stiffer penalties be introduced, together with greater powers of obtaining access to company documents and other potentially incriminating evidence.

Anti-competitive practices

Various trade practices which may have the effect of restricting or eliminating competition in a market may be investigated both by the OFT itself and (if necessary) by the MMC, and prohibited if they are found to be unduly restrictive of competition. The Competition Act, 1980 provides for the investigation of particular anti-competitive practices on an *individual* basis, as opposed to their investigation only as part of a wider 'monopoly' reference, which had been the case before. Recent cases in which the OFT have found offence to the public interest include the refusal of two trade magazines to accept advertisements for amusement machines and video games which gave price information (this affected the ability of distributors offering lower prices to compete in the market); the refusal of Southern Vectic Omnibus (which owns the only bus station in Newport, Isle of Wight) to let other operators use the station; and Black and Decker's policy of refusing to supply retailers who sell its power tools and workbenches below recommended prices.

Resale price maintenance (RPM)

Manufacturers' stipulation of the resale prices of their products is generally prohibited in the UK, although under the Resale Prices Act 1976, it is possible for a manufacturer to obtain exemption by satisfying the RPC that, on balance, RPM confers net economic benefit (by, for example, benefiting consumers through greater convenience). The major objection to RPM is that it deprives customers of the benefits of lower prices by preventing lower-cost retailers from cutting prices to win sales at the

expense of less efficient retailers. The Act makes one concession to manufacturers, allowing them legally to prevent a retailer from pricing products
as a 'loss leader' (that is, selling the product at below bought-in cost as an
inducement to encourage customers to visit the retailer's outlet). In many
cases, manufacturers have replaced RPM by 'recommended retail prices' as
a 'guide' to retailers in setting their own prices.

Consumer protection

In addition to the above, the OFT also has other responsibilities with
regard to the protection of consumers' interests generally, including taking
action against unscrupulous trade practices such as false description of
products and prices ('Trade Descriptions Acts, 1968 and 1972) and inaccur-
ate weights and measures (Weights and Measures Act, 1963), and the
regulation of consumer credit (Consumer Credit Act, 1974). Table 9.2
gives details of convictions by the courts under various areas of consumer
legislation.

Table 9.2   Convictions under selected consumer legislation

Convictions under:	Number		Fines/compensation £000	
	1990	1991	1990	1991
Trade Descriptions Acts	1284	1304	978	851
Weights & Measures Act	238	363	127	166
Food and Drugs Act	1966	1390	1377	1046
Consumer Credit Act	75	156	76	156

Source: Office of Fair Trading

In sum, the UK has developed a comprehensive legislative framework for
maintaining competitive markets, though there are some weaknesses in
application, critics would argue.

The selection of particular monopoly cases for investigation and not
others is one issue. Why, for example, was coffee chosen for investigation
but not also tea? Why, was a case such as 'electrical contracting services
at exhibition halls in London' investigated, given its narrow focus and
limited regional impact? Clearly, it is not possible to discern fully what
'inside information' the OFT was privy to (for example, complaints from
customers, distributors, smaller suppliers, etc.) which led it to decide the
need for a fuller investigation.

Mergers and restrictive agreements have been another area of concern.
As Table 9.1 shows, only a very small proportion of those mergers and
takeovers falling within the scope of the legislation have actually been
referred to the Commission for detailed report, and only a small number
of these have been vetoed. As a result, UK concentration levels in general

have shown a marked increase. However, it is important to view this issue in the context of the United Kingdom's membership of the European Community. As a result of the elimination of tariffs and quotas and the removal of various 'internal' barriers to trade (under the Single European Act, 1986 – the so-called '1992' initiative) many sectors of UK industry have been exposed to growing competition both from imports and from EC companies (and multinationals from the USA, Japan, etc.) who have established an investment presence in the UK market.

In the case of restrictive agreements, it is clear from the work of the OFT in uncovering unregistered (and hence, illegal) cartels that the problem of clandestine collusion between suppliers remains a serious threat to the maintenance of competitive markets. Currently, however, the authorities have only limited powers to detect and uncover such agreements, while critics maintain that the 'penalties' available to deter and punish offenders are wholly inadequate.

9.2.3 Competition policy in the European Community (Union)

A key objective of the European Community is to secure the economic benefits of free trade through the creation of a 'common market', providing for the unrestricted movement of goods, services, capital and people. Initially, under the Treaty of Rome, attention was focused on the elimination of governmental restrictions on inter-state trade, such as tariffs and quotas. Latterly, under the Single European Act, the intention has been to sweep away obstacles to trade arising from historical differences in EC states' policies and practices covering, for example, taxation rates, descriptions of goods, technical specifications and standards, labelling and packaging regulations. The general intention is to remove the fragmentation of the EC into national markets and to create a 'level playing field', so that firms can produce and sell their products throughout the EC without discrimination.

Competition policy is seen as the main tool to ensure that the EC remains undistorted by suppliers' attempts to seal off markets. Competition policy in the EC covers three main areas of application: cartels, monopolies/dominant firms and mergers, and employs a mix of non-discretionary and discretionary control measures.

Cartels

Article 85 of the Treaty of Rome prohibits cartel agreements (that is, 'formal' collusion) and 'concerted practices' (that is, 'informal' collusion) between firms relating to price-fixing, limitations on production and investment, market sharing, etc., whose effect is to restrict competition and inter-state trade within the EC. Certain other agreements (for example, those providing for joint technical R & D, or specialisation of production), may be exempted from the general prohibition of cartels, *provided* they do not restrict inter-state competition and trade. Firms found guilty of illegal cartelisation by the European Commission's Competition Directorate can be fined up to 10 per cent of their annual sales turnover.

The main problems faced by the authorities in this area are detection of illegal conspiracies and, despite greater powers to fine companies than in the UK, deterrence. To date, the Commission has unearthed a number of major cartels, including those of dyestuffs, quinine, polypropylene, low-density polyethylene (LdPE), polyvinyl chloride (PVC), soda ash and glass. The 1988 plastics cases (LdPE and PVC), for example, involved twenty-three European chemical producers who were fined ECU 60 million (around £39 million) for illicit price-fixing and production/market sharing. The price-fixing took place in the late 1970s and early 1980s, when the plastics sector was in recession, with weak demand leading to problems of over-capacity, low prices and low profitability. Together, the cartel members supplied 90 per cent and 80 per cent of the EC's annual consumption of PVC and LdPE, respectively. Directors of the companies involved met regularly in hotels in Switzerland to establish 'posted prices' for the two materials, which were then generally accepted as the market price. Additionally, members were allocated production quotas based on capacity, but this part of the arrangement worked less successfully, because of 'cheating'. Documents obtained by the Commission revealed details of more than twenty attempted joint price increases between 1976 and 1984. Details of this case came about as a result of a previous investigation by the Commission into price-fixing in respect of another plastics material, polypropylene. In this case, fifteen producers of polypropylene were fined £36 million for illicit price-fixing.

In addition, to pan-EC conspiracies, the Commission has also attempted to break up cartels affecting principally an individual EC state. Italy's three leading flat glass producers (two of which are subsidiaries of French and US companies) were fined £9 million for conspiring to fix prices and terms of sale for glass sold to the Italian building industry. They also rigged prices and organised illicit quotas for deliveries to the car industry. While Italy represents only 20 per cent of the EC's flat glass market, the Commission felt the cartel was all the more serious in view of the fact that its members belonged to multinational groups which together account for over 50 per cent of the EC's supply of flat glass. Obviously, the possibility of similar cartels operating elsewhere in the EC could not be ruled out.

Dominant firms

Article 86 of the Treaty of Rome is directed primarily at the activities of large firms which are not subject to effective competition. Dominance refers to a degree of market power which enables firms to pursue courses of action which are largely unchecked by competitors' actions. As in the United Kingdom, there is no rule against dominance as such (i.e., high market shares) but the *abuse* of a dominant position is prohibited. Cases of 'abusive' conduct investigated by the European Commission include:

- *Predatory pricing*: pricing at levels below cost in order to discipline or eliminate a competitor. In 1985 the chemical company Akzo was found to have abused its dominant position in the supply of peroxides (50 per cent EC market share) by threatening a smaller UK rival, ECS (1 per cent of the market), that unless it withdrew from this particular sector of the market it would retaliate with overall price reductions and selective price cuts aimed at ECS's customers. Akzo was fined ECU 10m. (£7.14m.) by the European Commission,

- *Predatory rebates:* In 1988 BPB, Europe's largest and at that time sole United Kingdom plasterboard manufacturer, was fined ECU 3.15m. (£2m.) for using illegal means to stop imported Spanish plasterboard being sold in the United Kingdom. BPB had sought to protect its home market by giving 'fidelity rebates' to builders' merchants so that they would buy exclusively from BPB,

- *Marketing restrictions/price discrimination*: in 1991, Toshiba was fined ECU 2m. (£1.4m.) for using illegal agreements to keep photocopier prices artificially high in some EC countries. The company had obliged dealers in seven countries not to export machines to other EC countries where the company was selling identical goods at higher prices,

- *Restrictive supply contracts*: As a result of a European Commission ruling (1989), seven industrial gas companies were forced to abandon supply contracts which limited customers' commercial freedom. L'Air Liquide and BOC were held to have abused their dominant positions by obliging customers to buy exclusively from them over fixed periods, to use their storage equipment, to promise not to resell their gases, and to provide details of competitors offering lower prices,

- *Access to facilities*: in 1988 the Commission ruled that the Belgian national airline, Sabena, had hampered operations of the British airline, London European Airways, by refusing it access to its computerised reservation system. This refusal had been motivated by the fact that London European had undercut Sabena's fares and had also chosen not to employ Sabena for the ground handling of its aircraft at Brussels Airport,

- *Tying arrangements*: in 1987 Hilti AG, the largest European manufacturer of power-actuated tools, was fined ECU 6m. (£2.7m.) for illegally limiting the expansion of other manufacturers of nails, by tying the sales of nails to the sale of cartridges supplied by itself.

Mergers

In 1990 the EC introduced its first direct powers to control mergers and takeovers. Under the EC's merger regulation, the Commission can investigate mergers involving companies with a combined worldwide turnover of ECU 5b. (around £3.7b.) and if the aggregate EC-wide turnover of the companies concerned is greater than ECU 250m. (except when each of the companies has more than two-thirds of its turnover in a single member state). The Commission's main remit is to prevent mergers and takeovers which are likely to restrict competition and trade within the EC.

Before the introduction of these new powers, the Commission could only take action against mergers if they constituted (under Article 86) an abuse of a dominant position, or if state subsidies were involved. In 1988, for example, the Commission ruled against a bid by a consortium of three UK brewers to take over Irish Distillers (IDC), on the grounds that the consortium was in a dominant position in the EC market and that their intention of sharing out IDC's brands between them would be anti-competitive; while, earlier, the Commission forced the UK government to scale down the debt write-offs for Rover, the car group sold to British Aerospace. British Airway's takeover of British Caledonian was approved by the Commission subject to further releases of air slots by British Airways, to overcome problems of dominance on certain air routes.

In 1991, the Commission made its first decision under the new rules – it vetoed a joint bid for the ailing Canadian aircraft producer, de Havilland, (owned by the US concern Boeing), by two state-owned enterprises, France's Aerospatiale and Italy's Alenia. The deal would have given the joint venture 50 per cent of the world market and 65 per cent of the EC market for commuter planes with 20–70 seats, a level of concentration considered by the Commission to be unduly anti-competitive.

More recently, the European Commission approved Nestlé's takeover of Perrier, subject to Nestlé agreeing to sell a number of Perrier's mineral water brands to competitors in order to reduce the combined group's dominance of the French market, while it has allowed Air France to keep its 37 per cent stake in the Belgian airline Sabena, subject to handing over a number of flight slots to a competitor on the Brussels-Paris route.

Competition policy versus industrial policy in the EC

The de Havilland case has particular significance for an ongoing debate within the EC as to the respective roles of competition policy and industrial policy. In theory, both are concerned with the same ends, that is, greater efficiency and benefits for consumers. In practice there are problems in respect of the means employed – greater concentration may help efficiency (through economies of scale effects, etc.) but by reducing competitive pressures, efficiency incentives may be blunted and consumers' interests neglected or 'abused' by powerful suppliers. Thus, more competition rather than less may be the preferred means of securing an efficient industrial performance.

This has been given an added twist in the context of the EC's economic status *vis-à-vis* its major international competitors, the USA and Japan. There are those governments (the French and Italian, in particular, who have long traditions of interventionist policies) who see the need to promote large 'national champions' to meet and beat foreign competitors (a kind of 'united we stand, divided we fall' ideology) and who would restrict access to the European market. Aligned against these are governments who see the maintenance of effective competition within the EC as a cornerstone of domestic policy towards industry, and who favour a relatively open door policy in respect of trade and investment relations with non-member countries.

The de Havilland case highlights the inconsistencies which can arise when there is no clear-cut stance – thus, while vetoing the de Havilland takeover, the Commission had earlier approved a merger of Aerospatiale's helicopter business with that of Germany's Messerschmitt-Bolkow-Blöhm, creating a group with 50 per cent of the EC market for civilian helicopters.

The political problem of securing agreement on a common, coherent policy in respect of industry remains in flux and is unlikely to be resolved in the near future.

QUESTIONS

1 Indicate the rationale underlying the use of industrial policy. What forms can industrial policy take?
2 Outline some of the initiatives taken over the years in the UK as part of industrial policy.
3 Discuss some of the current features of industrial policy in the EC.
4 Discuss the advantages and disadvantages of the discretionary and non-discretionary approaches to competition policy.
5 Examine the control of dominant firms/monopolies under UK and EC competition policy.
6 Indicate the approach to the control of mergers and takeovers in the United Kingdom and EC, and discuss some of the problems involved in evaluating the likely effects of a merger on market efficiency.
7 Outline UK and EC competition policy in respect of the control of restrictive trade agreements and cartels. How can the problem of secret and illegal collusion be tackled more effectively?

Chapter 10

The dynamics of market processes
Case applications

The following cases provide an opportunity to analyse the 'forces driving competition' in a market and the interrelationships between market structure, conduct and performance. The United Kingdom plasterboard industry supplies an intermediate or producers' good and has become highly price competitive with the recent entry of two new manufacturers; the United Kingdom coffee industry supplies a final or consumers' product and is characterised by product differentiation competition between brand manufacturers and price-based competition between 'own label' suppliers.

10.1 THE UNITED KINGDOM PLASTERBOARD INDUSTRY

10.1.1 Introduction

The United Kingdom plasterboard industry was transformed in the late 1980s from one dominated by a single supplier facing limited competition from imports, to one characterised by more competitive supply conditions with the entry of two new producers. The industry was investigated by the Monopolies and Mergers Commission (MMC) in 1990, which concluded that the industry had become highly competitive and that 'there are no facts which currently operate, or may be expected to operate, against the public interest' (para. 1.8). A previous report by the Commission on the industry in 1974 had found certain practices of BPB, the monopoly supplier of plasterboard, to operate against the public interest. In particular, BPB was forced to abandon its zonal system of uniform delivered prices and various restrictions on customers who wished to buy direct rather than through builders' merchants. In 1988 BPB was fined ECU 3m. (around £2m.) by the European Commission under Article 86 of the EC Treaty for impeding imports into the United Kingdom by offering financial inducements to builders' merchants who agreed to buy their plasterboard *exclusively* from BPB.

10.1.2 Materials, products and customers

Plasterboard is a flat sheet which consists of a core containing gypsum plaster, sandwiched between two sheets of heavy paper known as plaster-board liner. A number of standardised types of plasterboard are produced (baseboard, wallboard, etc.), varying in thickness, width, length and texture according to particular user applications. Plasterboard is used extensively in both domestic and commercial buildings as an internal lining for walls, an internal partition within buildings, a ceiling lining material and a roof lining material. In a number of uses, plaster which is applied 'on the spot' to surfaces represents a competitive material to plasterboard, but plasterboard has been gaining market share because of its greater con-venience and versatility.

Gypsum is of two types: natural gypsum, which is mined in the United Kingdom and in countries such as France and Spain, and gypsum obtained as a by-product from other processes, in particular power station desulphu-risation (DSG). BPB Industries, the leading United Kingdom producer of plasterboard, is the sole United Kingdom supplier of natural gypsum, and it is also the only United Kingdom supplier of lining paper.

In 1990 United Kingdom plasterboard sales totalled £197m., having fallen from £222m. the previous year with the onset of recessionary conditions in the house-building market.

Most end-users of plasterboard make their purchases through builders' merchants, who form the largest customer group for the plasterboard producers. In 1990 there were around 1,750 builders' merchants, the largest of which operate on a nationwide multi-outlet basis. Other customers include large DIY groups, national house and factory builders and dryliner contractors who in the main buy direct from the producers. Buying power has become more concentrated in recent years and this, together with the entry of new producers, has served to increase discount competition. According to an MMC survey of builders' merchants and direct users, many of them have adopted a policy of multi-sourcing and, given the standardised nature of plasterboard products, are readily prepared to switch their custom to obtain lower prices.

10.1.3 Market structure

Seller concentration

Until 1989, BPB Industries was the sole United Kingdom manufacturer of plasterboard, accounting for upwards of 95 per cent of United Kingdom supplies of plasterboard. Import penetration was limited by the low value added nature of the product and relatively high shipping costs. In April 1989 and September 1989 two new producers, Knauf and RPL, respectively, opened up greenfield manufacturing plants in the United Kingdom. Table 10.1 gives market-share details and shows a deconcentration of the market as the new entrants have established a greater market presence.

Table 10.1   Market shares: UK plasterboard market

	1986/87 million sq.m	%	1987/88 million sq.m	%	1988/89 million sq.m	%	1989/90 million sq.m	%
BPB	143.3	97.0	161.0	96.3	174.6	90.6	138.4	76.0
RPL	–	–	0.4	0.2	8.5	4.4	22.2	12.2
Knauf	–	–	–	–	1.6	0.8	11.2	6.2
Others	4.4	3.0	5.8	3.5	8.0	4.2	10.2	5.6
	147.7	100.0	167.2	100.0	192.7	100.0	182.0	100.0

Source: MMC

The development of BPB's dominant position

The production of plasterboard originated in the USA. It was introduced into the United Kingdom in 1917 by British Plaster Board Ltd, now called BPB Industries plc. Initially market penetration was slow, as the building industry regarded plasterboard as an inferior substitute to traditional wet plastering, but the product gained acceptance in the 1930s.

At this time BPB expanded its interests into plaster production and gypsum-mining by acquiring seven companies. BPB also acquired three of its plasterboard competitors in 1936, 1939 and 1944, and in so doing became the United Kingdom's largest producer. The remaining producers were ICI and Plaster Products, the latter being acquired by BPB in 1955. In the 1950s a new entrant, Bellrock, appeared. By 1969 the market shares of the three producers were BPB 78 per cent, ICI 11 per cent and Bellrock 11 per cent. In 1968 BPB acquired Bellrock (this takeover was 'vetted' by the then Board of Trade under new powers contained in the 1968 Monopolies and Mergers Act, and was allowed to proceed without reference to the Monopolies Commission). Also in 1968 ICI notified the Board of Trade that it was withdrawing from the market, and offered to sell its machinery to BPB. No objection was raised to this and the transaction was completed, leaving BPB as the monopoly supplier.

Over the years, BPB has expanded into mainland Europe and is a leading producer of plasterboard in Italy, Germany, France, the Netherlands, Spain and Austria, as well as having interests in gypsum-mining and plaster production. The company is now the largest plasterboard manufacturer in Europe.

The entrants

RPL is a joint venture company owned 51 per cent by Redland, a United Kingdom-based supplier of building materials (roof tiles, bricks, aggregates, etc.) and 49 per cent by CSR, which is the largest producer of plasterboard in Australia. The company's first plant, at Bristol, came on-stream in September 1989. (RPL intends to build a second plant at some future date.) RPL had already begun to build up its sales and distribution network in 1987 to 'prime' the market and supplied this operation by importing plasterboard from its joint venture companies in the Netherlands and Norway.

Knauf, with its headquarters in Germany, is the second largest plasterboard manufacturer in Europe, after BPB. It has three plants in Germany and one each in Austria, France, Greece and Spain. Knauf started importing plasterboard in August 1988 in order to prime the market before production at its first United Kingdom plant, at Sittingbourne, came on-stream in April 1989. A second plant was opened at Immingham in September 1990.

Market entry: background to the decision to set-up United Kingdom capacity

RPL told the MMC that it had decided to enter the United Kingdom market 'because they believed that, given the existing high margins, unpopular monopoly conditions and prospects for future growth, there would be considerable potential for a *second* supplier to establish a sound and profitable business in the market' (para. 7.2). When RPL announced its decision to enter the market in September 1987, 'it was not aware that Knauf also intended to begin production' (para. 7.3).

RPL had intended to establish two plants to give it national coverage, but Knauf's entry put it in a dilemma by causing overcapacity and BPB to cut prices: 'RPL believed [when it had originally planned its entry] that the addition of 60m. sq. metres of plasterboard could be absorbed by the likely growth of the market' (para. 7.6). This had exacerbated its losses during its start-up phase and raised a question-mark over the viability of setting up a second plant.

Knauf had been 'eyeing up' the market for some time, but 'the acquisition of a German competitor by BPB in 1987 had probably accelerated its decision to enter' (para. 7.27). Knauf, like RPL, was interested in establishing two United Kingdom plants. At the time of the MMC report the company's second plant had been given the go-ahead and was under construction.

Potential barriers to entry

Various possible barriers to entry were cited, including the *capital costs* required to build an optimal-sized plant (estimated at £20–30 million – see section 10.1.5) and the need to acquire *technical expertise* in producing plasterboard. These were not particular problems for RPL or Knauf, which were both backed by 'deep pocket' parents, while in the case of Redland plasterboard know- how was provided by its joint-venture partner (with Redland providing marketing expertise and established contacts in the building materials market).

RPL and Knauf told the MMC that the main potential barrier to a new entrant concerned the availability of locally sourced materials and the marketing difficulties of persuading the large multiple merchants to stock new entrants' products.

- *Access to inputs*: the production of plasterboard requires the input of gypsum and liner paper. BPB is the only company mining natural gypsum in the United Kingdom. An alternative base material is DSG, which is produced as a by-product of power generation. BPB has contracted to buy the entire output of the first United Kingdom power station (Drax) which will produce DSG.

  RPL and Knauf currently source gypsum from abroad. According to data supplied to the MMC, RPL and Knauf are at an (undisclosed) cost disadvantage compared to BPB. RPL relies entirely on Spanish gypsum. The cost of this is around £11.30 per tonne, of which £6.80 is accounted for by shipping and port charges. Knauf uses DSG sourced from German power stations at around £10.50 per tonne (to which must be added £2 per tonne drying costs).

  RPL told the MMC it was concerned that BPB had taken a majority stake in a Spanish holding company which controlled most of the gypsum mined in Spain, including supplies to RPL. Thus, 'it would be indirectly dependent on BPB for the supply of gypsum' (para. 7.20). Additionally, RPL was concerned that BPB, having secured DSG supplies from Drax, would similarly pre-empt supplies from other power stations as they became available.

  Liner paper is the single largest element of manufacturing costs (around 22 per cent). BPB owns all the current production of liner paper in the United Kingdom. RPL obtains its liner paper from a Swedish paper producer in which it has a 51 per cent stake; Knauf imports liner paper from a German paper manufacturer, partly owned by Knauf's parent. Again, the entrants have been required to absorb the extra expense of importing liner paper compared to BPB.

- *Access to customers*: Knauf maintained that many of the larger builders' merchants purchased exclusively from BPB. Some merchants were prepared to take a proportion of their needs from Knauf and RPL but 'rarely more than 10 per cent. Merchants seemed unwilling to risk their relationship with BPB to any greater extent than that' (para. 7.39).

The MMC surveyed builders' merchants' procurement policies and concluded: 'The evidence indicates that the new entrants, pricing at levels lower than BPB, could expect to have an impact on the market provided that the quality of their product was satisfactory' (para. 4.62). This has been the case 'as shown by the number of merchants who purchase from them and by the fact that, amongst the merchants who do not, they are considered realistic alternatives to BPB' (para. 4.65).

With regard to special project work, where large contractors bypass merchants and buy direct from the manufacturer, two factors were, according to Knauf, preventing its market penetration: loyalty to BPB's 'Gyproc' brand name, but more particularly the cross- subsidisation by BPB of the ancillary products (such as steel supports) used in special projects.

10.1.4 Market conduct

Pricing policies: general

Given the commodity nature of plasterboard, competition in this market (post-entry) has been largely based on price.

Plasterboard prices edged upwards between 1985 and the end of 1988, but by less than the United Kingdom's average inflation rate. BPB cut its prices in January 1989, January 1990 and again in June 1990, reflecting its attempt to limit the market penetration of the new entrants. In real terms, BPB's prices for standard wallboard and baseboard products were 25 per cent lower in January 1990 compared to January 1985. On 4 June BPB introduced a further range of discounts to merchants of between 15 and 22½ per cent as compared with the 'standard' merchant discount of 10 per cent (which itself had been increased from 5 per cent in 1989).

BPB informed the MMC that its long-term pricing strategy was to keep increases in plasterboard prices below rises in the retail price index and the building materials index in order 'to support a strategy of developing the market for new applications' (para.4.76 – note MMC's conclusion, however, that BPB's prices – prior to entry – were 'unreasonable' – see section 10.1.5).

BPB's pricing policy since 1974 has been conditioned by the under-takings given to the OFT, following the MMC's first investigation of the industry. The undertakings mean that BPB's ex-works prices for a given type of product are the *same* throughout the country, and that its delivered prices for these products *add* to the ex-works price a transport charge reflecting delivery costs (previously BPB had operated a zonal system of *uniform* delivered prices which meant that customers further from a given regional plant were subsidised by customers more proximate to the plant).

For pricing purposes, BPB categorises plasterboard in many different ways (by type; by thickness and width; by length; by finishing), leading to a complex pricing structure (quoting some 2,880 different prices!).

RPL's strategy had been to set its published prices at approximately 2 per cent below BPB's. Delivered prices were set to take into account delivery costs and prices charged by competitors. Until BPB's June 1990 increase in discounts, RPL's standard discount had been the same as BPB's (10 per cent), but RPL also offered 'special' rebates on larger orders and various trade promotions (e.g. reduced delivery charges, free packs). RPL responded to BPB's increased discounts of June 1990 by increasing its trade discount on all plasterboard products from 10 to 15 per cent.

Knauf also generally aims to undercut BPB's published prices 'in order to gain entry into the market' (para. 4.92). Its pricing also took into account transport costs from its Sittingbourne plant and the intensity of competition from BPB and other suppliers. Knauf offers a 'standard' merchant discount (initially 10 per cent, but increased to 15 per cent following BPB's June 1990 discount increase), but does not offer further discretionary discounts to customers.

With regard to national coverage and related delivery charges, single- or dual-plant operators (such as RPL and Knauf) are at some disadvantage compared to BPB, which is a multi-plant operator, currently servicing the British market from five major works.

BPB's reaction to entry

RPL said that BPB had responded to the new entry by increasing the prices of products not sold by the new entrants, such as specialist boards and plasters, and reducing the prices on products supplied by the new entrants.

BPB had also offered additional discounts and rebates to encourage buyers to remain loyal and offered low metal prices on mixed board/metal contracts which 'tended to suggest that BPB was cross-subsidising between products' (para.7.9).

Moreover, RPL believed that BPB charged delivery prices which reflected transport costs from the nearest plant to the customer, rather than from the plant which in fact manufactured the product. 'This enabled BPB to supply the South of England with products made in the Midlands while charging prices as if the product originated in the South-East' (para. 7.11).

BPB introduced major price-cuts on 4 June 1990 (during the course of the MMC inquiry) which RPL considered to be predatory. RPL believed that these price cuts had reduced BPB's average net margins on all its plasterboard products to a level such that RPL believed that BPB could not be earning an adequate return on capital employed ... RPL did not believe that the selling prices were sustainable in the long term given that cost inflation was running at about 7 per cent and therefore concluded that the latest price cuts represented a further attempt by BPB to drive the new entrants out of the market.

(para. 7.13)

As noted above, the general fall in plasterboard prices had increased RPL's losses during the start-up phase of its operations.

Knauf complained to the MMC that BPB had reacted to its entry by lowering its prices in Germany very significantly (by around 30 per cent over a period of twelve months). This, Knauf suggested, was designed to cut its cash flow, with a view to preventing Knauf from building a second United Kingdom plant. BPB also simultaneously lowered the price of plaster in Germany and raised plaster prices in the United Kingdom.

Knauf told the MMC that it had anticipated a fall in plasterboard prices in the United Kingdom in response to new entry and that its 'business plans in the short to the medium term took this expectation into account' (para. 7.31). Knauf considered that it could survive because, like itself, 'its competitors would not be operating profitably at those levels and in due course prices would rise again' (para. 7.31). Knauf, as a private company with no external borrowings, took a long-term view of its investments – it did not expect a payback on investments for between twelve and fifteen years. It was, thus, not going to be 'pressurised' into leaving the market.

Overall, the MMC concluded on the entry issue:

> even in the face of keen competition by BPB, RPL and Knauf may be expected to remain viable competitors. They have invested substantial capital in starting-up manufacture; the financial position of their parents is strong; and each of them has built up a sound customer base' ... we conclude that BPB's latest price cuts were not predatory. BPB's resulting realised prices exceed total average costs; the cuts are explicable as a competitive action by BPB in a market which is under threat, particularly at a time of excess capacity; and having regard to the structure of the market it is implausible to suppose that BPB considered that the cuts were likely to drive out either RPL or Knauf.

(paras 9.84 and 9.85)

10.1.5 Market performance

Ideally, an industry's output should be produced in plants of optimal scale, thus allowing market supply costs to be minimised. If plant sizes are suboptimal, or because of an imbalance of market supply and demand, optimal sized plants are under-utilised, then actual supply costs may be higher than attainable cost levels. Ideally, customers should be charged prices which are consistent within the real economic costs of supplying a product, including a 'normal' profit return to suppliers for providing risk capital.

In the plasterboard market, the entry of two new United Kingdom producers has had a salutary effect on market performance by leading to lower market prices and profitability, but it has also created a problem of over-capacity.

Costs and capacity

Estimates of the minimum efficient scale for plasterboard production were provided by RPL, Knauf and BPB. Knauf suggested an annual production rate of 20 million square metres of plasterboard, while RPL cited the higher figure of 25 million square metres. BPB considered that costs per square metre of plasterboard would continue to fall as scale increased (as lower running costs offset higher capital costs), but above the capacity range of 20 to 30 million square metres, further falls in cost per square metre were considered to be 'modest'. Table 10.2 gives details of the nominal capacity of the plants operated by BPB, Knauf and RPL in 1990, together with details of the capacities of two further plants yet to come on-stream. It is apparent from these data that the industry's output is being produced in plants of minimal optimal scale.

However, because of an over-capacity problem, some of these plants were only barely breaking-even. According to estimates submitted to the MMC by the companies 'the minimum economic output lies in the range of 60–70 per cent of plant capacity' (para. 9.48).

Table 10.2   Plant capacities (9.5mm basis), 1990: UK plasterboard market

		Million square metres
BPB	East Leake	63.0
	Kirby Thore	53.5
	Robertsbridge	36.4
	Sharpness	25.7
	Sherburn	51.1
		229.7
RPL	Bristol	38.2
Knauf	Sittingbourne	46.0
		313.9
(RPL Rainham – planned)		(29.2)
(Knauf Immingham – under construction)		(24.0)

Source: MMC

The industry's overall capacity-utilisation rate in 1989–90 was around

58–63 per cent (nominal United Kingdom plasterboard capacity = 314 million square metres compared to industry sales in 1989 of 193 million square metres and 182 million square metres in 1990).

Prices and profits

Table 10.3 gives details of BPB's turnover, profits and its return on capital employed for the financial years 1985–90. For the years 1985–9 (that is, *before* the entry of RPL and Knauf) BPB's profits were well in excess of the norm of the building materials industry in general. The MMC commented thus:

> We accept that part of the explanation was improved efficiency, coupled with high and rapidly expanding United Kingdom demand in the last few years which has enabled BPB to run all its plasterboard plants at high levels. In part, however, we believe that the explanation was that BPB was able to charge its customers prices for plasterboard higher than would have been the case in conditions of more normal competition and this, we find, was a step taken by BPB to exploit the monopoly situation.
> (para. 9.105)

Table 10.3   BPB's turnover, profits and ROCE

			£ million		
	1985/ 86	*1986/ 87*	*1987/ 88*	*1988/ 89*	*1989/ 90*
Turnover	141.6	155.5	181.8	200.9	155.5
Profit before interest and tax	40.4	53.4	67.1	73.7	33.6
Return on average capital employed (%)	34.0	41.5	46.8	42.9	17.2

Source: MMC

The entry of Knauf and RPL, together with recessionary conditions in the United Kingdom market after 1989, had severely dented BPB's profitability, and the MMC felt that while an upturn in demand would enable prices to rise, the ability of BPB to exploit this to the disadvantage of customers was now constrained by the presence of competitors. Some rise in prices was considered desirable in any case, it was suggested to the MMC by Knauf and RPL, to provide them with a 'reasonable' return on their investment in United Kingdom capacity.

A point of concern in the MMC inquiry was whether these new competitors could survive the price-cuts imposed by BPB, which Knauf and RPL felt were instigated primarily 'to oust them from the market'. The MMC concluded, however, as noted earlier, that BPB's increased discounts to merchants introduced in June 1990 were primarily to defend its market position, rather than as a deliberate predatory act to remove competition. In particular, BPB was still trading profitably at the new price levels and had not sold plasterboard at below production cost in order to impose losses on its rivals. The MMC duly noted the 'deep-pocket' backing of the two entrants' parent companies and the fact that the entrants had quickly established a market reputation. Accordingly, the MMC was confident that the earlier monopoly conditions had now been swept away 'and that there was now no reason to suppose that they will return in the foreseeable future' (para. 9.105)

10.1.6. Postscript

Redland

In 1990 Redland ended its joint venture with CSR, exchanging its 51 per cent holding in RPH for a 20 per cent stake in a new joint venture company, Lafarge Plâtreurope, formed in association with Lafarge Coppée, a French building materials supplier. At the same time the new joint venture company acquired CSR's 49 per cent holding in RPH for cash. 'Our plasterboard operations could not escape being squeezed between falling demand and a marked increase in total industry capacity. In these circumstances we decided it would be preferable to broaden our competitive position in this activity[. . . by forming a joint venture with a major European-based supplier]' (Annual Report, 1990). In 1991, however, after incurring further losses, Redland sold its stake to Lafarge Coppée, thus exiting the plasterboard market.

10.2 THE UNITED KINGDOM COFFEE INDUSTRY

The United Kingdom coffee market is characterised by product differentiation competition between manufacturers of branded products who have been increasingly exposed to competition from cheaper 'own-label' brands offered by the leading supermarket groups. In 1991 the Monopolies and Mergers Commission reported on the industry and concluded that the consumer had benefited from the availability of a very large number of brands providing a wide choice of price and quality combinations.

10.2.1 Products and customers

Coffee is supplied in two main forms: 'roast and ground' which needs to be prepared in a percolator, filter machine or cappuccino/espresso machine; and 'instant' or 'soluble' coffee which requires the user merely to add hot water in a cup. Instant coffee accounts for around 90 per cent of United

Kingdom consumption of coffee, a figure which is much higher than for most other countries. The types of instant coffee consumed in the United Kingdom comprise spray-dried granules, freeze-dried granules and powders (Table 10.4), these being supplied in both caffeinated and decaffeinated form. Freeze-dried granules have become more popular in recent years (freeze-drying preserves more of a coffee's flavour) as has the decaffeinated form (reflecting some customers 'healthier' life-style). In 1990 there were over 200 coffee brands available on the market.

Table 10.4   Sector share of the instant coffee market

	%	
	1986	*1990*
Spray-dried granules	58	58
Freeze-dried granules	18	28
Powders	24	14

Source: MMC

In 1990 the United Kingdom retail instant coffee market was worth around £600m., having peaked in the late 1980s. Although coffee has gained ground at the expense of tea in recent years (in 1970 3.7 cups of tea were drunk for every cup of coffee; in 1989 the ratio was around 2 to 1) the market for coffee is now mature. Although the share of sales between suppliers is determined by the pattern of primary demand, in part the availability of brands is influenced by the procurement and stocking policies of the major supermarket groups, who account for around 80 per cent of purchases from manufacturers, supplying either manufacturers' branded items or providing retailers with own label brands.

10.2.2 Market structure

Suppliers

The supply of instant coffee in the United Kingdom is dominated by Nestlé, whose 'Nescafé' portfolio of brands accounted for some 47 per cent by volume and 56 per cent by value of total retail sales in 1990. For a while in the 1960s and 1970s the company's market share came under threat from other brand suppliers, in particular by General Food's 'Maxwell House' and Brooke Bond's 'Red Mountain', and the emergence of a plethora of retailers' own label brands. At the end of the 1970s Nestlé's market share had been reduced to under 40 per cent, but it has since regained its preponderant position in the market by astute marketing and new product launches. In contrast to the experiences of many other branded grocery products, Nestlé has managed to reverse the trend towards cheaper retailers' own label brands, whose collective market share has been reduced from around 33 per cent by volume in 1980 to around 25 per cent of the market by volume, and 15 per cent by value in 1990.

Table 10.5 gives details of the overall market shares of the suppliers of instant coffee and their main brand shares in 1990. As indicated above, instant coffee is supplied both under the brand name of the manufacturer and also to retailers for sale as an own label brand. Nestlé produces only for itself, as does Brooke Bond. Around three-quarters of GFL's coffee is

Table 10.5   Market shares by suppliers and major brands, 1990: UK coffee market

	%	
	Value	*Volume*
Nestlé	56.0	47.5
Nescafé	40.8	35.7
Nescafé decaffeinated	2.9	2.4
Nescafé Gold Blend	7.1	5.3
Nescafé Gold Blend decaffeinated	2.4	1.7
Nescafé Blend 37	1.3	1.0
Others	1.5	1.4
GFL (General Foods)	24.7	24.9
Branded sales:	19.5	18.0
Maxwell House	8.7	8.7
Maxwell House decaffeinated	0.5	0.5
Kenco	2.3	1.8
Kenco decaffeinated	1.1	0.8
Café Hag	4.0	3.3
Other	2.9	2.9
Own label	5.2	6.9
Brooke Bond	5.7	5.7
Red Mountain	4.6	4.6
Red Mountain decaffeinated	0.7	0.7
Other	0.4	0.4
Lyons Tetley	8.3	12.8
Own label	8.3	12.8
Other Suppliers	5.3	9.1
Total	100.0	100.0
Brand Analysis		
Nestlé	56.0	47.5
GFL	19.5	18.0
Brooke Bond	5.7	5.7
Other branded	3.5	4.7
Own label	15.3	24.1

Source: MMC

sold under its brand name, the remainder being supplied as own label. Lyons Tetley supplies almost exclusively own label brands.

- *Nestlé*: the company, which is Swiss-owned, pioneered the establishment of the industry in the United Kingdom in 1939 when it launched its original 'Nescafé' brand. Over the years it has added to its brand portfolio and is represented in all the main market segments (brands: Nescafé; Nescafé Gold Blend; Nescafé Blend 37; Nescafé Alta Rica; Nescafé Cap Colombie; Nescafé Fine Blend; Nescafé Elevenses; Nescafé Nescore). The company has production plants at Hayes and Tutbury.

- *GFL*: General Foods, which is American-owned, entered the United Kingdom market in 1947 with the acquisition of an established coffee producer, Alfred Bird. In 1954, it launched its main US brand, 'Maxwell House', in the United Kingdom. In 1981 it 'added to its United Kingdom brands by acquiring Hag AG, the Dutch supplier. The company became a subsidiary of the tobacco group Philip Morris in 1985 and was reconstituted in 1989, following Morris's acquisition of the Kraft food group (brands: Maxwell House; Café Hag; Masterblend; Mellow Bird; Brim). The company has a production plant at Banbury.

- *Brooke Bond*: the company, an established United Kingdom supplier of tea, entered the coffee market in 1965 with the launch of 'Crown Cup'. In 1985 Brooke Bond was acquired by the Anglo-Dutch food and detergents group, Unilever. The company's main brand is 'Red Mountain', launched in 1982 (other brands: Café Mountain; Brazilian Choice). Brooke Bond imports made-up coffee from Europe and Brazil which it then packages for retail sale at its Redbourn and Trafford Park factories.

- *Lyons Tetley*: the company is a subsidiary of Allied Lyons, the United Kingdom brewing and food group. Lyons entered the market in 1961 with 'Lyons Instant Coffee'. The product failed, however, and in order to use the spare capacity at its Greenford plant, the company turned to supplying own label brands. In 1965 Lyons acquired Sol Café, another own label supplier, and in 1982 it purchased Tenco, an American-owned company, which packaged own-label brands. The company is now the largest United Kingdom own-label supplier, although it also supplies some branded coffee for sale in cash-and-carry outlets.

- *Other suppliers*: Fine Foods International (German-owned) is the largest of the minor suppliers; it sources coffee from its parent company ready packed and supplies own label retailers. Gold Crown Foods (United Kingdom) imports coffee which it packages at its Liverpool factory for sale as own label. S. Daniels entered the market in 1978 selling under the brand name of 'Vendona'; the company imports coffee, which since 1989 it has packed in its United Kingdom factories. The Food Brands Group supplies coffee under the 'Percol' brand name, which was launched in the United Kingdom in 1989; coffee supplies are sourced

from the Swiss company Jacobs Suchard (now owned by Philip Morris).
Douwe Egberts is a subsidiary of the Dutch concern Sara Lee/DE NV
(itself owned by Sara Lee of the USA); the company entered the United
Kingdom market in 1984 with its 'Moccona' brand. McCormick supplies
'Camp', the only liquid coffee brand.

• *Own-label retailers*: the main own label retailers are the leading supermarket groups – Sainsbury, Tesco, Safeway, Gateway and Asda.

The condition of entry

As noted above, a number of new suppliers have entered the market, the
latest being Douwe Egberts and Food Brands, as well as an increasing
number of own label brands (for example, Aldi of Germany, a recent
entrant to the United Kingdom market, offers four types of own label).

The ease of entry into the industry depends on the method of entry
adopted. Entry by establishing a new greenfield instant coffee plant would
require a capital investment of some £30–£50m. for a spray-dried coffee
plant and some £35–£60m. for a freeze-dried coffee plant, although these
figures would be reduced if a plant was installed at an existing food
manufacturing site. These sums would not be a problem for a 'deep-pocket'
entrant. Nestlé indicated that the minimum efficient scale of operation for
a spray-dried plant was in the order of 5,000 tonnes per annum, equivalent
to around 10 per cent of the United Kingdom market. An alternative entry
strategy would be to import ready-made coffee for packaging in the United
Kingdom or importation of the complete product, as have Food Brands
and Douwe Egberts.

In either case, large-scale entry into the main market segments would
(given a relatively static overall demand for coffee) require an entrant to
win market share from established firms. In this context, it was suggested
to the MMC that advertising posed a particularly serious problem for
entrants. Advertising and promotional costs for a typical national launch
were in the order of £4.5m., but this in itself would not be a particular
problem for a 'deep-pocket' entrant, nor is it out of line with those for
any other branded grocery product. Smaller newcomers such as Food
Brands and Douwe Egberts have not sought to compete head-to-head with
Nestlé in the main market segments but have focused on the premium
sector, obtaining widespread distribution for their brands without heavy
television advertising. At the other end of the market, major food retailers
have launched their 'captive' own label brands into mainly the low-price
sector. The development of the own label sector has provided coffee
producers with greater opportunities for entry as a specialist supplier of
own-labels, as was the case with Sol Café (now part of Lyons Tetley).

The MMC concluded that it was not so much the high level of advertising in the industry *per se* (see Section 10.2.3) which represented a serious

barrier to entry, but the need for entrants' brands to match or exceed the quality of Nescafé's brands which was the key factor in successful entry. The fact that major new brands such as 'Red Mountain' and 'Maxwell House' had failed to undermine the dominant position of Nescafé, despite heavy advertising support, was due to their inability to outperform Nescafé in terms of quality and value-for-money attributes. A number of coffee suppliers indicated that there were proprietary methods of manufacture which enabled some existing suppliers to produce coffee of superior quality: 'Most suppliers agreed that the quality of Nescafé products could not be easily replicated by other manufacturers' (para. 2.117).

The MMC concluded:

> In our view there are several means of entry to the market. Entry has indeed occurred and, although new entrants may be reluctant to compete directly with Nestlé for a large market share, there is no evidence that entry has been deterred by Nestlé's strong position in the market, or that Nestlé has taken action to prevent such entry.
>
> (para. 7.51)

10.2.2 Market conduct

Pricing policies

A number of stages are involved in pricing instant coffee. Suppliers set a wholesale list price for their products; their customers, in the main retailers, purchase at these prices less a discount; retailers, in turn, set retail prices to customers.

It was suggested to the MMC that competition between suppliers could be described 'as being on the basis of value-for-money rather than price alone' (para. 2.65).

The pricing system adopted by the leading suppliers is similar. Suppliers' price lists show the price per case for each product, with customers qualifying for discounts off this list price according to quantities purchased and other factors. Most suppliers offer a 'basic' discount related to quantity purchased, but there are variations based on product size (200 gram jars v. 100 gram jars) and type of product (freeze-dried v. spray-dried). Discounts can also reflect 'allowances' to retailers for providing in-store displays and promotions and special rebates (so-called 'overriders' and 'retrospective bonuses') may be paid to encourage the placing of large orders. The MMC found that the extent of these discounts varied substantially between suppliers: 'The discount off list price for Maxwell House, for example, was more than double the discount for Nescafé' (para. 2.77).

Table 10.6 lists the average retail prices of manufacturers' brands of 100-gram jars and a sample of own label brands sold in major supermarkets in

June 1990. It can be seen that there is a very wide range of prices are available. In the regular granulated sector the brand leader, 'Nescafé', was priced at £1.39, 5p more expensive than its chief competitor, 'Maxwell House'; 'Café Mountain' was similarly priced at £1.39. Retailers' own label brands, of varying qualities, cost between 20p and 30p less than 'Nescafé'. In the freeze-dried sector the brand leader 'Nescafé Gold Blend' was priced at £1.69, as were its main competitors, 'Nescafé Blend 37', 'Kenco' and 'Continental Gold'.

Table 10.6   Prices for 100-gram jars, June 1990 (£s): UK coffee market

Average at major supermarkets	Nestlé	GFL	Brooke Bond	Other manufacturers	Own-label (OL)
0.52				Vendona Chicory (S. Daniel – O)	
0.53					OL – O
0.59				Vendona S/B Powder (S. Daniel – P)	
0.68					OL – O
0.73				Vendona Classic Granules (S. Daniel – G)	
0.79				Grandos Instant (FFL – G)	
0.86					OL – P
0.89					OL – PD
0.92				Camp Chicory (McCormick – L)	
0.94				Vendona Gold (S. Daniel – F)	
1.09					OL – F
1.15				Grandos Expresso (FFL – F)	
1.19			Choice (P)		OL – G
1.27	Nescafé Fine Blend (P)				
1.29		Birds Mellow (P) Maxwell House (G)			OL – G OL – GD
1.34		Maxwell House (P)			
1.39	Nescafé (G)		Café Mountain (G)		
1.47		Master Blend (G)			
1.49					OL – FD
1.59			Red Mountain (F)		

Table 10.6   continued

Average at major supermarkets	Nestlé	GFL	Brooke Bond	Other manufacturers	Own label (OL)
	Nescafé Decaffeinated (GD)	Café Hag (GD)		Continental Gold (Douwe – F)	
1.69	Nescafé Gold Blend (F) Nescafé Blend 37 (F)	Maxwell House Decaffeinated (GD) Kenco (F)		Percol Decaffeinated (Food Brands – GD)	
1.72				Percol Café Mocha (Food Brands – P)	
1.74				Percol Café Expresso (Food Brands – P)	
1.89		Café Hag Select (FD)	Red Mountain Decaffeinated (FD)	Percol Sp Decaffeinated (Food Brands – FD)	
1.95	Nescafé Gold Blend Decaffeinated (FD) Nescafé Cap Colombie (F) Nescafé Alta	Kenco Decaffeinated (FD)			
2.55	Rica (F)				

Type code	F (Freeze-dried)	P (Powder)
	FD (Freeze-dried decaffeinated)	PD (Powder decaffeinated)
	G (Granules)	O (Other mixtures)
	GD (Granules decaffeinated)	L (Liquid)

Source: MMC

Retail surveys indicate that because instant coffee is part of many consumers' regular grocery shopping, consumers are highly aware of coffee prices and are in a position to compare the prices of different brands both within and between stores. As a consequence, retail prices for equivalent brands tend to be very similar in all the major supermarkets. The keenness of coffee pricing by these groups is reflected in the fact that the coffee brands sold in these outlets are priced only marginally higher than those to be found in the stores of 'cut-price' retailers such as Kwik-Save and Budgens.

The MMC duly noted that the price structure for coffee reflected gradations in the quality of product supplied and that consumers' perceptions of differences in quality between brands offered suppliers scope to 'add value' to their brands. Thus, as noted above, the brand leader 'Nescafé' has been able to sustain a 5p price premium over its closest branded competitor, 'Maxwell House', and a 20–30p price premium over own label while *increasing* its market share. 'Nescafé's market share by value increased from 37 per cent to 56 per cent over the period 1980–90, while over the same period 'Maxwell House' market share fell from 17 per cent to under 10 per cent. The MMC was satisfied that there was vigorous price competition between coffee brands and that given the wide spectrum of price-quality combinations available, ranging from 'basic' own label brands to premium-priced 'specialities', there was no question but that consumers had been given sufficient freedom of choice to make their preferences felt in the market-place. The MMC concluded: 'Consumer preference for the leading Nestlé brands, particularly for Nescafé, reflects therefore the outcome of consumer choice among a wide range of alternatives and a preference for a perceived higher quality at a somewhat higher price' (para. 7.64).

Product differentiation

The leading coffee products are strongly branded and their successful marketing has required a substantial investment and expertise in developing an appropriate brand: 'The branding of the product is a complex mixture of taste positioning, advertising, packaging, pricing, trade and promotional terms in order to develop a differentiated product' (para. 2.49).

Advertising plays a key role in developing a brand, by serving to communicate the qualities and characteristics of the brand, to create favourable associations in the consumer's mind and to communicate the benefits of the brand compared with competitors' products. The two main coffee suppliers rely extensively on advertising and promotions to support their brands. Table 10.7 shows the total amount spent on advertising and promotion by Nestlé, GFL and Brooke Bond over the period 1985–9 and the amount spent on television advertising in 1989. Television advertising accounts for about half of the advertising and promotional spending at Nestlé and GFL. The remainder is taken up by various 'value added' promotions, a substantial proportion of which consist of lump-sum payments to retailers for providing in-store displays and special promotions. Nestlé spends only slightly more on advertising than GFL, though it has twice the market share. Nestlé, it will be noted, sells all its brands using the 'umbrella' name of 'Nescafé' which it feels confers 'considerable spill-over gains between advertising different Nescafé brands' (para. 2.60). GFL's brands, by contrast, are promoted on a stand-alone basis.

Table 10.7   Advertising and promotion spending, 1985–9 (£ million): UK coffee market

	Date launched	1985	1986	1987	1988	1989 TV	1989 Total	Cumulative 1985–9
Nestlé		14.7	19.3	24.5	29.3	15.3	29.9	117.7
Nescafé	1939	9.3	12.3	15.7	18.4	6.9	18.5	74.2
Blend 37	1955	0.7	1.0	1.3	1.3	1.4	1.8	6.1
Gold Blend	1965	4.2	5.1	6.4	8.3	6.6	8.4	32.4
Fine Blend	1973	0.3	0.5	0.6	0.6	–	0.4	2.4
Nescore	1975	0.1	0.1	0.1	–	–	–	0.3
Elevenses	1977	0.1	0.1	0.1	0.1	–	–	0.4
Alta Rica/Cap Colombie	1985	–	0.2	0.3	0.6	0.4	0.8	1.9
GFL		10.6	19.1	21.1	28.2	17.5	27.6	106.6
Maxwell House	1954	8.1	11.4	14.2	16.8	8.2	14.5	65.0
Café Hag	1979	1.5	1.9	2.2	4.7	4.1	5.9	16.2
Mellow Birds	1972	1.0	1.8	1.8	1.8	0.5	1.3	7.7
Kenco	1988	–	–	–	2.7	4.7	5.6	8.3
Master Blend	1986	–	4.0	2.9	2.2	–	0.3	9.4
Brooke Bond		2.1	3.2	4.5	6.3	2.7	5.8	21.9
Red Mountain	1982	1.4	2.7	4.4	6.2	2.7	5.6	20.2
Other		0.7	0.5	0.1	0.2	–	0.2	1.7

Source: MMC

Maintaining the market position of established brands requires close attention to marketing mix details. A good illustration of the branding process is provided by 'Nescafé'. Nestlé told the MMC that in the 1960s it had 'set about developing the instant coffee market away from a commodity milk modifier to a more discerning appreciation of coffee quality' (para. 2.52). Its marketing department was charged with making 'Nescafé' synonymous with 'quality' in terms of its physical properties, its presentation and the perception of the brand by consumers. In 1981 a 'new improved' Nescafé was developed, containing a more expensive, higher-quality blend of coffee beans. The relaunch in 1981 was combined with a new label and a new advertising campaign. Nestlé indicated that it strongly believed that 'long- term advertising campaigns were a cumulative investment that made a major contribution to the establishment of the brand in the minds of consumers' (para. 2.52).

Over the longer term, the maintenance and extension of a company's market position requires it to pay particular attention to product updates, repositioning opportunities, withdrawal and the introduction of new brands. Table 10.8 gives details of product launches, relaunches, etc. in the coffee market. 'Nescafé' was launched in 1939 and its major rival, 'Maxwell House' was introduced into the United Kingdom market in 1954. In 1970

Table 10.8 Brand developments, major suppliers, 1939–90: UK coffee market

	Nestlé	GFL	Brooke Bond	Other
1939	L Nescafé			
1947		GF acquires Alfred Bird brands		
1954		L Maxwell House		
1955	L Blend 37			
1960				L Lyons Instant Coffee
1963				W Lyons Instant
1965	L Gold Blend		L Crown Cup	Lyons acquires Sol Café (own label)
1970	R Nescafé Granulated	R Maxwell House Granulated		
1972		L Mellow Birds	L Brazilian Blend	
1973	L Fine Blend			
1975	L Nescore			
1976		L Coffee Time		
1977	L Elevenses			
1978	L Gold Blend Decaffeinated	L Brim		L Vendona brands (S. Daniels)
1979		GF acquires Hag brands		
1981	R Nescafé	L Café Hag for general distribution		
1982	L Good Day		L Red Mountain R Brazilian Choice (Blend)	Lyons acquires Tenco (own label)
1984	L Gold Blend roast and ground	L Master Blend roast and ground		L Douwe Egberts Moccona
1985	W Good Day			
1986	L Nescafé Decaffeinated R Blend 37/ Gold Blend	L Master Blend light and rich		
1987	L Blend 37 roast and ground	GF acquires Kenco	R Red Mountain	
1988		L Kenco Regular and Decaffeinated	L Red Mountain Decaffeinated	

Table 10.8 continued

	Nestlé		GFL	Brooke Bond	Other
1989	R Nescore Decaffeinated	L	Maxwell House Decaffeinated		L Percol brands (Food Brands) L Douwe Egberts Continental Gold
1990		L	Maxwell House Classic		

Key L = Launch
   R = Relaunch
   W = Withdrawal

Source: MMC

both Nestlé and GFL brought out spray-dried granular versions of these brands. In 1981, as noted above, a quality-enhanced version of 'Nescafé' was introduced.

In the freeze-dried sector, 'Nescafé Gold Blend' was introduced in 1965. It was not until 1982 that a branded rival appeared with the launch of Brooke Bond's 'Red Mountain'. GFL entered this sector only in 1988 with its 'Kenco' brand. In the late 1980s several new freeze-dried products were launched, including various 'Percol' brands (from Food Brands) and two brands by Douwe Egberts.

The powdered sector is more heterogeneous. GFL offers a powdered version of Maxwell House and introduced Mellow Birds in 1972, while Nestlé is represented by 'Nescafé Fine Blend' (launched in 1973) and 'Nescafé Elevenses' (launched in 1977); Brooke Bond introduced 'Brazilian Blend' in 1972 and launched a reformulated version of this product in 1982 under a new brand name 'Brazilian Choice'. The leading suppliers have withdrawn a number of unsuccessful brands in this sector, for example, 'Good Day' (in 1985) and 'Coffee Time' (in 1989).

In the decaffeinated sector, Nestlé launched 'Nescafé Gold Blend' in 1978. GFL, having acquired Hag AG in 1979, introduced the company's leading brand 'Café Hag' nationally in 1981. This brand is now market leader. Decaffeinated versions of established brands have been introduced by Nestlé ('Nescafé' in 1986), Brooke Bond ('Red Mountain' in 1988) and GFL ('Maxwell House' in 1989).

10.2.3 Market performance

Prices and selling costs

The conventional market theory objection to product differentiation is that it is used by suppliers as a substitute for price competition, since product differentiation offers a more permanent and 'safer' way of improving a company's market position and profitability than price competition, which if pursued aggressively reduces everybody's profits. This view, however, needs to be tempered by the fact that in many markets, including that for coffee, advertising and price are used in combination as part of a broader-based marketing-mix strategy; that is, they are not either/or options, but are deployed *in tandem* to support 'value-for-money' competition. The leading coffee producers supply a range of brands serving particular market segments and operate a price structure to reflect gradations in quality and different types of coffee. Advertising of established brands is used as a means of 'competitive maintenance', reminding customers of the quality of the brand and reassuring customers of the value of the product to them. In this sense advertising is pro-competitive, rather than restrictive of competition. Similarly, although conventional market analysis depicts advertising as a barrier to entry, in reality it is an essential means of supporting the launch of a new brand onto the market. Again, advertising can have a pro-competitive impact, in this case serving as an 'entry facilitator'. As emphasised earlier (see Chapter 8), studies indicate that it is not advertising *per se* which acts as a major barrier to entry. A more critical element in the entry equation is the need for entrants to offer customers innovative new brands which will induce them to switch their purchases away from established brands in sufficient numbers so as to enable the entrant to win a viable market share. Out-performing efficient, innovative established producers is difficult, as the experiences of Lyons Tetley and Brooke Bond bear out.

Coffee producers spend large sums of money on advertising their products, but the amount leading suppliers spend on advertising *per se* is much less than for many other consumer-product industries. Table 10.9 shows advertising-sales ratios for a number of branded consumer goods markets in 1990. The MMC did not consider the amount of expenditure on coffee advertising to be excessive, and was satisfied that it was a manifestation of 'workable competition'.

Table 10.9   Advertising–sales ratios: selected markets, 1990

	%
Toothpaste	15.2
Shampoos	14.1
Washing powder	11.0
Breakfast cereals	10.3
Cough remedies	9.2
Margarine	8.5
Sauces and pickles	8.2
Coffee	7.6
Soup	7.0

Source: *Advertising Statistics Yearbook*

Choice and product quality

Overall, the MMC was of the opinion that the thrust of competition in the coffee market had benefited consumers by providing them with an extensive variety of brands and improvements in product quality. The MMC concluded:

> The market research studies we have seen confirm that quality has improved over time, and that most participants in the market are continuing to improve the quality of their products. Given the continuing choice available to customers, with a wide spectrum of price and quality alternatives, these improvements in quality would appear to accord with consumer preferences. Nestlé has indeed increased its market share at the expense of own label by offering higher quality and better value-for-money, despite higher prices. The increasing success of its brands, particularly of Nescafé, given the extent of choice available, reflects Nestlé's success as a competitor in offering a reliable product at a quality and price in accordance with consumer preferences.
>
> (para. 7.66)

Profitability

Table 10.10 provides details of the rate of return on capital employed achieved by the leading suppliers for the period 1985–9. Nestlé's profits were considerably higher than the average rate of profitability for manufacturing industry in general and for food companies in particular. High rates of profitability may be justified by superior efficiency, the need to generate funds to finance capital investment and research and development, and to reward suppliers for taking risks. The MMC is required to assess whether a particular dominant company's profit rate is indeed a 'reasonable' reward in this regard, or whether it has 'abused' its market power by overcharging customers. In practice, of course, it is difficult to draw a fine distinction between what is reasonable or unreasonable. As regards Nestlé, the MMC was 'satisfied' that the company's profits had been earned in the context of a highly competitive market and reflected its commercial success in outperforming its rivals, rather than its ability to exploit a monopoly position protected from competition. The company's profitability 'has arisen in a market with a wide degree of consumer-choice and effective competition' (para. 7.87);

> there is sufficient competition on prices to set a ceiling to the prices that can be charged by Nestlé. Nestlé's only advantages stem from its success as a competitor; it has increased its market share by offering a good quality product, its advertising is more effective, its leading brands are stronger, and in a number of ways it appears to have been more efficient than its competitors.   (para. 7.78)

Table 10.10   Return on capital employed, 1985–9: UK coffee market

	1985	1986	% 1987	1988	1989
Nestlé	49.5	64.9	98.9	118.1	113.7
GFL	27.6	35.7	37.2	33.0	29.2
Lyons Tetley	47.3	35.3	33.1	22.2	10.0
Brooke Bond	(loss)	(loss)	(loss)	8.9	2.6

Source: MMC

The MMC concluded:

It may be regretted that no other firm has to date proved as effective a competitor as Nestlé, but this is no reason, we feel, to conclude that Nestlé's performance is against the public interest and Nestlé is, in our view, a highly effective and successful competitor in their market: its high profitability need not lead us to penalise that success in a market characterised by such a wide degree of choice. Its high profitability should indeed be seen as an incentive for other firms to compete in this lucrative market.

(para. 7.79)

Even so, in other cases where profits have been similarly high (for example, colour film, household detergents, salt, contraceptives) the MMC has recommended price-cuts or the imposition of price controls to ensure 'fair' prices. The MMC did in fact consider the possible impact of such a course of action in the coffee case, but rejected it, observing that although this 'could offer some short-term benefits in the form of price reductions' it would carry the considerable risk (given the lower profitability of Nestlé's competitors) 'of there being less choice, poorer quality and weaker competition in the long run. The interests of consumers who already have the option of purchasing cheaper coffee should they so choose, are in our view best served by the maintenance of competition' (para. 7.80). Whether or not lower prices by Nestlé would serve to eliminate such competition is, of course, a moot point. (In the colour film case, following the instigation of price-cuts by the dominant supplier, Kodak, that company's only United Kingdom rival at the time, Ilford, was forced to exit the market as a brand supplier, leaving Kodak as monopoly supplier facing limited competition (at the time) from imports and own-label brands.)

10.2.4 POSTSCRIPT

In February 1994 Allied Lyons withdrew from the UK coffee market, selling its soluble coffee interests to General Foods. Allied's decision to exit from the coffee market followed a strategic decision to concentrate its resources on its larger branded tea business.

QUESTIONS

10.1 Plasterboard

1 (a) What factors can lead to an increase in concentration in a market?
  (b) What is a 'concentration ratio'? Why might a concentration ratio overstate or understate the degree of competition/monopolisation present in a market?
  (c) Account for the growth in concentration in the plasterboard market down to the late 1980s.
2 (a) Outline some of the main potential barriers to entry operating in a market.
  (b) What potential barriers to entry exist in the plasterboard market?
  (c) What factors encouraged RPL and Knauf to enter the United Kingdom market?
3 (a) Comment on the pricing strategies of RPL and Knauf.
  (b) How did BPB react to new entry? Do you consider BPB's behaviour to have been a 'reasonable' response, or predatory?
4 (a) What is meant by the 'minimum efficient scale' of operation?
  (b) To what extent has the addition of new capacity in the plasterboard market served to compromise the achievement of cost-effective rates of capacity utilisation?
5 (a) What is meant by the concept of 'normal' profit?
  (b) Indicate some of the difficulties in distinguishing between 'normal' and 'excessive' profits.
  (c) How do these considerations apply to BPB's profitability?

10.2 Coffee

1 Account for the continuing dominance of Nestlé in the coffee market.
2 (a) Examine the proposition that advertising can act as a barrier to entry.
  (b) What evidence is there that advertising by established firms is a strong barrier to entry in the coffee market?
3 Why do oligopolists tend to prefer product differentiation competition to price competition?
4 Examine the role of advertising and sales promotion as a source of competitive advantage (a) generally and (b) in the particular case of coffee.
5 Examine the role of new product development in maintaining competitive advantage (a) generally and (b) in the particular case of coffee.
6 Evaluate the MMC view that competition in the coffee market was strong and had benefited consumers as evidenced by the wide spectrum of coffee brands and prices on offer.

7 Is there a case for imposing price-cuts/controls on Nestlé in view of the company's extremely high level of profitability?

Bibliography

Text references

Baumol, W. J. (1967) *Business Behavior, Value and Growth*, New York: Harcourt, Brace and World.

Boston Consulting Group (1968) *Perspectives on Experience*, Boston.

Buckley, P., Pass, C. L. and Prescott, K. (1992) *Servicing International Markets*, Oxford: Blackwell.

Comanor, W. S. and Wilson, T. (1967) 'Advertising, Market Structure and Performance', *Review of Economics and Statistics*, 49.

Galbraith, J. K. (1967) *The New Industrial State*, Boston: Hamish Hamilton.

Jewkes, J., Saward, D. and Stillerman, R. (1969) *The Sources of Invention*, London: Macmillan.

Marris, R. (1964) *The Economic Theory of Managerial Capitalism*, London: Macmillan.

Pavitt, K., Robson, N. and Townsend, J. (1987) 'The Size Distribution of Innovating Firms in the UK 1945–1983', *Journal of Industrial Economics*, 35: 297–316.

Porter, M. E. (1980) *Competitive Strategy: Techniques for Analyzing Industries and Competitors*, New York: Free Press.

Porter, M. E. (1985) *Competitive Advantage: Creating and Sustaining Superior Performance*, New York: Free Press.

Pratten, C. F. (1971) *Economies of Scale in Manufacturing Industry*, Cambridge: Cambridge University Press.

Scherer, F. M. (1990) *Industrial Market Structure and Economic Performance*, Chicago: Rand McNally.

Schumpeter, J. (1965) *Capitalism, Socialism and Democracy*, London: Allen and Unwin.

Williamson, O. E. (1968) 'Economics as an Antitrust Defence: The Welfare Trade-Offs', *American Economic Review*, 58.

Further reading

Students are recommended to consult the following books for a more in-depth treatment of the subject matter:

George, K. D., Joll, C. and Lynk, E. L. (1992) *Industrial Organization* (4th edn.), London: Routledge.

Hay, D. A. and Morris, D. J. (1991) *Industrial Economics and Organization* (2nd edn.), Oxford: Oxford University Press.

Index